CISCO

Course Booklet

CCNA Discovery

Designing and Supporting Computer Networks

Version 4.0

Cisco | Networking Academy
Mind Wide Open

ciscopress.com

CCNA Discovery Course Booklet Designing and Supporting Computer Networks, Version 4.0

Cisco Networking Academy

Copyright© 2010 Cisco Systems, Inc.

Published by:
Cisco Press
800 East 96th Street
Indianapolis, IN 46240 USA

Printed in the United States of America

First Printing   October 2009

Library of Congress Cataloging-in-Publication Data is on file.

ISBN-13: 978-1-58713-257-5

ISBN-10: 1-58713-257-5

Warning and Disclaimer

This book is designed to provide information about routing and switching. Every effort has been made to make this book as complete and as accurate as possible, but no warranty or fitness is implied.

The information is provided on an "as is" basis. The authors, Cisco Press, and Cisco Systems, Inc. shall have neither liability nor responsibility to any person or entity with respect to any loss or damages arising from the information contained in this book or from the use of the discs or programs that may accompany it.

The opinions expressed in this book belong to the author and are not necessarily those of Cisco Systems, Inc.

Publisher
Paul Boger

Associate Publisher
Dave Dusthimer

Cisco Representative
Erik Ullanderson

**Cisco Press
Program Manager**
Anand Sundaram

Executive Editor
Mary Beth Ray

Managing Editor
Patrick Kanouse

Project Editor
Bethany Wall

Editorial Assistant
Vanessa Evans

Cover Designer
Louisa Adair

Composition
Mark Shirar

CISCO

Trademark Acknowledgments

All terms mentioned in this book that are known to be trademarks or service marks have been appropriately capitalized. Cisco Press or Cisco Systems, Inc., cannot attest to the accuracy of this information. Use of a term in this book should not be regarded as affecting the validity of any trademark or service mark.

Feedback Information

At Cisco Press, our goal is to create in-depth technical books of the highest quality and value. Each book is crafted with care and precision, undergoing rigorous development that involves the unique expertise of members from the professional technical community.

Readers' feedback is a natural continuation of this process. If you have any comments regarding how we could improve the quality of this book, or otherwise alter it to better suit your needs, you can contact us through email at feedback@ciscopress.com. Please make sure to include the book title and ISBN in your message.

We greatly appreciate your assistance.

Americas Headquarters
Cisco Systems, Inc.
San Jose, CA

Asia Pacific Headquarters
Cisco Systems (USA) Pte. Ltd.
Singapore

Europe Headquarters
Cisco Systems International BV
Amsterdam, The Netherlands

Cisco has more than 200 offices worldwide. Addresses, phone numbers, and fax numbers are listed on the Cisco Website at **www.cisco.com/go/offices.**

CCDE, CCENT, Cisco Eos, Cisco HealthPresence, the Cisco logo, Cisco Lumin, Cisco Nexus, Cisco StadiumVision, Cisco TelePresence, Cisco WebEx, DCE, and Welcome to the Human Network are trademarks; Changing the Way We Work, Live, Play, and Learn and Cisco Store are service marks; and Access Registrar, Aironet, AsyncOS, Bringing the Meeting To You, Catalyst, CCDA, CCDP, CCIE, CCIP, CCNA, CCNP, CCSP, CCVP, Cisco, the Cisco Certified Internetwork Expert logo, Cisco IOS, Cisco Press, Cisco Systems, Cisco Systems Capital, the Cisco Systems logo, Cisco Unity, Collaboration Without Limitation, EtherFast, EtherSwitch, Event Center, Fast Step, Follow Me Browsing, FormShare, GigaDrive, HomeLink, Internet Quotient, IOS, iPhone, iQuick Study, IronPort, the IronPort logo, LightStream, Linksys, MediaTone, MeetingPlace, MeetingPlace Chime Sound, MGX, Networkers, Networking Academy, Network Registrar, PCNow, PIX, PowerPanels, ProConnect, ScriptShare, SenderBase, SMARTnet, Spectrum Expert, StackWise, The Fastest Way to Increase Your Internet Quotient, TransPath, WebEx, and the WebEx logo are registered trademarks of Cisco Systems, Inc. and/or its affiliates in the United States and certain other countries.

All other trademarks mentioned in this document or website are the property of their respective owners. The use of the word partner does not imply a partnership relationship between Cisco and any other company. (0812R)

Contents at a Glance

Contents

Command Syntax Conventions

The conventions used to present command syntax in this book are the same conventions used in the IOS Command Reference. The Command Reference describes these conventions as follows:

- **Boldface** indicates commands and keywords that are entered literally as shown. In actual configuration examples and output (not general command syntax), boldface indicates commands that are manually input by the user (such as a **show** command).

- *Italic* indicates arguments for which you supply actual values.

- Vertical bars (|) separate alternative, mutually exclusive elements.

- Square brackets ([ ]) indicate an optional element.

- Braces ({ }) indicate a required choice.

- Braces within brackets ([{ }]) indicate a required choice within an optional element.

About This Course Booklet

Your Cisco Networking Academy Course Booklet is designed as a study resource you can easily read, highlight, and review on the go, wherever the Internet is not available or practical:

- The text is extracted directly, word-for-word, from the online course so you can highlight important points and take notes in the "Your Chapter Notes" section.

- Headings with the exact page correlations provide a quick reference to the online course for your classroom discussions and exam preparation.

- An icon system directs you to the online curriculum to take full advantage of the images, labs, Packet Tracer activities, and dynamic Flash-based activities embedded within the Networking Academy online course interface.

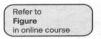

Refer to **Figure** in online course | Refer to **Lab Activity** for this chapter | Refer to **Packet Tracer Activity** for this chapter | Refer to **Interactive Graphic** in online course. | Go to the online course to take the quiz.

The Course Booklet is a faster, economical paper-based way to help you succeed with the Cisco Networking Academy online course.

Welcome

Welcome to the CCNA Discovery course, Designing and Supporting Computer Networks. The goal of this course is to assist you in developing the skills necessary to design small Enterprise LANs and WANs. The course provides an introduction to collecting customer requirements, translating those requirements into equipment and protocol needs, and creating a network topology which addresses the needs of the customer. It will also familiarize you with how to create and implement a design proposal for a customer. This course prepares you with the skills required for entry-level Pre-Sales Support and entry-level Network Design jobs.

More than just information

This computer-based learning environment is an important part of the overall course experience for students and instructors in the Networking Academy. These online course materials are designed to be used along with several other instructional tools and activities. These include:

- Class presentation, discussion, and practice with your instructor
- Hands-on labs that use networking equipment within the Networking Academy classroom
- Online scored assessments and grade book
- Packet Tracer 4.1 simulation tool
- Additional software for classroom activities

A global community

When you participate in the Networking Academy, you are joining a global community linked by common goals and technologies. Schools, colleges, universities and other entities in over 160 countries participate in the program. You can see an interactive network map of the global Networking Academy community at http://www.academynetspace.com.

The material in this course encompasses a broad range of technologies that facilitate how people work, live, play, and learn by communicating with voice, video, and other data. Networking and the Internet affect people differently in different parts of the world. Although we have worked with instructors from around the world to create these materials, it is important that you work with your instructor and fellow students to make the material in this course applicable to your local situation.

Keep in Touch

These online instructional materials, as well as the rest of the course tools, are part of the larger Networking Academy. The portal for the program is located at http://cisco.netacad.net. There you will obtain access to the other tools in the program such as the assessment server and student grade book), as well as informational updates and other relevant links.

Mind Wide Open®

An important goal in education is to enrich you, the student, by expanding what you know and can do. It is important to realize, however, that the instructional materials and the instructor can only facilitate the process. You must make the commitment yourself to learn new skills. Below are a few suggestions to help you learn and grow.

1. Take notes. Professionals in the networking field often keep Engineering Journals in which they write down the things they observe and learn. Taking notes is an important way to help your understanding grow over time.

2. Think about it. The course provides information both to change what you know and what you can do. As you go through the course, ask yourself what makes sense and what doesn't. Stop and ask questions when you are confused. Try to find out more about topics that interest you. If you are not sure why something is being taught, consider asking your instructor or a friend. Think about how the different parts of the course fit together.

3. Practice. Learning new skills requires practice. We believe this is so important to e-learning that we have a special name for it. We call it e-doing. It is very important that you complete the activities in the online instructional materials and that you also complete the hands-on labs and Packet Tracer® activities.

4. Practice again. Have you ever thought that you knew how to do something and then, when it was time to show it on a test or at work, you discovered that you really hadn't mastered it? Just like learning any new skill like a sport, game, or language, learning a professional skill requires patience and repeated practice before you can say you have truly learned it. The online instructional materials in this course provide opportunities for repeated practice for many skills. Take full advantage of them. You can also work with your instructor to extend Packet Tracer, and other tools, for additional practice as needed.

5. Teach it. Teaching a friend or colleague is often a good way to reinforce your own learning. To teach well, you will have to work through details that you may have overlooked on your first reading. Conversations about the course material with fellow students, colleagues, and the instructor can help solidify your understanding of networking concepts.

6. Make changes as you go. The course is designed to provide feedback through interactive activities and quizzes, the online assessment system, and through interactions with your instructor. You can use this feedback to better understand where your strengths and weaknesses are. If there is an area that you are having trouble with, focus on studying or practicing more in that area. Seek additional feedback from your instructor and other students.

Explore the world of networking

This version of the course includes a special tool called Packet Tracer 4.1®. Packet Tracer is a networking learning tool that supports a wide range of physical and logical simulations. It also provides visualization tools to help you to understand the internal workings of a network.

The Packet Tracer activities included in the course consist of network simulations, games, activities, and challenges that provide a broad range of learning experiences.

Create your own worlds

You can also use Packet Tracer to create your own experiments and networking scenarios. We hope that, over time, you consider using Packet Tracer – not only for experiencing the activities included in the course, but also to become an author, explorer, and experimenter.

The online course materials have embedded Packet Tracer activities that will launch on computers running Windows® operating systems, if Packet Tracer is installed. This integration may also work on other operating systems using Windows emulation.

CHAPTER 1

Introducing Network Design Concepts

Introduction

Refer to
Figure
in online course

1.1 Discovering Network Design Basics

1.1.1 Network Design Overview

Refer to
Figure
in online course

Computers and information networks are critical to the success of businesses, both large and small. They connect people, support applications and services, and provide access to the resources that keep the businesses running. To meet the daily requirements of businesses, networks themselves are becoming quite complex.

Network Requirements

Today, the Internet-based economy often demands around-the-clock customer service. This means that business networks must be available nearly 100 percent of the time. They must be smart enough to automatically protect against unexpected security incidents. These business networks must also be able to adjust to changing traffic loads to maintain consistent application response times. It is no longer practical to construct networks by connecting many standalone components without careful planning and design.

Building a Good Network

Good networks do not happen by accident. They are the result of hard work by network designers and technicians, who identify network requirements and select the best solutions to meet the needs of a business.

Refer to
Figure
in online course

Network users generally do not think in terms of the complexity of the underlying network. They think of the network as a way to access the applications they need, when they need them.

Network Requirements

Most businesses actually have only a few requirements for their network:

- The network should stay up all the time, even in the event of failed links, equipment failure, and overloaded conditions.

- The network should reliably deliver applications and provide reasonable response times from any host to any host.

- The network should be secure. It should protect the data that is transmitted over it, as well as data stored on the devices that connect to it.

- The network should be easy to modify to adapt to network growth and general business changes.

- Because failures occasionally occur, troubleshooting should be easy. Finding and fixing a problem should not be too time-consuming.

Fundamental Design Goals

When examined carefully, these requirements translate into four fundamental network design goals:

- Scalability

- Availability

- Security

- Manageability

1.1.2 The Benefits of a Hierarchical Network Design

Refer to **Figure** in online course

To meet the four fundamental design goals, a network must be built on an architecture that allows for both flexibility and growth.

Hierarchical Network Design

In networking, a hierarchical design is used to group devices into multiple networks. The networks are organized in a layered approach. The hierarchical design model has three basic layers:

- *Core Layer* - Connects Distribution Layer devices

- *Distribution Layer* - Interconnects the smaller local networks

- *Access Layer* - Provides connectivity for network hosts and end devices

Advantages Over Flat Networks

Hierarchical networks have advantages over flat network designs. The benefit of dividing a flat network into smaller, more manageable blocks is that local traffic remains local. Only traffic that is destined for other networks is moved to a higher layer.

Layer 2 devices in a flat network provide little opportunity to control broadcasts or to filter undesirable traffic. As more devices and applications are added to a flat network, response times degrade until the network becomes unusable.

Refer to **Figure** in online course

The *Cisco Enterprise Architectures* can be used to further divide the three-layer hierarchical design into modular areas. The modules represent areas that have different physical or logical connectivity. They designate where different functions occur in the network. This modularity enables flexibility in network design. It facilitates implementation and troubleshooting. Three areas of focus in modular network design are:

- *Enterprise Campus* - This area contains the network elements required for independent operation within a single campus or branch location.

- *Server Farmlink* - A component of the enterprise campus, the data center server farm protects the server resources and provides redundant, reliable high-speed connectivity.

- *Enterprise Edge* - As traffic comes into the campus network, this area filters traffic from the external resources and routes it into the enterprise network. It contains all the elements required for efficient and secure communication between the enterprise campus and remote locations, remote users, and the Internet.

Refer to
Figure
in online course

The modular framework of the Cisco Enterprise Architectures has the following design advantages:

- It creates a *deterministic network* with clearly defined boundaries between modules. This provides clear demarcation points so that the network designer knows exactly where the traffic originates and where it flows.

- It eases the design task by making each module independent. The designer can focus on the needs of each area separately.

- It provides scalability by allowing enterprises to add modules easily. As network complexity grows, the designer can add new functional modules.

- It enables the designer to add services and solutions without changing the underlying network design.

Refer to
Interactive Graphic
in online course.

Full Screen Activity

Drag the characteristics of the hierarchical model and the Cisco Enterprise Architectures to the correct locations, then click Check.

1.1.3 Network Design Methodologies

Refer to
Figure
in online course

Large network design projects are normally divided into three distinct steps:

Step 1: Identify the network requirements.

Step 2: Characterize the existing network.

Step 3: Design the network topology and solutions.

Identifying Network Requirements

The network designer works closely with the customer to document the goals of the project. Goals are usually separated into two categories:

- Business goals - Focus on how the network can make the business more successful

- Technical requirements - Focus on how the technology is implemented within the network.

Characterizing the Existing Network

Information about the current network and services is gathered and analyzed. It is necessary to compare the functionality of the existing network with the defined goals of the new project. The designer determines whether any existing equipment, infrastructure, and protocols can be re-used, and what new equipment and protocols are needed to complete the design.

Designing the Network Topology

A common strategy for network design is to take a *top-down approach*. In this approach, the network applications and service requirements are identified, and then the network is designed to support them.

When the design is complete, a prototype or proof-of-concept test is performed. This approach ensures that the new design functions as expected before it is implemented.

Refer to
Figure
in online course

A common mistake made by network designers is the failure to correctly determine the scope of the network design project.

Determining the Scope of the Project

While gathering requirements, the designer identifies the issues that affect the entire network and those that affect only specific portions. Failure to understand the impact of a particular requirement often causes a project scope to expand beyond the original estimate. This oversight can greatly increase the cost and time required to implement the new design.

Impacting the Entire Network

Network requirements that impact the entire network include:

- Adding new network applications and making major changes to existing applications, such as database or DNS structure changes

- Improving the efficiency of network addressing or routing protocol changes

- Integrating new security measures

- Adding new network services, such as voice traffic, *content networking*, and *storage networking*

- Relocating servers to a data center server farm

Refer to
Figure
in online course

Impacting a Portion of the Network

Requirements that may only affect a portion of the network include:

- Improving Internet connectivity and adding bandwidth

- Updating Access Layer LAN cabling

- Providing redundancy for key services

- Supporting wireless access in defined areas

- Upgrading WAN bandwidth

These requirements may not affect many users or require many changes to the installed equipment. It is sometimes possible to integrate design changes into the existing network without disrupting the normal network operations for the majority of network users. This method reduces the costs associated with downtime and speeds the implementation of the network upgrade.

Refer to
Interactive Graphic
in online course.

Activity

Determine whether the requirement affects the entire network or only a portion of the network by placing a check in the appropriate column. Then click Check.

1.2 Investigating Core Layer Design Considerations

1.2.1 What Happens at the Core Layer?

Refer to
Figure
in online course

The Core Layer is sometimes called the *network backbone*. Routers and switches at the Core Layer provide high-speed connectivity. In an enterprise LAN, the Core Layer may connect multiple buildings or multiple sites, as well as provide connectivity to the server farm. The Core Layer includes one or more links to the devices at the enterprise edge in order to support Internet, Virtual Private Networks (*VPN*s), *extranet*, and WAN access.

Implementing a Core Layer reduces the complexity of the network, making it easier to manage and troubleshoot.

Goals of the Core Layer

The Core Layer design enables the efficient, high-speed transfer of data between one section of the network and another. The primary design goals at the Core Layer are to:

- Provide 100% uptime
- Maximize throughput
- Facilitate network growth

Core Layer Technologies

Technologies used at the Core Layer include:

- Routers or *multilayer switch*es that combine routing and switching in the same device
- Redundancy and *load balancing*
- High-speed and aggregate links
- Routing protocols that scale well and converge quickly, such as Enhanced Interior Gateway Routing Protocol (*EIGRP*) and Open Shortest Path First (*OSPF*) protocol

Refer to **Figure** in online course

Redundant Links

Implementing redundant links at the Core Layer ensures that network devices can find alternate paths to send data in the event of a failure. When Layer 3 devices are placed at the Core Layer, these redundant links can be used for load balancing in addition to providing backup. In a flat, Layer 2 network design, Spanning Tree Protocol (*STP*) disables redundant links unless a primary link fails. This STP behavior prevents load balancing over the redundant links.

Mesh Topology

Most Core Layers in a network are wired in either a *full mesh* or *partial mesh* topology. A full mesh topology is one in which every device has a connection to every other device. While full mesh topologies provide the benefit of a fully redundant network, they can be difficult to wire and manage and are more costly. For larger installations, a modified partial mesh topology is used. In a partial mesh topology, each device is connected to at least two others, creating sufficient redundancy without the complexity of a full mesh.

Refer to **Packet Tracer Activity** for this chapter

Packet Tracer Activity

Create and compare full mesh and partial mesh topologies between routers.

1.2.2 Network Traffic Prioritization

Refer to **Figure** in online course

Preventing Failures

The network designer must strive to provide a network that is resistant to failures and can recover quickly in the event of a failure. Core routers and switches can contain:

- Dual power supplies and fans
- A modular chassis-based design
- Additional management modules

Redundant components increase the cost, but they are usually well worth the investment. Core layer devices should have *hot-swappable* components whenever possible. Hot-swappable components can be installed or removed without first having to turn off the power to the device. Using these components reduces repair time and disruption to network services.

Larger enterprises often install generators and large *UPS* devices. These devices prevent minor power outages from causing large-scale network failures.

Reducing Human Error

Human errors contribute to network failures. Unfortunately, the addition of redundant links and equipment cannot eliminate these factors. Many network failures are the result of poorly planned, untested updates or additions of new equipment. Never make a configuration change on a production network without first testing it in a lab environment!

Failures at the Core Layer cause widespread outages. It is critical to have written policies and procedures in place to govern how changes are approved, tested, installed, and documented. Plan a back-out strategy to return the network to its previous state if changes are not successful.

1.2.3 Network Convergence

Refer to
Figure
in online course

The choice of a routing protocol for the Core Layer is determined by the size of the network and the number of redundant links or paths available. A major factor in choosing a protocol is how quickly it recovers from a link or device failure.

Convergence

Network convergence occurs when all routers have complete and accurate information about the network. The faster the *convergence time*, the quicker a network can react to a change in topology. Factors that affect convergence time include:

- The speed at which the routing updates reach all of the routers in the network
- The time that it takes each router to perform the calculation to determine the best paths

Selecting a Routing Protocol

Most dynamic routing protocols offer acceptable convergence times in small networks. In larger networks, protocols like RIPv2 may converge too slowly to prevent disruption of network services if a link fails. Generally, in a large enterprise network, EIGRP or OSPF provide the most stable routing solution.

Design Considerations

Most networks contain a combination of dynamic and static routes. Network designers need to consider the number of routes required to ensure that all destinations in the network are reachable. Large routing tables can take significant time to converge. The design of network addressing and summarization strategies in all layers affects how well the routing protocol can react to a failure.

Refer to **Packet Tracer Activity**
for this chapter

Packet Tracer Activity

Using the existing topology, add a new LAN segment to observe network convergence.

1.3 Investigating Distribution Layer Considerations

1.3.1 What Happens at the Distribution Layer?

Refer to
Figure
in online course

The Distribution Layer represents a routing boundary between the Access Layer and the Core Layer. It also serves as a connection point between remote sites and the Core Layer.

Distribution Layer Routing

The Access Layer is commonly built using Layer 2 switching technology. The Distribution Layer is built using Layer 3 devices. Routers or multilayer switches, located at the Distribution Layer, provide many functions that are critical for meeting the goals of the network design. These goals include:

- Filtering and managing traffic flows

- Enforcing access control policies

- Summarizing routes before advertising the routes to the Core

- Isolating the Core from Access Layer failures or disruptions

- Routing between Access Layer VLANs

Distribution Layer devices are also used to manage queues and prioritize traffic before transmission through the campus core.

Refer to **Figure** in online course

Trunks

Trunk links are often configured between Access and Distribution Layer networking devices. Trunks are used to carry traffic that belongs to multiple VLANs between devices over the same link. The network designer considers the overall VLAN strategy and network traffic patterns when designing the trunk links.

Redundant Links

When redundant links exist between devices in the Distribution Layer, the devices can be configured to load balance the traffic across the links. Load balancing increases the bandwidth available for applications.

Distribution Layer Topology

Distribution Layer networks are usually wired in a partial mesh topology. This topology provides enough redundant paths to ensure that the network can survive a link or device failure. When the Distribution Layer devices are located in the same wiring closet or data center, they are interconnected using Gigabit links. When the devices are separated by longer distances, fiber cable is used. Switches that support multiple high speed fiber connections can be expensive, so careful planning is necessary to ensure that enough fiber ports are available to provide the desired bandwidth and redundancy.

Refer to **Packet Tracer Activity** for this chapter

Packet Tracer Activity

Demonstrate the functions performed by the Distribution Layer devices.

1.3.2 Limiting the Scope of Network Failure

Refer to **Figure** in online course

A failure domain defines the portion of the network that is affected when either a device or network application fails.

Limiting the Size of Failure Domains

Because failures at the Core Layer of a network have a large impact, the network designer often concentrates on efforts to prevent failures. These efforts can greatly increase the cost to implement the network. In the hierarchical design model, it is easiest and usually least expensive to control the size of a failure domain in the Distribution Layer. In the Distribution Layer, network errors can be contained to a smaller area, thus affecting fewer users. When using Layer 3 devices at the Distribution Layer, every router functions as a gateway for a limited number of Access Layer users.

Switch Block Deployment

Routers, or multilayer switches, are usually deployed in pairs, with Access Layer switches evenly divided between them. This configuration is referred to as a building or departmental *switch block*. Each switch block acts independently of the others. As a result, the failure of a single device does not cause the network to go down. Even the failure of an entire switch block does not impact a significant number of end users.

Refer to **Packet Tracer Activity** for this chapter

Packet Tracer Activity

Turn off the devices and disable interfaces to see the resulting network failures.

1.3.3 Building a Redundant Network

Refer to **Figure** in online course

To reduce downtime, the network designer deploys redundancy in the network.

Redundancy at the Distribution Layer

Devices at the Distribution Layer have redundant connections to switches at the Access Layer and to devices at the Core Layer. If a link or device fails, these connections provide alternate paths. Using an appropriate routing protocol at the Distribution Layer, the Layer 3 devices react quickly to link failures so that they do not impact network operations.

Providing multiple connections to Layer 2 switches can cause unstable behavior in a network unless STP is enabled. Without STP, redundant links in a Layer 2 network can cause broadcast storms. Switches are unable to correctly learn the ports, so traffic ends up being flooded throughout the switch. By disabling one of the links, STP guarantees that only one path is active between two devices. If one of the links fails, the switch recalculates the spanning tree topology and automatically begins using the alternate link.

Rapid Spanning Tree Protocol (RSTP), as defined in IEEE 802.1w, builds upon the IEEE 802.1d technology and provides rapid convergence of the spanning tree.

Refer to **Figure** in online course

A high volume, enterprise server is connected to a switch port. If that port recalculates because of STP, the server is down for 50 seconds. It would be difficult to imagine the number of transactions lost during that timeframe.

In a stable network, STP recalculations are infrequent. In an unstable network, it is important to check the switches for stability and configuration changes. One of the most common causes of frequent STP recalculations is a faulty power supply or power feed to a switch. A faulty power supply causes the device to reboot unexpectedly.

1.3.4 Traffic Filtering at the Distribution Layer

Refer to **Figure** in online course

Access control lists (ACLs) are a tool that can be used at the Distribution Layer to limit access and to prevent unwanted traffic from entering the Core network. An *ACL* is a list of conditions used to test network traffic that attempts to travel through a router interface. ACL statements identify which packets to accept or which to deny.

Filtering Network Traffic

To filter network traffic, the router examines each packet and then either forwards or discards it, based on the conditions specified in the ACL. There are different types of ACLs for different purposes. Standard ACLs filter traffic based on the source address. Extended ACLs can filter based on multiple criteria including:

- Source address
- Destination address

- Protocols

- Port numbers or applications

- Whether the packet is part of an established TCP stream

Both standard and extended ACLs can be configured as either numbered or named access lists.

Complex ACLs

Standard and extended ACLs serve as the basis for other, more complex types of ACLs. Using Cisco IOS software, there are three complex ACL features that can be configured: dynamic, reflexive, and time-based.

Dynamic ACL - requires a user to use Telnet to connect to the router and authenticate. Once authenticated, traffic from the user is permitted. Dynamic ACLs are sometimes referred to as "lock and key" because the user is required to login in order to obtain access.

Reflexive ACL - allows outbound traffic and then limits inbound traffic to only responses to those permitted requests. This is similar to the `established` keyword used in extended ACL statements, except that these ACLs can also inspect UDP and ICMP traffic, in addition to TCP.

Time-based ACL - permits and denies specified traffic based on the time of day or day of the week.

Placing ACLs

Traffic that travels into an interface is filtered by the inbound ACL. Traffic going out of an interface is filtered by the outbound access control list. The network designer must decide where to place ACLs within the network to achieve the desired results.

Refer to **Interactive Graphic** in online course.

Full Screen **Activity**

Drag the correct ACL to the appropriate statement, then click Check.

Refer to **Packet Tracer Activity** for this chapter

Packet Tracer Activity

Place the ACLs onto the appropriate interface in the topology.

Refer to **Lab Activity** for this chapter

Lab Activity

Create an ACL to meet the conditions specified in the lab.

1.3.5 Routing Protocols at the Distribution Layer

Refer to **Figure** in online course

Another important function that occurs at the Distribution Layer is route summarization, also called route aggregation or supernetting.

Route Summarization

Route summarization has several advantages for the network, such as:

- One route in the routing table that represents many other routes, creating smaller routing tables

- Less routing update traffic on the network

- Lower overhead on the router

Summarization can be performed manually or automatically, depending on which routing protocols are used in the network.

Classless routing protocols such as RIPv2, *EIGRP*, OSPF, and *IS-IS*, support route summarization based on subnet addresses on any boundary.

Classful routing protocols such as RIPv1, automatically summarize routes on the classful network boundary, but do not support summarization on any other boundaries.

Refer to
Interactive Graphic
in online course.

Full Screen **Activity**

Drag the summary route to the appropriate location.

1.4 Investigating Access Layer Design Considerations

1.4.1 What Happens at the Access Layer?

Refer to
Figure
in online course

The Access Layer represents the edge of the network where end devices connect. Access Layer services and devices reside inside each building of a campus, each remote site and server farm, and at the enterprise edge.

Access Layer Physical Considerations

The Access Layer of the campus infrastructure uses Layer 2 switching technology to provide access into the network. The access can be either through a permanent wired infrastructure or through wireless Access Points. Ethernet over copper wiring poses distance limitations. Therefore, one of the primary concerns when designing the Access Layer of a campus infrastructure is the physical location of the equipment.

Wiring Closets

Wiring closets can be actual closets or small telecommunication rooms that act as the termination point for infrastructure cabling within buildings or within floors of a building. The placement and physical size of the wiring closets depends on network size and expansion plans.

The wiring closet equipment provides power to end devices such as IP phones and wireless Access Points. Many Access Layer switches have Power-over-Ethernet (*PoE*) functionality.

Unlike a typical wiring closet, inside a server farm or data center the Access Layer devices are typically redundant multilayer switches that combine the functionality of both routing and switching. Multilayer switches can provide firewall and intrusion protection features, as well as Layer 3 functions.

Refer to
Figure
in online course

The Impact of Converged Networking

The modern computer network consists of more than just personal computers and printers connecting to the Access Layer. Many different devices can connect to an IP network, including:

- IP telephones
- Video cameras
- Video conferencing systems

All of these services can be converged onto a single physical Access Layer infrastructure. However, the logical network design to support them becomes more complex due to considerations such as QoS, traffic segregation, and filtering. These new types of end devices, and the associated applications and services, change the requirements for scalability, availability, security and manageability at the Access Layer.

The Need for Availability

In early networks, high availability was usually present only at the network core, enterprise edge, and data center networks. With IP telephony, there is now an expectation that every individual telephone should be available 100% of the time.

Redundant components and *failover* strategies can be implemented at the Access Layer to improve reliability and increase availability for the end devices.

Refer to **Figure** in online course

Access Layer Management

Improving the manageability of the Access Layer is a major concern for the network designer. Access Layer management is crucial due to:

- The increase in the number and types of devices connecting at the Access Layer
- The introduction of wireless access points into the LAN

Designing for Manageability

In addition to providing basic connectivity at the Access Layer, the designer needs to consider:

- Naming structures
- VLAN architecture
- Traffic patterns
- Prioritization strategies

Configuring and using network management systems for a large converged network is very important. It is also important to standardize configurations and equipment when possible.

Following good design principles improves the manageability and on-going support of the network by:

- Ensuring that the network does not become too complex
- Allowing easy troubleshooting when there is a problem
- Making it easier to add new features and services in the future

Refer to **Packet Tracer Activity** for this chapter

Packet Tracer Activity

Explore different Access Layer functions.

1.4.2 Network Topologies at the Access Layer

Refer to **Figure** in online course

Most recent Ethernet networks use a star topology, which is sometimes called a hub and spoke topology. In a star topology, each end device has a direct connection to a single networking device. This single networking device is usually a Layer 2 or multilayer switch. A wired star topology in the Access Layer typically has no redundancy from individual end devices to the switch. For many businesses, the cost of additional wiring to create redundancy is usually too high.

The advantages of a star topology include:

- Easy installation
- Minimal configuration

The disadvantages of a star topology are significant:

- The central device represents a single point of failure.

- The capabilities of the central device can limit overall performance for access to the network.

- The topology does not recover in the event of a failure when there are no redundant links.

Ethernet star topologies usually have a combination of the following wiring:

- Twisted pair wiring to connect to the individual end devices

- Fiber to interconnect the access switches to the Distribution Layer devices

Refer to **Packet Tracer Activity** for this chapter

Packet Tracer Activity

Create an access layer star topology.

1.4.3   How VLANs Segregate and Control Network Traffic

Refer to **Figure** in online course

Using VLANs to Segregate Traffic

Using VLANs and IP subnets is the most common method for segregating user groups and traffic within the Access Layer network.

VLANs in the Past

With the introduction of Layer 2 switching, VLANs were used to create end-to-end workgroup networks. The networks connected across buildings or even across the entire infrastructure. End-to-end VLANs are no longer used in this way. The increased number of users and the volume of network traffic that these users generate is too high to be supported.

VLANs Now

Today VLANs are used to separate and classify traffic streams and to control broadcast traffic within a single wiring closet or building. Although large VLANs that span entire networks are no longer recommended, they may be required to support special applications, such as wireless roaming and wireless IP phones.

The recommended approach is to contain VLANs within a single wiring closet. This approach increases the number of VLANs in a network, which also increases the number of individual IP subnets. It is recommended practice to associate a single IP subnet with a single VLAN. IP addressing at the Access Layer becomes a critical design issue that affects the scalability of the entire network.

Refer to **Lab Activity** for this chapter

Lab Activity

Monitor traffic passing through a VLAN.

1.4.4   Services at the Network Edge

Refer to **Figure** in online course

Providing Quality of Service to Network Applications

Networks must provide secure, predictable, measurable and, at times, guaranteed services. Networks also need mechanisms to control congestion when traffic increases. Congestion is caused when the demand on the network resources exceeds the available capacity.

All networks have limited resources. For this reason, networks need QoS mechanisms. The ability to provide QoS depends on traffic classification and the assigned priority.

Classification

Before designing QoS strategies, it is necessary to classify applications based on specific delivery requirements. Classifying data at or near the source enables the data to be assigned the appropriate priority as it moves through the entire network. Segregating traffic with similar characteristics into classes, and then marking that traffic, is a function of the network devices at the Access and Distribution Layers. An example of this strategy is to place the voice traffic on an access switch into a single VLAN. The device then marks the traffic originating from the voice VLAN with the highest priority.

1.4.5 Security at the Network Edge

Refer to
Figure
in online course

Security Risks at the Access Layer

Many of the security risks that occur at the Access Layer of the network are the result of poorly-secured end devices. User error and carelessness account for a significant number of network security breaches.

How Can the Network Designer Improve Security?

Providing adequate security for end devices may not be in the scope of a network design project. Nevertheless, the designer needs to understand the network impact of a security incident, such as a worm or a trojan, at an end device. The designer can then better determine what network security measures to put in place to limit the effects on the network.

Permitting network access to only known or authenticated devices limits the ability of intruders to enter the network. It is important to apply wireless security measures that follow recommended practices.

Refer to
Lab Activity
for this chapter

Lab Activity

Use the SANS site to identify Internet security threats.

1.4.6 Security Measures

Refer to
Figure
in online course

Providing Physical Security

Physical security of a network is very important. Most network intruders gain physical entry at the Access Layer. On some network devices, like routers and switches, physical access can provide the opportunity to change passwords and obtain full access to devices.

Obvious measures, like locking wiring closets and restricting access to networking devices, are often the most effective ways to prevent security breaches. In high risk or easily accessible areas, it may be necessary to equip wiring closets with additional security, such as cameras or motion detection devices and alarms. Some devices, such as keypad locks, can record which codes are used to enter the secured areas.

Securing Access Layer Networking Devices

The simple measures below can provide additional security to networking devices at the Access Layer:

- Setting strong passwords
- Using SSH to administer devices
- Disabling unused ports

Switch port security and *network access control* can ensure that only known and trusted devices have access to the network.

Recommended Practice on Security

Security risks cannot be eliminated or prevented completely. Effective risk management and assessment can significantly minimize the existing security risks. When considering security measures, it is important to understand that no single product can make an organization secure. True network security comes from a combination of products, services, and procedures as well as a thorough *security policy* and a commitment to adhere to that policy.

Refer to
Lab Activity
for this chapter

Lab Activity

Learn the risks of allowing physical access to the network by unauthorized persons.

Refer to
Lab Activity
for this chapter

Lab Activity

Implement port security to prevent unauthorized access.

1.5 Investigating Server Farms and Security

1.5.1 What is a Server Farm?

Refer to
Figure
in online course

Most enterprise networks provide users with Internet-accessible services, like email and e-commerce. The availability and security of these services is crucial to the success of a business.

Server Farms

Managing and securing numerous distributed servers at various locations within a business network is difficult. Recommended practice centralizes servers in *server farm*s. Server farms are typically located in computer rooms and *data center*s.

Creating a server farm has the following benefits:

- Network traffic enters and leaves the server farm at a defined point. This arrangement makes it easier to secure, filter, and prioritize traffic.

- Redundant, high-capacity links can be installed to the servers as well as between the server farm network and the main LAN. This configuration is more cost-effective than attempting to provide a similar level of connectivity to servers distributed throughout the network.

- *Load balancing* and *failover* can be provided between servers and between networking devices.

- The number of high-capacity switches and security devices is reduced, helping to lower the cost of providing services.

Refer to **Packet
Tracer Activity**
for this chapter

Packet Tracer Activity

Observe and record the way in which traffic moves to and from the servers on the network.

1.5.2 Security, Firewalls, and DMZs

Refer to
Figure
in online course

Data center servers can be the target of malicious attacks and must be protected.

Attacks against server farms can result in lost business for e-commerce and business-to-business applications as well as information theft. Both local area networks (LANs) and storage area networks (*SAN*s) must be secured to reduce the chances of such attacks. Hackers use a variety of tools to inspect networks and to launch intrusion and denial of service (*DoS*) attacks.

Protecting Server Farms Against Attack

Firewalls are often deployed to provide a basic level of security when internal and external users attempt to access the Internet via the server farm. To properly secure server farms, a more thorough approach must be followed. Such an approach takes advantage of the strengths of the following network products that can be deployed in a server farm:

- Firewalls

- LAN switch security features

- Host-based and network-based intrusion detection and prevention systems

- Load balancers

- Network analysis and management devices

Refer to **Figure** in online course

Demilitarized Zones

In the traditional network firewall design, servers that needed to be accessed from external networks were located on a demilitarized zone (*DMZ*). Users accessing these servers from the Internet or other untrusted external networks were prevented from seeing resources located on the internal LAN. LAN users were treated as trusted users and usually had few restrictions imposed when they accessed servers on the DMZ.

Protecting Against Internal Attacks

Attacks originating on the internal network are now more common than attacks from external sources. As a result, the design of server farm security is different from the older DMZ model. A layer of firewall features and intrusion protection is required between the servers and the internal networks, as well as between the servers and the external users. An additional security layer between the servers may also be required.

The sensitivity of data stored on the servers and contained in the transactions traveling the network determines the appropriate security policy for the design of the server farm.

1.5.3 High Availability

Refer to **Figure** in online course

Providing High Availability

In addition to providing an extra layer of security, server farms are usually required to provide high availability for network applications and services. A highly available network is one that eliminates or reduces the potential impact of failures. This protection enables the network to meet requirements for access to applications, systems, and data from anywhere, at any time.

Building in Redundancy

To achieve high availability, servers are redundantly connected to two separate switches at the Access Layer. This redundancy provides a path from the server to the secondary switch if the primary switch fails. Devices at the Distribution and Core Layers of the server farm network are also redundantly connected. Spanning Tree Protocols, like Enhanced Rapid Spanning Tree Protocol (*RSTP+*), manage redundant Layer 2 links. Hot Standby Router Protocol (HSRP) and routing protocols provide support for Layer 3 redundancy and failover.

Virtualization

Many separate logical servers can be located on one physical server. The physical server uses an operating system specifically designed to support multiple virtual images. This feature is known as virtualization. This technology reduces the cost of providing redundant services, load balancing, and failover for critical network services.

Refer to **Packet Tracer Activity** for this chapter

Packet Tracer Activity

Set up redundant switch links in a server farm and observe what happens when one device fails.

1.6 Investigating Wireless Network Considerations

1.6.1 Considerations Unique to WLAN

Refer to
Figure
in online course

Understanding Customer Requirements

Before designing an indoor wireless LAN (*WLAN*) implementation, the network designer needs to fully understand how the customer intends to use the wireless network.

The designer learns about the network requirements by asking the customer questions. The answers to these questions affect how a wireless network is implemented. Examples of some of these questions are:

- Will wireless roaming be required?
- What authentication for users is needed?
- Will open access (hotspots) be provided for the guests?
- Which network services and applications are available to wireless users?
- What encryption technique can be used?
- Are wireless IP telephones planned?
- Which coverage areas need to be supported?
- How many users are in each coverage area?

If the designer does not get answers to the questions or fully understand the customer requirements, implementing a wireless LAN will be difficult, if not impossible. For example, the requirements to provide unsecured hotspots are significantly less complex to design than authenticated access to protected internal servers.

Refer to
Figure
in online course

Physical Network Design

In typical wireless network designs, most of the effort focuses on the physical coverage areas of the network.

The network designer conducts a site survey to determine the coverage areas for the network and to find the optimum locations for mounting wireless Access Points. The site survey results help determine the Access Point hardware, types of antennas, and the desired wireless feature sets. The designer determines that roaming between overlapping coverage areas can be supported.

Logical Network Design

Designing the logical network usually causes network designers the most difficulty. Customers often want to provide different levels of access to different types of wireless users. In addition, wireless networks must be both easy to use and secure. Resolving both the desired features and the constraints presents many different ways to design and configure wireless LANs.

An example of a complex wireless network design is a business that needs to offer the following services:

- Open wireless access for their visitors and vendors
- Secured wireless access for their mobile employees
- Reliable connectivity for wireless IP phones

1.6.2 Considerations Unique to WLAN

Refer to
Figure
in online course

Each type of wireless access requires unique design considerations.

Open Guest Access

When visitors and vendors are at a business site, they often require access to email and web sites. This type of access must be convenient to use, and typically is not Wired Equivalent Privacy (*WEP*) or Wi-Fi Protected Access (*WPA*) encrypted. To help guest users connect to the network, the Access Point service set identifier (*SSID*) is broadcast.

Many hotspot guest systems use DHCP and a logging server to register and record wireless use. Guest users typically access the wireless network by opening a browser window and agreeing to a specified usage policy. The guest registration system records the user information and hardware address and then begins logging the IP traffic. These systems require an application server to be installed on the same network or VLAN as the Access Points.

Secured Employee Access

Some WLAN devices do not support isolated guest access. To secure employee access, use an entirely separate WLAN infrastructure that does not include guest access. The recommended practice is to separate the internal users on a different VLAN.

Other wireless implementation recommended practices include:

- Non-broadcast SSID
- Strong encryption
- User authentication
- Virtual private network (*VPN*) tunneling for sensitive data
- Firewall and intrusion prevention

In areas where secured wireless is restricted to a few devices, MAC address filtering can be used to limit access.

1.7 Supporting WANs and Remote Workers

1.7.1 Design Considerations at the Enterprise Edge

Refer to
Figure
in online course

The enterprise edge is the area of the network where the enterprise network connects to external networks. Routers at the enterprise edge provide connectivity between the internal campus infrastructure and the Internet. They also provide connectivity to remote WAN users and services. The design requirements at the enterprise edge differ from those within the campus network.

Cost of Bandwidth

Most campus networks are built on Ethernet technology. However, WAN connectivity at the enterprise edge is usually leased from a third-party telecommunications service provider. Because these leased services can be expensive, the bandwidth available to WAN connections is often significantly less than the bandwidth available in the LAN.

QoS

The difference in bandwidth between the LAN and the WAN can create bottlenecks. These bottlenecks cause data to be queued by the edge routers. Anticipating and managing the queuing of data requires a Quality of Service (QoS) strategy. As a result, the design and implementation of WAN links can be complicated.

Security

Because the users and services accessed through the edge routers are not always known, security requirements at the enterprise edge are critical. Intrusion detection and stateful firewall inspection must be implemented to protect the internal campus network from potential threats.

Remote Access

In many cases, the campus LAN services must extend through the enterprise edge to remote offices and workers. This type of access has different requirements than the level of public access provided to users coming into the LAN from the Internet.

1.7.2 Integrating Remote Sites Into the Network Design

Refer to **Figure** in online course

Designing a network to support branch locations and remote workers requires the network designer to be familiar with the capabilities of the various WAN technologies. Traditional WAN technologies include:

- Leased lines
- Circuit-switched networks
- Packet-switched networks, such as Frame Relay networks
- *Cell-switched networks* such as Asynchronous Transfer Mode (*ATM*) networks

In many locations, newer WAN technologies are available, such as:

- Digital Subscriber Line (DSL)
- Metro Ethernet
- Cable modem
- Long-range wireless
- Multiprotocol Label Switching (MPLS)

Most WAN technologies are leased on a monthly basis from a telecommunications service provider. Depending on the distances, this type of connectivity can be quite expensive. WAN contracts often include service level agreements (*SLA*s). These agreements guarantee the service level offered by the service provider. SLAs support critical business applications, such as IP telephony and high-speed transaction processing to remote locations.

Refer to **Figure** in online course

In many companies, not every employee works on the main site premises. Employees who work offsite can include:

- Remote workers
- Mobile workers
- Branch employees

Remote workers usually work one or more days a week from home or from another location. Mobile workers may be constantly traveling to different locations or be permanently deployed at a customer site. Some workers are employed at small branch offices. In any case, these employees need to have connectivity to the enterprise network. As the Internet has grown, businesses have turned to it as a means of extending their own networks.

Virtual Private Networks

One very common connectivity option, especially for remote workers, is a virtual private network (*VPN*) through the Internet. A VPN is a private network that uses a public network to connect remote sites or users together. Instead of using a dedicated, real-world connection, such as leased lines, a VPN uses virtual connections routed through the Internet from the company private network to the remote router or PC.

Refer to
Interactive Graphic
in online course.

Full Screen

Activity

Roll over the photos to view information specific to that remote worker. Drag the connection type to the appropriate remote worker, then click Check.

1.7.3 Redundancy and Backup Links

Refer to
Figure
in online course

Redundant Links

Redundancy is required on WAN links and is vitally important to ensure reliable connectivity to remote sites and users.

Some business applications require that all packets be delivered in a timely fashion. For these applications, dropped connectivity is not an option. Providing redundancy on the WAN and throughout the internetwork ensures high availability for end-to-end applications.

For a WAN, backup links provide the required redundancy. Backup links often use different technologies than the primary connection. This method ensures that if a failure occurs in one system, it does not necessarily affect the backup system.

For example, a business that uses point-to-point WAN connections to remote sites can use VPNs through the Internet as an alternate strategy for redundancy. DSL, ISDN, and dialup modems are other connectivity options used to provide backup links in the event of a WAN failure. Although the backup links are frequently slower than the primary connections, they can be configured to forward only high-priority data and transactions.

Load Sharing

In addition to providing a backup strategy, redundant WAN connections can provide additional bandwidth through load sharing. The backup link can be configured to provide additional bandwidth all of the time or during peak traffic time only.

Refer to
Interactive Graphic
in online course.

Full Screen

Activity

Drag the connectivity option to the appropriate cloud for each network location.

Summary

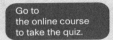

Quiz

Take the chapter quiz to check your knowledge.

Your Chapter Notes

CHAPTER 2

Gathering Network Requirements

Introduction

2.1 Introducing Cisco Lifecycle Services

2.1.1 The Lifecycle of a Network

Refer to
Figure
in online course

The world of networking is evolving. Networking is no longer just about connecting computers. Networking has become intelligent and plays a vital role in helping to improve business performance. Businesses are eager to expand their networks. Taking advantage of advances in technology, companies can add new services and increase productivity.

Cisco Lifecycle Services

Cisco Lifecycle Services is designed to support evolving networks. Cisco Lifecycle Services is a six-phase approach. Each phase defines the activities required to successfully deploy and operate Cisco technologies. It also details how to optimize performance throughout the lifecycle of a network.

The six phases of the Cisco Lifecycle Services are:

- The Prepare Phase
- The Plan Phase
- The Design Phase
- The Implement Phase
- The Operate Phase
- The Optimize Phase

This process is often referred to as *PPDIOO*, based on the first letters of each of the six phases.

Case Study: Sports Stadium Network

Refer to
Figure
in online course

The management organization of a stadium is working with the NetworkingCompany to renovate and update the stadium network. Over the years, the stadium network has grown. However, little thought was given to overall business goals and infrastructure design. Some new projects went ahead. But the network administrators did not have a realistic understanding of the bandwidth, traffic prioritization, and other requirements needed to support such an advanced and business-critical network. The stadium management now wants to add new high-tech features, but the existing network is not capable of supporting them.

Phases of the Network Lifecycle

NetworkingCompany representatives meet with the stadium management to discuss the process they intend to use to design the new network. Although the Design Phase is only one of the phases in the network lifecycle, all of the PPDIOO phases impact the design decisions.

In the Prepare and Plan phases, the network designer and stadium staff identify the business goals and technical requirements of the stadium organization as well as any design constraints. The requirements gathering that occurs during these phases influences the decisions made during the Design Phase.

The Implement Phase begins after the approval of the design. It includes the initial integration of the new design into the existing network.

During the Operate and Optimize phases, the stadium personnel analyze and monitor the network performance.

2.1.2 The Network Lifecycle Prepare Phase

Refer to **Figure** in online course

The Prepare Phase

During the Prepare Phase, the stadium management and NetworkingCompany staff define the following business goals:

- Improve customer experience
- Reduce costs
- Add additional services
- Support company expansion

These goals provide a foundation for a *business case*. The business case is used to justify the financial investment required to implement the technology change. The company considers possible business constraints, including budget, personnel, company policies, and schedule limitations.

After the business case is accepted, the NetworkingCompany staff assists in the development of the high-level technology strategy and solution.

This strategy identifies:

- Advanced technologies that support the new network solution
- Current and planned network applications and services, and their priorities based on business goals
- People, processes, and tools required to support the operations and management of the technology solution

The Prepare Phase is typically done before a company issues a Request For Proposal (*RFP*) or Request For Quotation (*RFQ*). RFPs and RFQs describe the requirements for the new network. They include information about the process that the company uses to purchase and install networking technologies.

2.1.3 The Network Lifecycle Plan Phase

Refer to **Figure** in online course

The Plan Phase

During the Plan Phase, the network designer performs a comprehensive site and operations assessment. This assessment evaluates the current network, operations, and network management infrastructure.

The NetworkingCompany staff identifies all physical, environmental, and electrical modifications. They assess the ability of the current operations and network management infrastructure to support the new technology solution. All changes to infrastructure, personnel, processes, and tools must be completed before the implementation of the new technology solution.

Custom applications that add to the feature and functionality requirements for the new network are also identified in this phase. The NetworkingCompany staff creates a document that contains all of the design requirements.

The Project Plan

In this phase, the NetworkingCompany staff and stadium management create a plan to help manage the project. The project plan includes:

- Tasks
- Timelines and critical milestones
- Risks and constraints
- Responsibilities
- Resources required

The plan needs to be within the scope, cost, and resource limits established in the original business goals. Both the stadium management and the NetworkingCompany assign individuals to manage the project.

Refer to **Lab Activity** for this chapter

Lab Activity

From the information provided, identify the business goals and constraints for the FilmCompany.

2.1.4 The Network Lifecycle Design Phase

Refer to **Figure** in online course

The Design Phase

In the Design Phase, the NetworkingCompany staff uses the initial requirements determined during the Plan Phase to direct its work.

The design requirements document supports the specifications identified in the Prepare and Plan phases for:

- *Availability*
- *Scalability*
- *Security*
- *Manageability*

The design must be flexible enough to allow for changes or additions as new goals or needs emerge. The technology must be integrated into the current operations and network management infrastructure.

Planning the Installation

At the end of the Design Phase, the network designer creates plans that guide the installation and ensure that the end result is what the customer requested. Plans include:

- Configuring and testing connectivity
- Implementing the proposed system

- Demonstrating the functionality of the network

- Migrating network applications

- Validating network operation

- Training end users and support personnel

During the Design Phase of the stadium network upgrade, the design of the network is completed. Any new equipment and technologies are specified and tested. A review of the proposed design confirms that the business goals are met. A final proposal is generated to continue with the implementation of the network upgrade.

Refer to
Interactive Graphic
in online course.

Full Page

Activity

MCSA - Write three or four questions about the prepare, plan and design phase.

2.1.5 The Network Lifecycle Implement Phase

Refer to
Figure
in online course

The Implement Phase

The Implement Phase begins after the NetworkingCompany completes the design and the customer approves it. The network is built according to the approved design specification. The Implement Phase verifies the success or failure of the network design.

Testing the New Network

Testing all or part of a new network solution in a controlled environment helps to identify and resolve any implementation issues before the actual installation.

After the issues have been resolved, the NetworkingCompany staff installs the new solution and integrates it into the existing network. When the installation is complete, additional testing is done.

System-level acceptance testing checks that the new network meets the business goals and design requirements. The results of this test are recorded and become part of the documentation provided to the customer. Any training required for the stadium staff needs to be completed during this phase.

Refer to
Interactive Graphic
in online course.

Full Screen

Activity

Drag the term to the appropriate definition, then click Check.

2.1.6 The Network Lifecycle Operate Phase

Refer to
Figure
in online course

The Operate Phase

The Operate and Optimize phases are ongoing. They represent the day-to-day operations of a network. The stadium staff monitors the network and establishes a *network baseline*. This monitoring helps the company achieve maximum scalability, availability, security and manageability.

After the new network is installed, stadium personnel manage the network to ensure that it is performing to the design specifications outlined in the Prepare and Plan phases.

Defining Policies and Procedures

Policies and procedures are needed to handle network issues, such as:

- Security incidents

- Configuration changes

- Equipment purchases

Updating these policies and procedures after an upgrade reduces downtime, operating costs, and change-related issues. If there are no policies and procedures in place, it is important to create them.

Lab Activity

Refer to **Lab Activity** for this chapter

Use Cisco Network Assistant to observe traffic.

2.1.7 The Network Lifecycle Optimize Phase

Refer to **Figure** in online course

The Optimize Phase

Optimizing the network is a continuous process. Its purpose is to improve network performance and reliability by identifying and resolving potential network problems before they happen. Doing this ensures that the business goals and requirements of the company are maintained. Common network problems that could be discovered in the Optimize Phase include:

- Feature incompatibilities

- Insufficient link capacity

- Device performance problems when multiple features are enabled

- Scalability of protocols

As business goals change, the technology strategy and operations may not adapt. At some point, a redesign may be required and the PPDIOO cycle starts again.

Refer to **Interactive Graphic** in online course.

Full Page

Activity

For each action listed on the left, place a check in the Prepare, Plan, Design, Implement, Operate, OR Optimize Phase column, then click Check.

2.2 Explaining the Sales Process

2.2.1 Respond to a Customer Request for a Proposal or Quote

Refer to **Figure** in online course

When a business or organization decides to upgrade or replace their existing network, they usually generate a Request for Proposal (RFP) or a Request for Quote (RFQ). In the PPDIOO model, this occurs at the end of the Prepare phase. RFPs and RFQs include specifications that define the format and content of the expected responses from the potential contractors. It is critical for contractors to follow the instructions contained within the document as accurately as possible. Not following the directions or missing sections of the request could mean that the project is awarded to another contractor.

In addition to the response format and content, RFPs and RFQs contain schedules that must be followed. The company that sent out the RFP may reject a late response.

Responding to the Request

Each section of the response document should be as detailed as possible. Unless otherwise indicated, the section numbers of the response document should correspond with the section numbers of the request. The response should be written with the target audience in mind. Technical terms and concepts need to be explained where necessary.

To ensure that the response document is easy to read, a table of contents is used to organize the material. An introductory letter is included to introduce the material.

2.2.2 Attend a Pre-bid Meeting

Refer to **Figure** in online course

Pre-bid Meeting

Prior to the deadline for submitting RFP responses, the customer may schedule an informational meeting. This meeting may be referred to as a pre-bid meeting or pre-submittal conference. The purpose of the meeting is to provide:

- An opportunity to review the project scope with the customer

- Additional information and documentation identified, but not included in the original RFP

- Clarification of formatting and project timeline details not included in the original RFP

The meeting enables the contractor to get an estimate of the number of other companies that are interested in submitting a bid on the project. If a pre-bid meeting is not scheduled, the information or documentation can be requested by contacting the appropriate personnel identified in the RFP.

2.2.3 Explain the Request for Proposal (RFP)

Refer to **Figure** in online course

The RFP

Businesses usually send a copy of the RFP to contractors. Occasionally the RFPs may be posted on the business web site. Responses to an RFP help the customer compare services, products, pricing, and support offered by the different contractors.

Typically an RFP for a network project includes:

- Business goals for the project

- Anticipated project scope

- Information on the existing network and applications

- Requirements for the new network.

- Business, technical, or environmental constraints

- Preliminary schedule with milestones and deliverables

- Legal contractual terms and conditions

When responding to an RFP, it is important that every item listed on the RFP is answered. The company that sent out the RFP may reject an incomplete proposal.

2.2.4 Explain the Request for Quote (RFQ)

Refer to **Figure** in online course

The RFQ

Businesses use an RFQ instead of an RFP when the technical specifications of the project are already known. If a business has a skilled networking support staff, the staff can write an RFQ to obtain the costs for the necessary services and equipment. An RFQ is usually much simpler to respond to than an RFP, because the costs associated with an RFQ can easily be obtained or estimated.

An RFQ can vary in content but will generally have three main parts. Like an RFP, the RFQ response may have formatting requirements. Proposal deadlines may be strictly enforced.

The same guidelines used to respond to an RFP should be followed when responding to an RFQ. Follow all directions precisely and submit the response before the deadline to ensure that it is considered.

Refer to **Interactive Graphic** in online course.

Full Page **Activity**

Drag the item on the right to the appropriate portion of the RFQ, then click Check.

2.2.5 Explain the Role of the Account Manager

Refer to **Figure** in online course

When the NetworkingCompany receives the RFP from the StadiumCompany, the task of responding to it is assigned to an account manager. NetworkingCompany account managers are responsible for maintaining a continuing relationship between the company and its customers. This relationship begins when an account manager first contacts a potential customer. It continues throughout all phases of the PPDIOO network lifecyle. Business customers rely on the knowledge and expertise of their account manager to help them determine network requirements. Gaining and keeping a customer's trust is critical to an account manager's success. The account manager assigned to the stadium account is responsible for ensuring a good business relationship between the StadiumCompany and the NetworkingCompany.

Communications Channel

The account manager serves as the primary NetworkingCompany contact for stadium management personnel. A good account manager needs excellent interpersonal skills and a thorough knowledge of the customer's business. The account manager communicates with the stadium management through face-to-face meetings, phone calls, email or a combination of more than one method, depending on the customer's preferences.

Refer to **Figure** in online course

Account Manager Responsibilities

In some companies, account managers are responsible for contacting all customers and potential customers within a geographic area or territory. Other companies assign account managers to accounts based on the customer's type of business. While specific duties may vary from position to position, most account managers are responsible for:

- Meeting their assigned sales and revenue goals
- Communicating information about new products or technologies to customers and potential customers
- Directing local sales, service and support teams
- Planning and budgeting for sales and support projects
- Responding to customer requests for proposals, demonstrations, quotations and information
- Negotiating and maintaining sales or service contracts

At the NetworkingCompany, account managers are required to take sales and customer management training, in addition to demonstrating basic networking skills.

2.2.6 Explain the Role of the Pre-Sales Systems Engineer

Refer to **Figure** in online course

The NetworkingCompany employs both pre-sales and post-sales technical staff to assist the account manager in providing support for their customers.

Pre-Sales Systems Engineer

Pre-sales systems engineers (sometimes called pre-sale technical support engineer) help the account manager and the customer to determine the need for upgrades or additions to the customer's network. Account managers rely on the technical expertise of the pre-sales systems engineers to ensure that any new equipment and services are appropriate for the customer's network needs. In the Plan and Design phases of the PPDIOO lifecycle, pre-sales systems engineers provide assistance to determine the technical requirements and feasibility of proposed network changes. These engineers, as well as network technicians who work with them, are responsible for:

- Evaluating the customer's current network

- Determining if a network upgrade or addition can meet the technical requirements

- Ensuring that the proposed changes can be integrated into the existing customer network

- Testing and evaluating proposed solutions

The pre-sales systems engineer assists the network designer in identifying problems with the existing network or possible problems that changes to the network may cause. Early identification and problem resolution is pivotal to a successful network upgrade or installation. The pre-sales systems engineer plays a vital role in creating an accurate response document to an RFP.

Training requirements for pre-sales systems engineers include network design courses, as well as network technology courses. Many pre-sales systems engineers are required to obtain network design certifications. An example of such certification is the Cisco Certified Design Associate (CCDA).

2.2.7 Explain the Role of the Network Designer

Refer to **Figure** in online course

A network designer needs a thorough understanding of the capabilities of all types of networking technologies and equipment. These skills enable the designer to provide customers with a network design that meets the customer requirements for scalability, availability, security and manageability. The designer is involved in the Plan and Design phases of the PPDIOO network lifecycle. In some smaller companies, a pre-sales systems engineer may also perform the role of network designer. In larger companies, there may be a team of network designers working on a single project. In this course, a single network designer will be used.

A good network designer takes the time to learn about the customer's business, in addition to the customer's network requirements. This helps the designer anticipate changes that might occur as the business grows and succeeds. A designer is responsible for:

- Analyzing customer goals and constraints in order to determine the technical requirements for the new design

- Evaluating the current installed network

- Selecting the technologies and equipment capabilities to meet the defined network requirements

- Diagramming the placement and interconnection of various network devices and services

- Designing and supervising proof-of-concept testing

- Assisting the account manager in preparing presentations to the customer

Refer to **Figure** in online course

At the NetworkingCompany, the design staff is made up of highly skilled network professionals. The network designer must stay up to date about technologies, as well as new design recommended practices.

The designer is required to obtain network design certifications, in addition to technical networking professional certifications.

The designer assigned to the stadium upgrade is a Cisco Certified Design Professional (CCDP). By obtaining this advanced certification, the designer has demonstrated the competencies necessary to design a complex network for the stadium company.

2.2.8 Explain the Role of the Post-Sales Field Engineer

Refer to **Figure** in online course

During the Implementation, Operation, and Optimize phases of the PPDIOO network lifecycle, the post-sales field engineer (sometimes called the post-sales technical support engineer) takes over the technical support responsibility from the pre-sales staff. It is usually a post-sales field engineer who is responsible for the smooth installation of new network equipment. Post-sales field engineers work with the customers to ensure that the network upgrade functions as designed.

Responsibilities of the Post-Sales Field Engineer

Responsibilities of the post-sales field engineer include:

- Provide installation assistance and acceptance testing.
- Support and organize troubleshooting of components or systems.
- Resolve technical problems the customer may encounter.
- Provide customer training and assistance with managing and configuring devices.

The post-sales field engineer helps develop recommended changes to the network design throughout the PPDIOO life cycle.

Training requirements for post-sales field engineers include basic and advanced networking technology courses. Some technologies, like IP voice, require the post-sales field engineer to take additional advanced training courses. A Cisco Certified Network Associate (CCNA) certification is considered a minimum requirement for most post-sales field engineer positions.

Refer to **Interactive Graphic** in online course.

Full Screen **Activity**

Drag a role to the appropriate activity, then click Check.

2.3 Preparing for the Design Process

2.3.1 Working with the Customer

Refer to **Figure** in online course

In designing the new network for the stadium, the NetworkingCompany interacts with personnel from the stadium offices. When the network designer and staff meet with the stadium personnel, it is important that they behave in a professional manner.

The Importance of Interpersonal Skills

Good interpersonal skills are critical when interacting with customers. A calm and courteous manner instills confidence in customers. The customer believes that the NetworkingCompany designer and staff can perform the necessary tasks.

The following skills are essential when working with clients:

- Listening and accurately summarizing information

- Corresponding with clients in a style, format, and level of detail appropriate for the intended audience

- Presenting well-organized technical material in a logical fashion

The ability to develop a good rapport with a client is crucial. Establishing a trusted business relationship eliminates many potential problems and contributes enormously to the success of the project for both companies.

2.3.2 Defining the Customer

Refer to
Figure
in online course

To create a comprehensive plan, the network designer needs to understand how the network users interact with the network resources and services. The designer gathers information about all internal and external access to the existing network infrastructure. Without full knowledge of who has access to the network, the designer may overlook some user requirements. As a result, the designer may present a design that is incomplete. Failure to submit an adequate design generates delays and increased costs.

Identifying Relevant Information

When gathering information on the infrastructure, the designer works with stadium personnel to identify all user groups. The customer's organizational chart is one of many components the designer must acquire. It is important to look beyond the organizational chart to determine all of the end users and stakeholders who access the customer network.

The stadium management identifies the following potential end users:

- Branch and field office staff

- Remote workers

- Sales and support personnel working off site

- Vendors, suppliers, and partners

- Board members

- Consultants and contractors

- Customers

Adding User Access

The designer also needs to assess the impact of adding new user groups to the network. Some end user groups that currently do not have network access may need access to new stadium network resources in the future.

The designer works with stadium management to identify:

- New user groups

- The type of access required

- Where access is allowed

- The overall impact on security

Including this information in the Plan and Prepare phases helps to ensure an accurate and successful new design.

Refer to
Lab Activity
for this chapter

Lab Activity

Create a network organization structure of the FilmCompany. Include all stakeholders in the structure - internal network users, IT organizations, external customers, suppliers, and partners.

2.3.3 Identifying Business Goals and Priorities

Refer to **Figure** in online course

The goal of every business is to be successful. Before beginning any network project, business managers analyze the feasibility of the project based on how it contributes to business success. They must consider:

- Profitability - Can the project reduce costs or help the business avoid costs in the future?
- Business growth and market share - Can the project help the business grow more efficiently or create competitive advantages?
- Customer satisfaction - Can the project improve the customer experience and increase customer loyalty?

This feasibility analysis enables the business managers to put together a list of high-level goals for the network project. The network designer notes these goals and records any issues or concerns that are mentioned.

Prioritizing Goals

In consultation with the stadium management, the designer prioritizes the business goals. The priorities are based on which goals present the best opportunities to contribute to the success of the business. For example, the relative importance of each goal can be rated as a percentage of the overall total of 100.

After the NetworkingCompany obtains the list of the prioritized business goals, the Plan Phase begins.

Refer to **Lab Activity** for this chapter

Lab Activity

To ensure that the information gathered is accurate, create a checklist of the business goals of the FilmCompany.

2.4 Identifying Technical Requirements and Constraints

2.4.1 Defining Technical Requirements

Refer to **Figure** in online course

After obtaining the prioritized business goals, the network designer determines the network functionality needed to meet each goal. The designer lists the business goals that must be met by the new design and then decides what is required technically to implement each change.

Determining the technical requirements enables the designer to establish the scope of the project. These requirements drive the selection of technologies, equipment, and management software.

Technical requirements include, but are not limited to:

- Improving network scalability
- Increasing network availability and performance
- Enhancing network security
- Simplifying network management and support

Refer to
Figure
in online course

The network designer works with the customer to create a prioritized list of technical requirements. This list provides direction for the following decisions:

- Selecting network equipment
- Choosing protocols
- Designing network services

This project list defines the project scope.

When discussing technical requirements with the customer, the designer considers the technical level of the audience. The customer may not clearly understand technical terms and jargon. Such terms should either be avoided or tailored to the level of detail and complexity that the customer can understand.

Refer to
Lab Activity
for this chapter

Lab Activity

Use the FilmCompany business goals to create and prioritize the technical requirements for the network.

2.4.2 Identifying Constraints

Refer to
Figure
in online course

Every company wants to have the most advanced and efficient network available. In reality, various business constraints affect network design. Common constraints include:

- *Budget* - Limited resources may require some compromises in design due to the costs of equipment, software, or other components.
- *Company policies* - The design must take into account the customer's existing policies regarding protocols, standards, vendors, and applications.
- *Scheduling* - The project time frame should be aligned with the customer schedules.
- *Personnel* - The availability of trained personnel at the implementation and operation phases might be a design consideration.

Constraints can and do affect network design and should be identified early in the PPDIOO lifecycle process. The relative importance of the constraints varies from project to project. Budget constraints are not always the main consideration for a large project.

For the stadium network project, the stadium management does not want the implementation to be scheduled during their sports season.

Refer to
Lab Activity
for this chapter

Lab Activity

Identify the constraints for the FilmCompany network project.

2.5 Identifying Manageability Design Considerations

2.5.1 Using the Top Down Design Approach

Refer to
Figure
in online course

There are two common approaches for network design: top-down and bottom-up.

Top-Down

The top-down approach adapts the network infrastructure to the needs of the organization. Top-down design clarifies the design goals and initiates the design from the perspective of the required applications and network solutions, such as IP telephony, content networking, and video conferencing. The PPDIOO methodology uses the top-down approach.

Bottom-Up

A common approach - but one that is not recommended - is the bottom-up design. In this approach, the network designer selects network devices and technologies based on previous experience rather than from an understanding of the organization. Because this approach does not include information on the business goals, the proposed network design may not be able to support the required applications.

2.5.2 Monitoring Network Operations

Refer to **Figure** in online course

After implementation, it is important to ensure that the network design specifications are met. The stadium network personnel monitor and manage the performance of the network. Network management includes the following functions:

- Managing configuration changes to the network

- Identifying network faults

- Monitoring performance levels

- Providing security and accounting management for individual and group usage of the network

A typical network management architecture consists of the following elements:

- Network Management System (*NMS*) - A system that uses an application to monitor and control managed network devices, such as CiscoWorks

- Network Management Protocol - A protocol that facilitates the exchange of information between network devices and the NMS, such as the Simple Network Management Protocol version 3 (*SNMP*v3)

- Managed Devices - Network devices that are managed by an NMS, such as a router or switch

- Management Agents - Software on managed devices that collect and store network management information

- Management Information - Data collected by the NMS

Refer to **Figure** in online course

CiscoWorks LAN Management Solution (LMS) is a suite of powerful management tools that simplify the configuration, administration, monitoring, and troubleshooting of Cisco networks. It integrates these capabilities into a best-in-class solution that provides the following benefits:

- Improves the accuracy and efficiency of the network operations staff

- Increases the overall availability of the network by simplifying configuration and quickly identifying and fixing network problems

- Maximizes network security through integration with access control services and audit of network-level changes

Refer to **Lab Activity** for this chapter

Lab Activity

Use a software program to monitor network performance.

2.5.3 Tools for Network Monitoring

Refer to
Figure
in online course

SNMP is the most common network management protocol to use. The protocol enables network administrators to gather data about the network and corresponding devices. SNMP management system software is available in tools such as CiscoWorks. SNMP management agent software is often embedded in operating systems on servers, routers, and switches.

SNMP has four main components:

- Management station
- Management agents
- Management Information Base (*MIB*)
- Network management protocol

As part of a network management system, SNMP tools can respond to network errors or failures in several ways. Generally, when a network fault occurs, or when predefined thresholds are met, the SNMP tools can react by:

- Sending an alert on the network
- Sending a message to a pager
- Sending an email to an administrator

Because stadium management may want to offer service level agreements to their vendors, they need to purchase network management software.

Refer to
Lab Activity
for this chapter

Lab Activity:

Investigate the capabilities and reports available in network monitoring software.

Summary

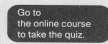

Quiz

Take the chapter quiz to check your knowledge.

Your Chapter Notes

CHAPTER 3

Characterizing the Existing Network

Introduction

Refer to **Figure** in online course

3.1 Documenting the Existing Network

Refer to **Figure** in online course

3.1.1 Creating a Network Diagram

Typically, the first step in installing a new network is to take a detailed look at the existing network. The NetworkingCompany designer examines the existing network to:

- Determine if the design goals are realistic and feasible

- Determine if the existing network meets the expectations for scalability, availability, security, and manageability

- Identify where new equipment, infrastructure upgrades, and new services can be integrated

- Ensure that old and new network devices, media, and functions can work together

Upgrading the Stadium Network

Like most organizations, the stadium has a pre-existing network. The management wants to install a new network to:

- Better manage its existing voice, video, and data networks

- Improve customer service

- Reduce costs

Refer to **Figure** in online course

The NetworkingCompany designer reviews the existing network documentation. The stadium IT department network documentation contains most of the information that the designer needs concerning network organization and services.

The network documentation should include:

- Logical and physical diagrams of the network

- Floor plans showing the location of wiring closets and wiring runs

- Inventory lists of installed network equipment

- Current network configuration files

- Inventory lists of network applications

Producing a Network Topology Map

As is the case with many businesses, the StadiumCompany's network documentation is not up-to-date. A new diagram will need to be created of the network as a whole, as well as the different segments that comprise it.

Network management programs collect information and produce a diagram of the current network. Cisco Network Assistant and CiscoWorks are two examples of network management programs.

Refer to **Figure** in online course

Cisco Network Assistant is used to obtain the information necessary to produce a diagram of the stadium network.

Obtaining Information About Devices and Data Routes

The NetworkingCompany staff can now log in to various network devices. The network designer uses standard Cisco IOS commands to obtain information about the devices and the routes that data takes through the network.

The Cisco IOS software offers useful commands to gain information from a router to create a network diagram. Some of these commands are:

- `show version`
- `show running-config`
- `show ip route`
- `show cdp neighbors detail`
- `show controllers`
- `show tech-support`

The `show tech-support` command can collect a large amount of information about a router. The output from this command varies depending on the router or switch platform and configuration.

Many of these same commands are used to gain information on a Cisco switch. Other useful switch commands include:

- `show vlan`
- `show vtp`
- `show spanning-tree`

Refer to **Interactive Graphic** in online course.

Full Page Custom Activity

Packet Tracer Activity

Refer to **Packet Tracer Activity** for this chapter

Use router and switch commands to investigate the existing network devices.

3.1.2 Diagramming the Logical Architecture

Refer to **Figure** in online course

After the information about the existing network is collected, the next task is to create or update one or more logical network diagrams.

Creating an Existing Network Overview Diagram

On the stadium network project, the first diagram that the network designer creates is a high-level view of all of the stadium network sites. The diagram shows:

- The main stadium network
- The souvenir shop

- The ticket outlet locations

- Connectivity to remote sites

- Connectivity to business partners

The designer diagrams the *WAN* connections between the networks and the equipment at each location where the WAN terminates.

This network diagram illustrates how the information flows from one area of the network to another. This helps the designer locate problem areas.

Creating Network Segment Diagrams

Next, the designer creates diagrams for the logical and physical layouts of the networks installed at each of the various sites.

Each diagram shows:

- The location of the network equipment and wiring closets

- The logical addressing information

- The naming information

Using these diagrams, the designer identifies where topology or equipment changes are needed. The designer evaluates the traffic flows and addressing structures.

Refer to **Figure** in online course

The network installed at the main stadium location is more complex than those at the individual remote sites. The network designer creates a separate logical diagram to illustrate all of the various LAN components and topologies. The diagram shows the traffic flows between the users and the servers.

Creating a Logical Diagram of the Main Stadium LAN

The designer creates a logical network diagram that shows the major pieces of networking equipment and how they interconnect. This diagram includes:

- Routers and switches

- Wireless Access Points

- Critical telecommunications equipment (CSU/DSU, modems, etc.)

- Firewalls and intrusion detection devices (*IDS*)

- Management stations

- Servers and server farms

All of the servers and services are included on the logical diagram. This is because their location can affect traffic patterns, bandwidth use, and security. The designer labels each of the connections with the bandwidth and type of cable or wireless device that is being used.

Refer to **Lab Activity** for this chapter

Lab Activity

Use Cisco Network Assistant and Cisco IOS commands to create a logical network diagram of the FilmCompany network.

3.1.3 Developing a Modular Diagram

Refer to **Figure** in online course

The stadium network has grown significantly from its initial design. The NetworkingCompany designer takes the logical diagram and organizes the network into a *modular block diagram*.

A modular block diagram is a simplified version of the network. The diagram shows the major functions in modular form. It helps the designer to determine the underlying architecture on which the network is built.

The designer compares the block diagram to the ideal network design represented by the Cisco *Enterprise Network Architectures*. The designer identifies areas that must be redesigned or upgraded.

The initial architecture of the stadium network is a large flat network. It has only two physical layers of switches. Some of the switches provide end device connectivity to the network and some interconnect other switches. Both layers are built using Layer 2 switches, which are not segmented by VLANs.

Server locations are at various points within the network.

Internet connectivity is provided through another router. Connectivity is protected by a firewall and IDS. Both of the remote locations connect to the stadium network through VPNs that terminate at the Internet router.

Refer to **Packet Tracer Activity** for this chapter

Packet Tracer Activity

Create a modular block diagram of an existing network to help identify weaknesses in the design.

3.1.4 Strengths and Weaknesses of the Existing Network

Refer to **Figure** in online course

The diagrams created by the network designer enable the NetworkingCompany staff to analyze the existing network for strengths and weaknesses.

Strengths of the Existing Stadium Network

The designer reviews the current voice and video network documentation to determine the locations of equipment and the various groups who use the services.

New Category 5e wiring was recently installed throughout the stadium complex. In addition, new single-mode fiber connects the wiring closets to the main telecommunications room. The available throughput provided by the existing cabling reduces the need for changes to the infrastructure of the stadium network. Additional wiring will only be done if it is required to install the new Access Points.

An area next to the wiring closet is ideally suited for the installation of a new data center to accommodate the server farm.

Refer to **Figure** in online course

After reviewing the diagrams and the existing equipment inventories, the network designer lists the strengths and weaknesses of the current stadium network:

Strengths:

- New wiring and adequate wiring closets
- Adequate space for a new data center
- Servers and PCs are current models and will not need to be replaced
- Some existing network switches and routers can be used in the new design

Weaknesses:

- Flat network design
- No Distribution Layer
- No true Core Layer

- Servers poorly located

- Multiple networks that can be difficult to maintain

- Inadequate IP addressing structure

- No dedicated bandwidth for WAN connectivity

- Poorly-implemented wireless

- Limited security implementations

Overcoming Weaknesses in Preparation for the Network Upgrade

The designer focuses on finding ways to overcome the weaknesses of the existing network. The designer proposes updating the network design with the necessary enhancements.

Equipment that will not be replaced during the upgrade is also evaluated. It is important to know that the hardware is working properly and that the software is up-to-date to ensure easy integration of new features into the network.

Refer to **Packet Tracer Activity** for this chapter

Packet Tracer Activity

Investigate the existing network and develop a list of strengths and weaknesses.

3.2 Updating the Existing Cisco IOS

3.2.1 Cisco CCO Features and Navigation

Refer to **Figure** in online course

The Cisco.com web site offers tools and online resources to help the NetworkingCompany staff obtain information about the stadium network equipment. The web site can help to resolve common technical problems. The tools and resources include the following:

- *Documentation* - Hardware and software configuration and verification, as well as troubleshooting Cisco products and technologies

- *Tools* - Troubleshooting, installation, assessment, and service requests

- *Downloads* - Software, specific file releases, and technical support applications

- *Communities and Training* - Information on the Networking Professionals Connection, attending Technical Support Seminars, and other training opportunities

- *News* - Current topics reported in the Cisco Technical Support Newsletter

Access to many of the features available on Cisco.com requires the creation of a Cisco.com registered user account. The level of access depends upon the type of user account and whether the user has a current SMARTnet maintenance contract.

3.2.2 Investigating the Installed Cisco IOS Software

Refer to **Figure** in online course

Before using the tools at Cisco.com, the NetworkingCompany staff requires the following information from the equipment inventory list:

- Model and type of device

- Installed memory

- Interfaces and slots

- Optional installed modules

- Current IOS software version and file name

The NetworkingCompany staff uses this information to determine which Cisco IOS software version is appropriate and which hardware options can be installed.

Using the `show version` Command

The technicians use the `show version` command on each device to verify that the inventory list is correct. The command will also help them to obtain any missing information.

The network designer then sends the staff a list of new features. These are features that the designer believes will be needed to support the expanded stadium network capabilities. Evaluating the new features list helps the staff to select an IOS software version that is appropriate for the new network.

Refer to
Lab Activity
for this chapter

Lab Activity

Use `show version` to fill out an inventory sheet for a Cisco switch and router.

Refer to
Figure
in online course

The NetworkingCompany staff and the stadium IT manager discuss how to upgrade the current network equipment with minimal disruption of day-to-day operations. They agree that the network switches and routers can be upgraded during scheduled maintenance on Sunday morning from 2:00 a.m. to 8:00 a.m. However, because of the large number of installed devices, the upgrade may take more than one Sunday morning to complete.

In the stadium network, three types of network devices will be included in the new design:

- 16 Cisco 2960 switches

- 1 Cisco 1841 router

- 3 non-Cisco routers

After the NetworkingCompany staff determines which Cisco IOS software versions and hardware components need to be installed, they are able to estimate the time necessary for the upgrades of the Cisco equipment. The non-Cisco routers will be updated at a later time.

IOS Software File Naming Conventions

IOS files need to be kept up-to-date to prevent security risks and to implement bug fixes. Some of the installed devices on the stadium network have outdated IOS versions.

*IOS file naming convention*s provide the version number and feature set of the IOS.

Refer to
Figure
in online course

When the Cisco IOS software on a switch or router is upgraded, the device needs to be rebooted. This process takes the device out of service for a short period of time. As with any upgrade, unforeseen problems may arise after the new hardware or IOS is loaded. Upgrades should be planned carefully. This will ensure that the network is not disrupted during normal operating hours.

Testing the Upgrade Process

To avoid as many problems as possible, the NetworkingCompany obtains a 2960 switch and an 1841 router. They use these devices to test the upgrade process before they attempt to upgrade the stadium equipment. Testing is a good practice, because there can be significant differences from one IOS version or hardware component to another.

Using test equipment enables the NetworkingCompany staff to verify that the updated system will operate as expected. They will be better able to estimate the length of time it will take to perform each upgrade.

3.2.3 Choosing an Appropriate Cisco IOS Image

Refer to
Figure
in online course

The NetworkingCompany staff needs to determine whether the current devices can support a Cisco IOS version with the necessary new network features. This is an important step in the upgrade process.

Using Feature Navigator

The Cisco.com web site provides tools to assist the NetworkingCompany staff in choosing the right IOS version. *Feature Navigator* is a web-based tool that helps to determine which features are supported by a specific IOS software image. Feature Navigator can also be used to find which IOS software images support a specific feature.

Feature Navigator allows searches by feature or release version. Under the release version section, the staff compares release versions side-by-side. Registered Cisco.com users can access Feature Navigator at http://www.cisco.com/go/fn.

IOS software is packaged in feature sets that support specific switch and router platforms. The staff uses Cisco Feature Navigator to determine which IOS releases are appropriate for the installed equipment. They use the inventory list and the list of necessary features that the network designer provided.

Refer to
Lab Activity
for this chapter

Lab Activity

Use Feature Navigator to select the correct Cisco IOS software for the FilmCompany network, and check that the device has enough *DRAM* and *flash memory* to support it.

Refer to
Figure
in online course

The NetworkingCompany staff identifies an appropriate Cisco IOS software image release. Having done so, the staff must check that each device has enough flash memory and *RAM* to support the new IOS files. If not, memory upgrades must be done before the new IOS can be installed.

The stadium company has a maintenance agreement that enables staff members to download the new IOS versions for their Cisco equipment. The NetworkingCompany staff asks the stadium management to ensure that they are in compliance with Cisco licensing agreements. They must verify that each Cisco device is included in the maintenance agreement.

The NetworkingCompany staff downloads the new IOS versions from Cisco.com. They can then be stored on a Trivial File Transfer Protocol (*TFTP*) server. Storing the files on a TFTP server enables the staff to load the software easily onto the routers and switches for the upgrade.

The **copy** command is used to transfer files from a TFTP server to a router or switch.

3.2.4 Download and Install Cisco IOS Software

Refer to
Figure
in online course

The stadium router and switches do not have a current Cisco IOS version. The necessary upgrades must be done manually by performing the following steps:

Step 1: Select a IOS Software Image

The first step in the upgrade procedure is to select an appropriate IOS software image version and feature set. The following factors need to be considered when selecting an IOS version:

- *Memory Requirement* - Ensure that the router has enough disk or flash memory to store the IOS. The router also needs sufficient memory (DRAM) to run the IOS. If the router does not have enough memory, the router may have problems when it boots under the new IOS.

- *Interface and Module Support* - Ensure that the new IOS supports all the current and new interfaces and modules to be installed in the router.

■ *Software Feature Support* - Compare the new IOS features with those used with the old IOS. Any new features required for the network upgrade need to be included.

The NetworkingCompany staff uses Feature Navigator to find the appropriate IOS versions for the installed equipment. They download and copy the IOS files to the download directory on the TFTP server. They also read the *release notes* to ensure that there are no unexpected changes or known issues with the release.

Refer to **Figure** in online course

Step 2: Identify the Device File System to Copy the Image

The NetworkingCompany staff uses the `show file systems` command output to locate the Cisco IOS files or images. Either this command or the `dir [file_system]` command can be used to find the free space available to store the new IOS images. If the devices do not have enough flash memory, memory upgrades should be implemented before the new IOS can be installed.

Step 3: Verify that the TFTP Server Has IP Connectivity to the Device

The TFTP server must have a network connection to the device. It must be able to ping the IP address of the device targeted for a TFTP software upgrade. To achieve this connection, the device interface and the TFTP server must have either an IP address in the same range or a default gateway configured.

Refer to **Figure** in online course

Step 4: Back Up the Current Configurations to Prepare for the Upgrade

The configuration files and current IOS from the router should be backed up before upgrading the Cisco IOS. The running configuration should be copied to the startup configuration. The startup configuration and the current IOS image should be backed up to a TFTP server. Some of the IOS releases add default configurations. These new configuration items may conflict with the current configuration.

Step 5: Copy the IOS Image to the Device

After the NetworkingCompany staff pings between the TFTP server and the device, they are ready to copy the IOS software image into flash memory. Before copying the image, the staff ensures that the TFTP server software is running. They confirm that the IOS image is in the appropriate TFTP server directory.

To upgrade the IOS from a TFTP server, the staff uses the `copy tftp flash` command.

The copy process takes several minutes. The `dir flash` command is used to check that the file has been transferred successfully.

To complete the upgrade, the NetworkingCompany staff reboots the device and observes the device bootup process.

The staff performs the upgrade on the test network devices. After completing the upgrade, they compare the resulting configurations to the saved configurations. The staff ensures that any differences between the configurations do not affect the stadium network operation.

Refer to **Packet Tracer Activity** for this chapter

Packet Tracer

Download the correct Cisco IOS and transfer the file to the Cisco router or switch using a TFTP server.

Refer to **Lab Activity** for this chapter

Lab Activity

Prepare a router to receive a new Cisco IOS and transfer the IOS to the router from a TFTP server.

3.2.5 The Router Startup Process

Refer to
Figure
in online course

The *bootup process* has three stages:

1. Performing the POST and Loading the Bootstrap Program

The power-on self test (*POST*) is a process that occurs on almost every computer when it boots. The POST is used to test the router hardware.

After the POST, the bootstrap program is loaded. The bootstrap program locates the Cisco IOS and loads it into RAM.

2. Locating and Loading the IOS Software

The location of the IOS file is specified by the value of the configuration register setting. The bits in this setting can instruct the device to load the IOS file from the following locations:

- Flash memory
- A TFTP server
- Another location indicated in the startup configuration file

To load the IOS normally from flash, the configuration register setting should be set to 0x2102.

3. Locating and Executing the Startup Configuration File or Entering Setup Mode

After the IOS is loaded, the bootstrap program searches for the startup configuration file (startup-config) in *NVRAM*. This file contains the previously saved configuration commands and parameters, including:

- Interface addresses
- Routing information
- Passwords
- Other configuration parameters

If no configuration file is located, the router prompts the user to enter setup mode to begin the configuration process.

If a startup configuration file is found, a prompt containing a hostname will display. The router has successfully loaded the IOS and the configuration file. The NetworkingCompany staff can begin using IOS commands on the router.

Refer to
Lab Activity
for this chapter

Lab Activity

Observe the startup process on an 1841 router.

3.3 Upgrading Existing Hardware

3.3.1 Investigating Installed Hardware Features

Refer to
Figure
in online course

After updating the Cisco IOS versions, the network designer needs to know what hardware upgrades can be performed on the existing devices so that they meet the new requirements. Upgrades may be needed that include high-speed or high-density modules and other available hardware options, such as rack mount kits.

Cisco.com offers datasheets for all of the devices that are installed in the stadium network. The NetworkingCompany staff uses these datasheets to create a list of the possible options for each device.

The staff uses the 1841 router datasheet to see what modules and interfaces are available for that model. A number of different types of modules fit the two option slots on the 1841, including:

- WAN interface cards (*WIC*s)
- High-speed WAN interface cards (*HWIC*s)
- Voice/WAN interface cards (*VWIC*s)
- Wireless WICs that can function as Access Points
- Gigabit Ethernet HWICs to provide fiber connectivity

The designer uses this list to determine which options are needed to meet the requirements of the new network.

3.3.2 Investigating Appropriate Hardware Options

Refer to
Figure
in online course

Hardware devices come with different capabilities. It is important to understand which technology and media a module in a given router would support. The network designer notes the technologies that are likely to be applicable in the new design for the stadium network.

To support the voice, video, and data traffic on the new network, the designer makes the following list of technologies and media:

- Gigabit Ethernet using fiber at the Core and Distribution Layers
- 100 Mbps connectivity using copper wire at the Access Layer
- Gigabit Ethernet using either copper or fiber in the data center
- High-speed serial connections to the two WAN sites
- High-speed digital subscriber line (*DSL*) to connect to the Internet

The designer compares this list to the list of available options in the documentation for the 1841 router on Cisco.com. The existing 1841 can support the necessary modules to connect to the WAN site and to the Internet.

Refer to
Interactive Graphic
in online course.

Full/Screen **Activity**

Lab Activity

Refer to
Lab Activity
for this chapter

Investigate the hardware options available on the 1841 Integrated Services Router.

3.3.3 Installing a New Hardware Option

Refer to
Figure
in online course

Installing Option Interface Cards in an 1841 Router

The NetworkingCompany staff goes to Cisco.com to locate the instructions for installing the option interface cards. The procedure to install these cards is as follows:

Step 1: Turn Off Power to the Router

The 1841 router option slots do not support *hot-swappable* option interface cards, which can be changed with the power on.

Step 2: Remove the Blank Faceplate from the Slot

Use either a Number 1 Phillips screwdriver or a small flat-blade screwdriver to unscrew the captive screws. Then remove the blank *faceplate* from the chassis slot.

Step 3: Install the Option Module

- To minimize the risk of static discharge and damage to equipment during the installation process, use a properly grounded antistatic wrist strap when working with electronic equipment.

- Handle the card by the edges to reduce the risk of damage from static discharge.

- Align the card with the guides in the chassis walls or slot divider and slide it gently into the slot.

- Push the card into place until the edge connector is secure. The faceplate should touch the chassis rear panel.

- Tighten the captive screws on the faceplate.

Step 4: Turn on Power to the Router and Check the New Configuration

- Connect a PC to the console port of the router and observe the initialization process.

- Check that the router recognizes the new option interface card.

- Note the interface designation that is given to the new device on the inventory sheet and the existing topology diagram.

Refer to **Packet Tracer Activity** for this chapter

Packet Tracer Activity

Add an option interface card to an 1841 router and observe the router startup and new interface designations.

3.4 Performing a Wireless Site Survey

3.4.1 Visiting the Customer Site

Refer to **Figure** in online course

The next step in characterizing the existing network is to evaluate the wireless LAN (WLAN) deployment in the stadium. Because of differences in the configurations, Access Point (AP) placement, and the physical environment, every WLAN is a unique installation.

Before the wireless network design is finalized, the NetworkingCompany staff performs a site survey to determine the best use and placement of the wireless networking components. The survey provides information needed to assist the network designer in determining the type, placement, and coverage areas for WLAN Access Points.

Wireless site surveys require that NetworkingCompany staff enter public spaces, offices, and other locations where business is being conducted.

Whenever the NetworkingCompany staff is on the stadium site, they are representing their company. When visiting a customer site, professional behavior and appropriate dress are important. The behavior and professionalism of the staff reflects positively on the ability of the NetworkingCompany to install the upgrade.

Refer to **Figure** in online course

When preparing for a wireless site survey, the NetworkingCompany staff should follow the NetworkingCompany guidelines.

These guidelines were prepared for the sports stadium site survey:

Preparation

- Schedule the site survey with the customer.

- Dress appropriately for the task.

- Wear or carry company credentials.

- Bring the proper equipment (create a standard checklist to ensure that all necessary materials are included).

- Notify stadium personnel when the staff will arrive and how long the site survey should take.

Site Survey

- Check in with the proper staff upon entry into the stadium.

- Work quickly and professionally to instill a sense of confidence in the customer.

- Answer questions politely and as completely as possible.

- Write down any questions that must be answered by other staff members.

- Inform the customer of the survey procedures.

- Report back to the customer staff before leaving the premises to inform them of the successful completion of the survey.

Security

Many companies have their own uniformed security guards who need to be aware of any visit. Businesses typically require a visitor to check in at the main office before accessing other areas. In high-security areas, it is extremely important to gain security clearance and be escorted if needed. High-security areas include government, aviation, and military locations.

Safety Guidelines

- Follow the recommended safety guidelines to ensure proper operation and safe use of the wireless devices.

- Obtain customer approval before touching or attaching devices to any existing networking equipment.

Refer to
Figure
in online course

When the NetworkingCompany schedules a wireless site survey, the customer may have site visit requirements for the staff to meet. Some companies may not have site visit requirements established if vendors do not routinely visit their locations. In this case, the NetworkingCompany technician must ask specific questions to help determine the site visit requirements when making the appointment.

Some site visit requirements may include:

- Access restrictions

- Clothing

- Safety equipment

- Identification Badges

- Hours of operation

- Security

- Prohibited items

Customer requirements may vary from site to site. NetworkingCompany staff must comply with customer requirements when preparing for a site visit.

Refer to
Lab Activity
for this chapter

Lab Activity

Set up an appointment to perform a wireless site survey.

3.4.2 Physical Network Considerations

Refer to
Figure
in online course

The stadium network is currently providing limited wireless access through two Access Points (APs). One AP is in the team office area. This AP is actually a small wireless router that was purchased by the team management. The other AP, an inexpensive older Cisco Aironet AP, is located in the stadium press box. This AP provides wireless access for the reporters.

In the proposed network design, the stadium network requires additional wireless hotspots in the stadium restaurant and luxury suites. In both locations, the stadium management plans to offer unsecured wireless access to the Internet.

The network designer has identified a list of possible sources of interference and some physical stadium infrastructure issues that might affect the RF coverage areas. During the site survey, the NetworkingCompany staff can check these areas to determine the actual impact on the wireless signals.

Areas of concern to the designer include:

- The many microwave ovens that are located in the concession areas and the luxury boxes
- Wireless telephones and headsets that are used by the reporters and newsmen
- Elevator shafts that are located near the outer areas of the restaurant and the luxury suites
- Thick concrete pillars and walls between the luxury suites

Refer to
Interactive Graphic
in online course.

Full Page Activity

3.4.3 Wireless Site Survey and Planning

Refer to
Figure
in online course

Performing a site survey consists of the following steps:

Step 1: Define Customer Requirements

The stadium may want to advertise the availability of wireless hotspots. The NetworkingCompany staff needs to determine the service level expectations. They also need to determine whether the stadium wants to support advanced wireless technologies, such as wireless IP phones.

Step 2: Identify Coverage Areas

The NetworkingCompany staff estimates the number of potential users in each coverage area. More importantly, the staff determines the expected peak usage during major events.

Step 3: Determine Preliminary AP Locations

The staff reviews the stadium plans and suggests possible AP locations. Then they determine how coverage can be provided, which areas need power, and how the APs will connect to the wired network.

Step 4: Measure Signal Strength

The staff temporarily installs an AP in a proposed location. Then they measure the received RF strength and possible causes of interference.

Refer to
Figure
in online course

The NetworkingCompany staff installs a temporary AP in the center of the restaurant, away from the kitchen. The AP does not need to be attached to the stadium network because only the wireless coverage is being tested.

The staff uses a laptop computer equipped with a site survey utility on a wireless NIC to perform the test.

The NetworkingCompany staff performs the following steps:

Step 1: Measure the signal strength and speed of a link as they walk away from the AP.

Step 2: Record the readings and measure the distances to the AP when the quality or link speed changes.

Step 3: Mark the areas where signals are acceptable on a floor plan.

The network designer uses the marked floor plan to determine the location of the APs and the wired network jacks that connect them to the network. Upon completing the third step, the designer must ensure compliance with all local, state, and national fire and electrical codes.

Refer to **Packet Tracer Activity** for this chapter

Packet Tracer Activity

Using a diagram that includes a floor plan of the FilmCompany, place APs at different locations.

Refer to
Lab Activity
for this chapter

Lab Activity

Perform a wireless site survey using an AP and the wireless NIC.

Refer to
Interactive Graphic
in online course.

Full Screen

Play the Cisco Wireless Explorer Game.

3.5 Documenting Network Design Requirements

3.5.1 Creating a Network Design Requirements Document

Refer to
Figure
in online course

The NetworkingCompany staff has now completed the Prepare and Plan phases of the network upgrade lifecycle. They are ready to create a Design Requirements document and begin the design of the new stadium network.

A Design Requirements document is a summary of all the major business and technical requirements for the new network design.

Much of the information needed to complete the Design Requirements document can be found in the Request for Proposal (RFP). The Design Requirements document contains the specifications for the proposed network upgrade.

The first two sections of the Design Requirements document are the Overall Project Goal and the Project Scope.

Overall Project Goal

This section states the overall goals of the upgrade. It also specifies how this upgrade will help the stadium management company become more successful.

Project Scope

This section outlines the physical areas, applications, and user groups affected by the network upgrade. It may list components of the network that are beyond the scope of the network upgrade, such as server or application updates.

Refer to
Figure
in online course

Two other important sections of the Design Requirements document are Network Requirements and Current State of the Network.

Network Requirements

This section details all of the business goals and technical requirements, constraints, user groups, and applications that influence the design of the proposed stadium network.

State of the Network

This section details the existing network and includes the following information:

Refer to
Figure
in online course

- Logical and physical diagrams

- Equipment lists

- Applications

- Strengths and weaknesses

The network designer needs to be aware of the existing network. This enables the designer to address its weaknesses and build on its strengths more efficiently.

The NetworkingCompany reviews the Design Requirements document in conjunction with the stadium management. They do this to ensure that there are no misunderstandings before proceeding with the design project.

3.5.2 Overall Project Goal

Refer to
Lab Activity
for this chapter

When writing an overall project goal, it is important to think about the primary purpose of the network design project. The overall goal needs to relate to the goals of the business, which are designed to make the business more successful.

In this section of the document, the NetworkingCompany designer describes the overall project goal of the stadium network upgrade. The designer takes into account all of the information obtained from interviews with the StadiumCompany president and discussions with other members of the stadium staff.

The NetworkingCompany obtains agreement from the stadium management on the overall goal of the project.

Lab Activity

Create an overall project goal statement for the FilmCompany.

Refer to
Figure
in online course

3.5.3 Project Scope

The second section of the Design Requirements document outlines the project scope. It details how much of the network is affected or changed as a result of the project.

It also defines the parts of the existing network that are not within the areas covered by the project. These out-of-scope areas are defined so that there is no misunderstanding between the NetworkingCompany and the StadiumCompany management.

The NetworkingCompany designer looks at the existing network topology and the services that it provides. The overall goal indicates that both the LAN and the WAN networks will need to be upgraded. The scope of this project impacts all of the users at the main stadium facility and at the two remote locations.

Refer to
Interactive Graphic
in online course.

Activity

Determine the scope of various network upgrade scenarios.

Lab Activity

Refer to
Lab Activity
for this chapter

Create a scope statement for the FilmCompany.

3.5.4 Business Goals and Technical Requirements

Refer to
Figure
in online course

The first two sections of the Design Requirements document are usually short and do not contain much detail. In contrast, the Network Requirements section is very detailed. This section helps drive the network design and implementation of new technologies.

The Network Requirements section has the following four subsections:

- Business Goals

- Technical Requirements

- Users

- Applications

Business Goals

The NetworkingCompany designer lists the goals in order of priority. The most important goals are listed first.

Technical Requirements

Refer to
Figure
in online course

The NetworkingCompany designer evaluates each of the business goals. The designer then determines the technical requirements to meet the goals. These requirements are outlined in the Technical Requirements section under the properties of scalability, availability, security, and manageability.

- *Scalability-* A business goal is to add new services, new users, and voice and video capability to the network. The network must be able to scale easily without a major redesign or disruption to services. The designer discusses and documents possible growth estimates with the stadium management.

- *Availability-* The addition of voice, security, video, and online ticketing requires the network to be available to users at all times. New applications need to be accessible to the remote sites and the main stadium location. The new ticketing and entry applications require very short transaction times. The addition of voice and video require that the network support QoS.

Refer to
Figure
in online course

- *Security-* A primary goal of all network upgrades is to improve security. The proposed stadium network will include firewalls, filtering, and an intrusion detection system (IDS) to protect it from access by unauthorized users. The services will be protected using a data center server farm.

- *Manageability-* The stadium management company does not want to increase the number of IT personnel to support the new network. Therefore, the network must be easy to manage and maintain. A network is easier to manage when networking standards are used during the design and installation. A management application is needed to provide the IT department with reports and alerts to help it support the network. Additionally, training for the stadium IT staff is required to manage and maintain the proposed network.

Users

In this section of the Design Requirements document, the different user groups and their access requirements are listed. The stadium management company plans for customers, vendors, team personnel, and remote workers to access the network. It makes similar provisions for the on-site management company personnel. Each of these groups may have specific requirements for network services. It is important to document these requirements so that they are considered in the network design.

Applications

The network traffic characteristics and requirements of various applications affect the design of the network. This section of the document describes the types of applications the network must support. Any specific network traffic requirements are listed as well.

Refer to
Interactive Graphic
in online course.

Activity

Lab Activity

Refer to
Lab Activity
for this chapter

Develop a Network Requirements section for the FilmCompany Design Requirements document.

3.5.5 Existing Network Characterization

State of the Existing Network

Refer to
Figure
in online course

The final section of the Design Requirements document includes the following information:

- All of the network diagrams that the NetworkingCompany creates to illustrate the existing network

- The names and IP addresses of servers and important networking components

- The existing network strengths and weaknesses and how they impact the business goals

The network designer creates a chart that lists each of the identified weaknesses, which business or technical goal is impacted, and how the weakness can be eliminated in the proposed network design.

The NetworkingCompany staff reviews the completed Design Requirements document. A meeting is then set up with the stadium management company officials. The purpose of the meeting is to obtain their agreement and authorization to continue with the design of the upgrade.

Refer to
Interactive Graphic
in online course.

Activity

Lab Activity

Refer to
Lab Activity
for this chapter

Analyze the existing FilmCompany network in relation to its business goals and technical requirements.

Summary

Quiz

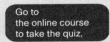

Take the chapter quiz to check your knowledge.

Your Chapter Notes

CHAPTER 4

Identifying Application Impacts on Network Design

Introduction

Refer to
Figure
in online course

4.1 Characterizing Network Applications

Refer to
Figure
in online course

4.1.1 The Importance of Application Performance

Most people who use network services know very little about the underlying network or network design. Their experience as users is based on how they interact with the applications that run on the network.

In the case of the sports stadium, network-based applications provide essential services to the fans, the teams, and the management. These services, and the network on which they reside, are among the business-critical elements ensuring that customer and user demands are met.

Gathering statistical information from routers, servers, and other network devices helps determine whether a system is functioning to manufacturer specifications. However, technical considerations alone do not determine success in the marketplace.

Success depends on how the customer, the suppliers, and the vendors view the performance of the network.

For end users, application performance is based on:

- Availability-Is the application working when they need it?

- Responsiveness-Is the application responding as quickly as expected?

For example, in the stadium, revenue from ticket sales, concessions, and souvenirs suffers when transaction processes are not available or are taking too long to complete.

Refer to
Figure
in online course

Stadium customers rate the convenience of an application by the length of time it takes to complete the transaction. They also expect the application to be available whenever they want to use it.

Applications for which fast response time is considered critical for the user include:

- Interactive kiosk services

- Point-of-sale ticket machines

- Concession registers

Applications considered critical by stadium personnel include:

- Emergency services
- Voice and video monitoring and transmission

Refer to
Figure
in online course

The measurement of application performance should combine user satisfaction with normal technical metrics, such as throughput on the network, or the number of successful transactions.

4.1.2 Characteristics of Different Application Categories

In an existing network, *application characterization* helps the network designer to incorporate business goals and technical requirements into the network design.

The application characterization process involves looking at the following aspects of network applications:

- How the applications work on the network
- The technical requirements of the application
- How applications interact with each other on the network

From the information gathered during the early phases of the design process, the designer determines which applications are considered business-critical. The designer estimates how these applications will function with the proposed network.

The characterization process provides information about network bandwidth usage and response times for specific applications. These parameters influence design decisions, including:

- Selection of the transmission medium
- Estimates of required bandwidth

Traffic from different types of applications results in varying network demands. The network designer recognizes four main types of application communication:

- *Client-to-client*
- *Client-to-distributed server*
- *Client-to-server farm*
- *Client-to-enterprise edge*

Refer to
Figure
in online course

On an existing network, the first step in characterizing applications is to gather as much information about the network as possible. This includes gathering information from:

- Organizational input
- Network audit
- Traffic analysis

Organizational Input

Organizational input consists of existing documentation about the network and verbal input from the stadium personnel. During the early phases of design, obtaining input is easy but not always reliable. For example, application changes such as upgrades or user-installed software may go undocumented or unnoticed.

Network Audit

A network audit gathers information about network devices, monitors traffic, and reveals details of the current network configuration.

Traffic Analysis

Traffic analysis provides information about how the applications and protocols use the network. It can reveal shortcomings in the network. For example, several high-bandwidth applications using the same medium can generate large amounts of traffic. This could be a potential weakness in the current design.

Cisco IOS Software Embedded Tools

Network-Based Application Recognition (*NBAR*) is a Cisco utility that conducts audits and traffic analysis. NBAR is a classification engine that recognizes a wide variety of applications. NBAR recognizes web-based and other difficult-to-classify protocols that utilize dynamic TCP and UDP port assignments.

Another tool is Cisco IOS *NetFlow*. NetFlow efficiently provides a set of services for IP applications. Services include:

- Network traffic accounting
- Usage-based network billing
- Network planning
- Security
- Denial of Service monitoring capabilities
- Network monitoring

NetFlow provides valuable information about network users and applications, peak usage times, and traffic routing.

Refer to
Lab Activity
for this chapter

Lab Activity

Use NetFlow to characterize the network applications being used on a network.

4.1.3 How Traffic Flow Affects Network Design

Refer to
Figure
in online course

As part of application characterization, it is necessary to determine the internal and external traffic flows on the network.

Internal Traffic

Internal traffic is generated by local hosts and is destined for other hosts within the campus network. Diagramming internal traffic flows can show areas where high bandwidth connections are needed, as well as identify possible bottlenecks where traffic might become congested. These diagrams assist the designer to select the appropriate equipment and infrastructure to support the traffic volumes.

External Traffic

External traffic is defined as traffic that is initiated by users outside the local network as well as traffic sent to destinations located on remote networks. Some types of external traffic, such as emergency services or financial services, require redundancy and present additional security concerns. The designer diagrams this traffic in order to determine the location of firewalls and DMZ networks, as well as the Internet connectivity requirements.

The designer analyzes internal and external traffic flows using NBAR and Netflow. To ensure that network bandwidth is used efficiently, NBAR can be used to identify and classify types of traffic in order to apply QoS mechanisms.

Refer to
Interactive Graphic
in online course.

full page activity

4.1.4 How Application Characteristics Affect Network Design

Refer to
Figure
in online course

The types of hardware installed on a network affect the performance of an application. A complex network, such as the sports stadium network, contains many different types of hardware. Each of these device types can introduce delay in application response speed to user requests. Delay affects customer satisfaction with the application performance. For example, applications used for voice and video can be affected by hardware delays, causing performance to degrade. Hardware delays can be caused by:

- Processing time that a router takes to forward traffic

- Older switches that are not able to handle traffic loads generated by modern applications

One way to ensure high performance is to use the top-down approach. The top-down approach adapts the design of the physical infrastructure to the needs of the network applications. Network devices are chosen only after a thorough technical requirements analysis.

Network applications on a modern network produce a range of packets. These packets are of various sizes, with distinct sets of protocols, different tolerances to delay, and other characteristics. When the service requirements of these different applications conflict with one another, performance problems can result. When adding a new application, the network designer needs to consider the impact on the performance of existing applications. The designer should consider the predicted application performance under varying configurations and network conditions.

Refer to
Interactive Graphic
in online course.

Full Page Activity

4.2 Explaining Common Network Applications

4.2.1 Transaction Processing

Refer to
Figure
in online course

Networked applications are now the backbone of business activity. To meet the business goals of the client, the network designer must ensure application performance. However, each application or traffic type and each particular mix of applications has different requirements, which can result in performance issues.

Some of the more common application types include:

- Transaction-processing applications

- Real-time streaming applications

- File transfer and email applications

- HTTP and web applications

- Microsoft domain services

Transaction-Processing Applications

Transaction-processing is a type of processing in which the computer responds immediately to user requests. Each request generated by the user is a transaction. These transactions can require additional operations to take place in response to the original request. For this reason, application transactions are a unique consideration in network design.

As an example of a transaction process, consider what happens when a customer purchases tickets online for an event at the sports stadium.

This single transaction generates all the following operations on the network:

- Web traffic from the client to the network
- Database transactions
- Customer order transaction
- Order processing transaction
- Shipping/delivery transaction

Refer to
Figure
in online course

Not all traffic that enters or exits a network is considered a transaction process. A valid transaction must meet the following criteria:

- It must be atomic.
- It must be consistent.
- It must be isolated.
- It must be durable.

Atomic Transaction

An *atomic transaction* guarantees that either all the tasks of a transaction are performed or none of them are. If the transaction is not fully processed, then the entire transaction is void.

Consistent Transaction

A consistent transaction ensures that incomplete transactions are not allowed. If an incomplete transaction occurs, the system returns to the state that it was in before the transaction began.

Isolated Transaction

An isolated transaction is kept secure from all the other transactions on the network. Security is a major network design consideration. Security options include the addition of access control lists (ACLs), *encryption*, and firewalls to the network topology.

Durable Transaction

A durable transaction guarantees that once the transaction is completed, the transaction will not be undone - even after a system failure. A durable design for transaction processes requires redundancy at multiple levels. These levels include the Physical Layer connections, servers, switching devices, and routers.

Refer to
Figure
in online course

The network designer evaluates redundancy and security tools that support transaction-processing applications.

Redundancy

Incorporating transaction applications requires the designer to consider the impact of each transaction on the network. This process is crucial, because additional cabling or devices may be needed to provide the redundancy or available throughput that these transactions require. Adding redundancy to a network brings the following advantages:

- Reduction or elimination of network downtime

- Increased availability of applications

Networks with redundancy eliminate the problem of single points of failure. If a path or device fails, the redundant path or device can complete the process or transaction. Servers that handle transaction processes have an alternate path to receive or deliver traffic. This helps ensure that the application is available when the customer requests it.

Network devices can also be configured for redundancy. Two common protocols are:

- Rapid Spanning Tree Protocol (*RSTP*)

- Hot Standby Routing Protocol (*HSRP*)

RSTP prevents Layer 2 switching loops that can occur with redundant switches.

HSRP can provide Layer 3 redundancy in the network. HSRP provides immediate or link-specific failover and a recovery mechanism.

Redundant links and devices can be implemented in the proposed stadium network design at both the Distribution and Core Layers.

> Refer to
> **Figure**
> in online course

Security

Security is always a major consideration. It affects not only the transaction processes, but all applications and traffic within an internal network and an external network. Protecting the privacy and integrity of transaction information and the transaction database should be the focus of security considerations. The network designer analyzes the potential for the transaction data to be accessed inappropriately or altered.

VPNs use a process called tunneling. Tunneling is often referred to as "port forwarding". It is the transmission of data through a public network that is intended for a private network. Tunneling is accomplished by encapsulating the private network data and protocol information within the public network transmission units.

Intrusion detection systems (IDS) are used to monitor network traffic for suspicious activity. If suspicious activity is detected, an IDS alerts the system or administrator. An IDS can be configured to block the user source IP address from accessing the network.

Firewalls filter traffic based on a set of criteria. The complexity of the firewall configuration can cause delays. The potential impact of delays should be considered in the design of a network.

ACLs can filter potentially harmful traffic that is trying to enter the network and block specific traffic from exiting the network. These access controls can slow the transaction process. The time-sensitive nature of some transactions should be considered when configuring ACLs.

4.2.2 Real-Time Streaming and Voice

> Refer to
> **Figure**
> in online course

Real-time Applications

When designing the network to accommodate real-time applications, the network designer must consider how the network infrastructure will affect application performance.

These considerations include the physical elements of the infrastructure:

- Hardware devices and connections

- Network topology

- Physical redundancy

Logical considerations include how the configuration of QoS and security solutions affect traffic. All of these considerations affect how the designer will implement network solutions, such as *IP telephony* services.

Real-time streaming applications present unique requirements for the network design. The only real-time application currently in use in the stadium is video surveillance. IP telephony is included in the proposed network upgrade. Traffic from these applications must be forwarded with the least latency and jitter possible.

When determining the business goals and technical requirements for the customer, all aspects of the network should be analyzed to ensure proper implementation and support of the real-time applications.

Refer to **Figure** in online course

Infrastructure

To support the existing and proposed real-time applications, the infrastructure must accommodate the characteristics of each type of traffic.

The network designer must determine whether the existing switches and cabling can support the traffic that will be added to the network. Cabling that can support gigabit transmissions should be able to carry the traffic generated and not require any changes to the infrastructure. Older switches may not support Power over Ethernet (PoE). Obsolete cabling may not support the bandwidth requirements. The switches and cabling would need to be upgraded to support these applications.

VoIP

When introducing *VoIP* to a network that uses traditional telephones, it is important to remember that VoIP uses voice-enabled routers. These routers convert analog voice from traditional telephone signals into IP packets.

Once converted into IP packets, the router sends those packets between corresponding locations. Voice-enabled routers must be added to the design.

IP Telephony

In IP telephony, the IP phone itself performs voice-to-IP conversion. Voice-enabled routers are not required within the enterprise network. IP phones can use *Cisco Unified Communications Manager* as a server for call control and signaling. The stadium network requirements include IP telephony.

Refer to **Figure** in online course

Real-time Video Protocols

To transport streaming media effectively, the network must be able to support applications that require delay-sensitive delivery. Real-Time Transport Protocol (*RTP*) and Real-Time Transport Control Protocol (*RTCP*) are two protocols that support this requirement.

RTP and RTCP enable control and scalability of the network resources by allowing QoS mechanisms to be incorporated. These QoS mechanisms provide valuable tools for minimizing latency issues for real-time streaming applications. These tools include priority queuing, custom queuing, *low latency queuing*, and class-based weighted fair queuing.

One of the technical requirements of the stadium is to allow video of the events held in the stadium to be viewed in real-time from anywhere in the stadium.

4.2.3 File Transfer and Email

Refer to **Figure** in online course

File transfers put high-volume traffic onto the network. This traffic can have a greater effect on throughput than interactive end-to-end connections. Although file transfers are throughput-intensive, they typically have low response-time requirements.

Some of the characteristics of file transfer traffic include:

- *Unpredictable bandwidth usage* - this type of traffic is usually user initiated and therefore cannot be reliably predicted.

- *Large packet size* - FTP and other file transfer traffic uses large packet sizes for efficient transfer. These large packets can cause delay for other types of traffic when the network becomes congested.

As part of the initial characterization of the network, it is important to identify the number of users that use file transfers on a regular basis. FTP is not the only type of file transfer traffic usually present on a LAN. Copying files from shared network drives and downloading large files using http have similar characteristics to FTP.

From this information, the network designer can anticipate the throughput requirements. If these requirements exceed the network capacity, it is necessary to implement QoS measures to ensure the performance of delay-sensitive applications.

Refer to
Figure
in online course

Email

Email is one of the most popular network services. With its simplicity and speed, email has revolutionized how people communicate. Yet, to run on a computer or other end device, email requires several applications and services. Two common Application Layer protocols are Post Office Protocol (POP) and Simple Mail Transfer Protocol (SMTP).

Email Client Processes

Email users typically access their email service using an application called an email client. The email client enables users to compose and send messages, then places received messages into the user's mailbox.

Email Server Processes

The email server also transfers and delivers mail to the email client.

Although a single email does not generate significant traffic, it is possible for mass emails to be transmitted that inundate the network or servers with traffic.

Refer to
Figure
in online course

Supporting File Transfer and Email Applications

Customers expect immediate access to their emails and to the files that they are sharing or updating.

To help ensure this availability, the network designer takes the following steps:

- Securing file and mail servers in a centralized location, such as a server farm.

- Protecting the location from unauthorized access by physical and logical security measures.

- Creating redundancy in the server farm that ensures that if one device fails, all files are not lost.

- Configuring redundant paths to the servers.

Refer to
Lab Activity
for this chapter

Lab Activity

Analyze network traffic using NBAR.

4.2.4 HTTP and Web Traffic

Refer to
Figure
in online course

HTTP and Web Traffic

Hypertext Transfer Protocol (*HTTP*) is one of the protocols in the TCP/IP suite that was originally developed to publish and retrieve web pages. It is now used for distributed collaborative information systems. HTTP is used across the World Wide Web for data transfer. It is one of the most widely used application protocols.

HTTP specifies a request/response protocol between a client, typically a web browser, and a server.

When a client sends a request message to a server, the HTTP protocol defines the message types used by the client. The protocol also specifies the message types that the server uses to respond.

This process would appear to be a minor consideration in the design process. However, if the server that is being accessed is used for e-commerce or to store customer information, the security and redundancy issues become even more important.

Refer to
Figure
in online course

Network Media

To support HTTP and web traffic, it is necessary to have Layer 3 devices that can control the internal and external traffic flows. In a network audit, the inbound traffic should be considered part of the network baseline testing.

Redundancy

Servers usually have redundant components and power sources. They may be equipped with two or more NICs connected to separate switches.

Security

Security features such as ACLs, firewalls, and IDS, are also used to prevent unauthorized traffic from being sent in to or out of the protected networks. As with the other application servers, the HTTP server should be located at the ISP or in the centralized server farm for added physical security and redundancy.

4.2.5 Microsoft Domain Services

Refer to
Figure
in online course

The stadium uses Microsoft Active Directory Services. Therefore, the network designer must consider both server-to-server and server-to-client communications. Microsoft servers support many different types of services that rely on high speed communications between the servers themselves. These services, such as Active Directory replication, must be considered when relocating servers during a network redesign.

Ports used by Microsoft Domain Services

Microsoft servers and clients communicate with each other using a set of TCP and UDP ports. These ports are used for various Microsoft services, including authentication and authorization. Many Microsoft-specific services generate local broadcast packets on these ports, as well as unicast requests. Common TCP and UDP ports that must be open for Microsoft Domain Services to operate correctly include:

UDP 53 - DNS Services

UDP 67 - DHCP

UDP 123 - Windows Time Service

TCP 135 - Remote Procedure Call (RPC)

UDP 137 - NetBIOS Name Resolution

UDP 138 - NetBIOS Datagram Service

TCP 139 - NetBIOS Session Service

TCP 389 and UDP 389 - LDAP Service

TCP 445 - Server Message Blocks (SMB)

TCP 1433 - Microsoft SQL over TCP

Active Directory and DNS

When a Microsoft Windows 2003 Server is installed in a network, there is very tight integration between Active Directory Services and DNS. Active Directory requires DNS to locate domain controllers, which provide authentication and authorization services. Windows 2003 Domain Controllers must be DNS servers as well. This DNS service can provide the main DNS for an organization, or may be in addition to Internet DNS services located on non-Windows servers. Microsoft design guides also recommend that DCHP be integrated with DNS. This ensures that a simultaneous entry is created in the DNS file when a PC or device receives an IP address via DHCP.

Refer to Interactive Graphic in online course.

full Screen Actiivty

4.3 Introducing Quality of Service (QoS)

4.3.1 What Is Quality of Service and Why Is It Needed?

Refer to Figure in online course

Quality of service (*QoS*) refers to the capability of a network to provide preferential service to selected network traffic. The primary goal of QoS is to provide priority, including dedicated bandwidth, controlled jitter and latency, and reduced packet loss.

When creating QoS policies for an organization, it is important to focus on which traffic needs preferential treatment. Network designers must consider how QoS issues affect not only the devices on a network but also the applications that use the network.

Users perceive service quality based on two criteria:

- The speed with which the network reacts to their requests

- The availability of the applications they want to use

QoS helps to manage these issues for traffic flows within the network infrastructure and for the applications that use the network.

Some Cisco devices, such as routers, have built-in QoS mechanisms.

Refer to Figure in online course

Some applications are extremely sensitive to bandwidth requirements, packet delays, network jitter, and possible packet loss. These applications include real-time IP telephony and streaming video.

IP Telephony Requirements

The requirements of IP telephony illustrate many of the problems of real-time applications in a converged network. Voice traffic requires more than a simple connection between users. The quality of the transmissions is extremely important. When delays occur, voices break up and words become distorted.

To avoid substandard transmission quality, IP telephony requires that QoS mechanisms be in place. Voice packets must not have a one-way delay greater than 150 ms. It is critical in the deployment of IP telephony solutions that voice packets have low latency and low jitter at each hop along a given path.

Streaming Video Requirements

Streaming video is a video feed that is usually sent from prerecorded files. It can be distributed in a live broadcast converting the video into a compressed digital signal and then transmitted by a special web server. This media stream is sent as a multicast so multiple users can view the stream at the same time.

In a network without QoS, all packets receive the same treatment, and real-time applications suffer.

QoS does not actually create more bandwidth. Instead, it prioritizes bandwidth use to support the applications, such as IP telephony, that need it most. To do this, QoS uses traffic queues to help manage priority traffic on converged networks.

4.3.2 Traffic Queues

Refer to
Figure
in online course

Voice and Data Traffic

In a converged network, constant, small-packet voice traffic competes with larger, irregular data flows from server updates and file transfers. Although typically the packets carrying voice traffic on a converged network are small, delays that occur while they traverse the network will cause poor voice quality.

Data from real-time applications, such as IP telephony, must be processed at the same rate as it is sent, and there is no time to retransmit packets with errors. Therefore, VoIP uses UDP as a best-effort transport protocol.

Conversely, packets carrying file transfer data typically are large. These packets use the error-checking and retransmission features of TCP to survive delays and packet drops.

It is possible to retransmit part of a dropped data file, but it is not feasible to retransmit part of a voice conversation. For this reason, critical, time-sensitive, voice and video traffic must have priority over data traffic.

QoS Mechanisms

Mechanisms must be in place to provide QoS priority. The priorities for traffic can be high, medium, normal, and low. Traffic queues are only one of the QoS mechanisms available for prioritizing traffic on the network. Traffic queues assist in providing secure, predictable, and guaranteed services. Even a brief network outage on a converged network can seriously disrupt business operations.

Refer to
Figure
in online course

Hardware and Software Queues

Queues are used to manage traffic flow with QoS. Hardware queues store traffic as it is received and send packets out in the order received, on a first-come first-served basis. The hardware queue is sometimes referred to as the transmit queue, or *TxQ*. This is the physical queue where packets wait for forwarding based on their priority.

Software queues allow the packets to be sent out based on the priority set by the network designer or administrator. The queues are based on the QoS requirements. Priority queuing (*PQ*) and custom queuing (*CQ*) are examples of software queues.

Implementing QoS in Traffic Queues

To implement QoS on a network, the designer follows three basic steps to ensure that traffic is properly prioritized:

Step 1: Identify Traffic Requirements

Determine the QoS requirements needed for the different types of traffic such as voice, mission-critical applications, and which low priority traffic can be marked as best-effort.

Step 2: Define Traffic Classes

After traffic has been identified, it can be placed in appropriate classes, such as voice traffic, which has the highest priority, followed by mission-critical applications. All other traffic can be prioritized as normal or low depending on the purpose of the data. Packets are marked to indicate the class to which they belong.

Step 3: Define QoS Policies

The last step is to define the *QoS policies* to be applied to each class. These policies include scheduling traffic queues and rules for managing congestion.

4.3.3 Priorities and Traffic Management

Refer to
Figure
in online course

Many methods are available for managing traffic on a network. One method is priority queuing (PQ). As part of implementing QoS on a network, Priority queuing classifies traffic as high, medium, normal, or low priority. Priority queuing can then be applied to these QoS classes.

Priority queuing is useful for time-sensitive, mission-critical protocols. PQ works by establishing four output interface queues - high, medium, normal, and low - each serving a different level of priority. These queues are configurable for the following characteristics:

- Queue type
- Traffic assignment
- Size

Incoming traffic is classified, marked to indicate its class, and forwarded.

Traffic is assigned to the various queues based on QoS policies defined in a priority list. These policies can be based on protocol, port number, or other criteria established for the designated traffic type. They represent a set of filters that separate different traffic types into the four class-based queues.

Refer to
Figure
in online course

Cisco is incorporating tools to assist with the configuration of QoS. One of those tools is Auto-QoS, which is available as part of the Cisco IOS software.

Cisco AutoQoS provides a simple, intelligent Command Line Interface (CLI). This CLI enables LAN and WAN QoS for VoIP on Cisco switches and routers.

Auto QoS incorporates the Cisco best practices for implementing quality of service and makes it easy for customers to configure their networks to support high priority traffic, such as voice or video.

Cisco AutoQoS can reduce the deployment cost and time frame by as much as two-thirds, when compared to a manual approach.

Refer to
Lab Activity
for this chapter

Lab Activity

Rank traffic based on given scenarios specific to the stadium case study.

4.3.4 Where Can QoS Be Implemented?

Refer to
Figure
in online course

When configuring QoS features, the network administrator can select the specific network traffic, prioritize it according to its relative importance, and use congestion-management techniques to provide preferential treatment. QoS can be implemented at the Access, Distribution, and Core Layers of a network.

Layer 2 Devices

Layer 2 switches at the Access Layer can support QoS based on IEEE 802.1p Class of Service (CoS). The Layer 2 switch QoS uses classification and scheduling to prioritize sending frames from the switch into the network.

Layer 3 Devices

Layer 3 devices can support QoS based on physical interface, IP addresses, logical port numbers, and QoS bits in the IP packet. QoS in Distribution and Core Layer devices must be supported in both directions of traffic flow.

Classification and Marking

Classification is the process by which traffic is grouped. Classifications are made based on how traffic is marked or by protocol. Traffic can be marked by Layer 2 class of service, an IP precedence, or a Differentiated Services Code Point (*DSCP*) value:

- Class of service (CoS) is the first 3 bits of an 802.1q VLAN tag.

- IP precedence is the first 3 bits of the Type of Service (*ToS*) byte in the IP header.

- DSCP can be assigned by the router or switch. It is the first 6 bits in the ToS byte in the header.

Classification and marking allow the partitioning of traffic into multiple priority levels, or classes of service.

Refer to Lab Activity for this chapter

Lab Activity

Set up a Priority Queue to mark packets. Use NetFlow to view packet markings. Create a list of possible areas for QoS and redundancy inclusion.

4.4 Examining Voice and Video Options

4.4.1 Converged Network Considerations

Refer to Figure in online course

Modern networks can support converged services where video and voice traffic are merged with data traffic. The network in the stadium is a typical example.

Managing Converged Networks

Control methods for voice and video traffic on converged networks are different from control methods for other traffic, such as web-based (HTTP) traffic.

Quality of Service (QoS) on Converged Networks

All networks perform better when QoS controls:

- Delay and jitter

- Bandwidth provisioning

- Packet loss parameters

Converged networks require strong performance and security features to manage the conflicting requirements of their traffic. For this reason, QoS mechanisms are mandatory.

4.4.2 Requirements of an IP Telephony Solution

Refer to Figure in online course

One of the technical requirements of the stadium network is to upgrade to an IP telephony solution.

IP Telephony Design Considerations

The proposed network design must include:

- Power and capacity planning

- Identifying contending traffic flows
- Selecting the components for the IP telephony solution

The components of an IP telephony solution can include:

- IP phones
- Gateway
- Multipoint control unit (MCU)
- Call agent
- Application servers
- Video endpoint
- Software telephone

Other components, such as software voice applications and interactive voice response (*IVR*) systems, provide additional services to meet the needs of enterprise sites.

Refer to
Figure
in online course

Isolating Traffic

If both the client PC and the IP phone are on the same VLAN, each will try to use the available bandwidth without considering the other device. The simplest method to avoid a conflict is to use separate VLANs for IP telephony traffic and data traffic.

Benefits of Separate VLANs

Using separate VLANs provides these benefits:

- QoS can prioritize the IP telephony traffic as it crosses the network.
- Network administrators can identify and troubleshoot network problems more easily when phones are on separate IP subnets and VLANs.

The proposed stadium network upgrade, including the IP telephony solution, requires the development of a more efficient IP addressing scheme and a VLAN structure. The network designer should add this information to the Design Requirements document.

Refer to
Figure
in online course

The stadium management wants to replace their digital telephone system with IP telephony.

Traditional Telephony

Traditional business telephone systems are typically built around a central control unit, called a private branch exchange (*PBX*). The PBX routes voice calls via analog or digital lines, depending on the type of device. For example, an analog fax machine or analog phone uses an analog line, and a digital desktop phone uses a digital line. In traditional telephony, the physical address of the phone is dependent on the wire to which it is connected. Consequently adding, moving, or changing telephones requires a significant amount of manual configuration. Most businesses have a separate wiring infrastructure to support their telephone network in addition to the infrastructure that supports their data network.

The stadium company has a digital PBX system that operates over a separate infrastructure.

VoIP

Cisco uses the term VoIP when using voice-enabled routers to convert analog voice from traditional telephones into IP packets and route those packets between locations. Within the IT industry, VoIP is used interchangeably with IP telephony. With VoIP, the PBX connects to a voice-enabled router. It does not connect to a *PSTN* or to another PBX. Businesses use VoIP to reduce costs by consolidating WAN links, decreasing long distance calling charges and reducing the number of support staff.

Refer to
Figure
in online course

IP Telephony

IP telephony replaces traditional phones with IP phones and uses Cisco Unified Communications Manager, which is a server for call control and signaling. IP telephony has the following features:

- Integrates voice and voice-messaging applications that connect via the IP network rather than via the analog or digital systems.

- Uses an IP phone to perform voice-to-IP conversion.

- Creates peer-to-peer relationships between the phones involved in a conversation rather than centrally routing calls as a PBX does.

The network designer and customer can incorporate VoIP or IP telephony onto the existing data network, creating a converged network.

The stadium company expects to gain the following benefits of IP telephony:

- Simplified administration of office moves, additions, and changes

- Additional applications, such as directories and web pages, to the telephony system

- Reduced cost to manage the separate infrastructures

Refer to
Interactive Graphic
in online course.

Full Screen Activity

4.4.3 Video - Live and On-Demand

Refer to
Figure
in online course

Higher bandwidths enable network users to have audio and video on their computer systems. Video can be viewed as live video or as Video on Demand (*VoD*).

Live Video

Live video, or *streaming video*, enables users to see content before all the media packets are inside their computer system. Streaming media files do not have a waiting period for viewing; they are available immediately as a continuous stream of data packets. Streaming video eliminates the need to store large media files or to allocate storage space for the files before playing them. A live video feed is often sent using multicast packets to many users at the same time.

VoD

With VoD, users can either stream or download all of the content to their computer cache before they view it. Downloading the complete video file before viewing is also called store-and-forward. This method minimizes the load on system resources. Installing a server to direct streaming media into a computer cache allows users to retain the content and view it at a later time. VoD is sent using unicast packets to the specific user requesting the video.

The stadium managment requires streaming video and VoD. This creates additional traffic on the network. Placing the servers for video storage inside the server farm makes it easier to manage troubleshooting, redundancy, and security.

Refer to
Interactive Graphic
in online course.

Full Screen

4.4.4 Supporting Remote Workers with Voice and Video

Refer to
Figure
in online course

Technology developments allow greater flexibility to workers in terms of how and where to work. At the stadium, for example, workers connect to the central site from several remote sites.

To take advantage of central site resources and communications, a teleworker, branch office, or mobile user typically has at least one WAN connection to the central site. The bandwidth requirements for the WAN connection depend on the type of network resources that the users need to function in their job. If remote workers are part of the IP telephony network, a call manager system may need to be located remotely. The network designer considers whether the remote workers require access to video resources simultaneously. This access impacts bandwidth. For example, streaming video may be used for a corporate meeting. These design decisions require assessing the bandwidth at the central site WAN connection as well.

Permanent Link or On Demand?

The network designer decides whether it is better to use permanent or on-demand links to the central site. The designer works with the customer to consider cost, security, and availability requirements.

Refer to
Figure
in online course

A high-speed Internet connection is a good solution for teleworkers. It is easy to set up in remote offices and is also available in many hotels. The stadium management plans to provide an Internet connection using wireless APs in the luxury boxes and the stadium restaurant.

Sometimes, asynchronous dialup connections are the only remote access solution available to travelers. Employees who travel can use a PC with a modem and the existing telephone network to connect to the company.

WAN connections at telecommuter sites can have the following features:

- Asynchronous dialup
- ISDN BRI
- Cable modems
- DSL
- Wireless and satellite
- VPN

Refer to
Lab Activity
for this chapter

Lab Activity

Investigate the impact of multicast streaming video traffic on a network.

4.5 Documenting Applications and Traffic Flows
4.5.1 What Is a Traffic Flow?

Refer to
Figure
in online course

Traffic Flow

Traffic flow on a network is similar to the traffic flow on city streets. Just as cars move from one location to another throughout the city, traffic generated from applications moves from one location in the network to another.

A car on the street travels from a starting point to a destination. Similarly, a traffic flow created by an application travels as a unidirectional stream of packets between a source and a destination. The path is typically defined by a Network Layer IP address. Depending on the QoS and policies configured in the network, the path can be influenced by other information such as Transport Layer source and destination port numbers. For example, a host sends a request for a file to a server in one flow. The server processes the request and returns the file to the host in another flow.

Traffic Control

Without some form of traffic control, such as traffic signs or alternate roads to maintain the flow, traffic on the streets becomes congested. Networks also need a way to control traffic flows. QoS mechanisms are designed to ensure the smooth flow of application traffic on the network.

Application Traffic Flows

The flow of application traffic in and out of a portion of the network can be minimal at times and significantly higher at others. For instance, in the sports stadium, early morning traffic may include email requests, Internet access, and file uploads to the stadium servers. Afternoon traffic might include VoIP, email, file transfers, and transaction processes from ticket sales.

If the network designer does not correctly estimate the volume of application traffic during the initial design of the stadium network, all applications could experience network congestion and degraded performance. Customers at concession stands and ticket purchasing kiosks might encounter significant delays or even an inability to access the applications. Customer satisfaction would diminish.

To aid in visualizing current and future traffic on the network, the designer creates a diagram of traffic flows. The first step is to identify the projected applications on the network. This information is gathered from the following sources:

- Customer input
- Network audit
- Traffic analysis

The designer documents these applications and associated hardware in a network diagram.

It is extremely important to identify traffic flows between hosts. The network designer uses the contents of logical or physical diagrams to plan the design to accommodate both existing and new applications traffic.

The network designer generally uses a design program, such as *MS Visio*, to create a diagram that shows the identified applications and the logical topology of the network.

After the diagram of applications, devices, and traffic flow is created, the designer analyzes the proposed design and identifies where the network can be improved.

From the logical diagram, the designer identifies possible areas of congestion. The designer then determines the equipment needed to handle the traffic flowing from host to host and from host to server.

In the stadium, the logical topology diagram shows the traffic flows from host to host and from host to servers. The connection of the devices also shows the applications that will be used. The traffic generated between the hosts is relatively minor when compared to the traffic generated from the hosts to the servers.

Lab Activity

Identify the traffic flows for the FilmCompany. Use NetFlow to identify the applications and the destination of traffic.

4.5.2 Diagramming Internal (Intranet) Traffic Flows

The stadium network serves a complex organization that has many operational areas. The management offices, servers, vendors, and ticket offices are all a part of the larger network.

Each LAN within the stadium handles traffic being sent from host to host and host to server. General file transfers from host to host and email traffic do not consume large amounts of bandwidth.

However, the daily backups to the server consume large amounts of bandwidth and need to be analyzed during the design phase.

All traffic flows, from both the internal and external networks, must be carefully assessed when designing a new network or proposing upgrades for an existing network. This assessment poses unique challenges for the network designer:

- Traffic within the internal network is easy to identify. This traffic can be used to estimate utilization of the network.

- Traffic from external sources is difficult to characterize. The designer needs to estimate the bandwidth requirements for external traffic flows.

Refer to Lab Activity for this chapter

Lab Activity

Using NetFlow, diagram the flow of traffic from host to host and host to server within a LAN segment of the FilmCompany.

4.5.3 Diagramming Traffic Flows To and From Remote Sites

Refer to Figure in online course

After all sections of the internal LAN have been characterized and diagrammed, the network designer focuses on the remote sites and VPNs.

The amount of traffic sent to or received from a remote site can be small. In the stadium network, the traffic flows may be small, but they are primarily transactional processes sent from the ticket office to the servers located at the stadium. Because these applications are mission-critical, it is important to identify the flows for QoS, redundancy, and security purposes.

As with the LAN topology, the remote devices that generate traffic on the network need to be identified. All switches and routers that are used to connect the remote sites to the stadium are part of the path that the application traffic takes.

The network designer should calculate the amount of traffic flowing from the remote sites as part of the external traffic flows into the stadium network. The designer should also determine if any ACLs or firewalls will interfere with the flow of appropriate traffic.

Refer to Lab Activity for this chapter

Lab Activity

Using NetFlow, diagram the flow of traffic to and from remote sites of the FilmCompany.

4.5.4 Diagramming External Traffic Flows

Refer to Figure in online course

Although most of the traffic in the existing stadium network is internal, the network designer must consider the external traffic that is destined for the Internet.

Diagramming the Internet is impossible, considering the number of devices that are connected to it. However, it is possible to determine:

- The outgoing traffic flows destined for the Internet. An example of outgoing traffic in the stadium network is users in the stadium who require access to external resources, such as online sports news.

- The incoming traffic flows from the Internet to locally-provided services. An example of incoming traffic is customers purchasing tickets online who need access to the internal servers to process the purchases.

By determining the traffic flows associated with the Internet, internal or external, the designer can assess the need for redundancy and security to facilitate the traffic that is generated.

Refer to
Lab Activity
for this chapter

Lab Activity

Using NetFlow, diagram the FilmCompany External traffic flows.

4.5.5 Diagramming Extranet Traffic Flows

Refer to
Figure
in online course

The stadium has a remote site and a vendor that is allowed to access the internal network through VPNs. These VPNs permit access to the stadium internetwork via secure, encrypted connections. The stadium also has a web-based e-commerce server that allows customers to buy tickets. This server is protected using *SSL*.

The trusted vendor and customers are using IPSec to secure traffic flows into the stadium network.

Refer to
Lab Activity
for this chapter

Lab Activity

Using NetFlow, diagram the FilmCompany Extranet traffic flows.

Summary

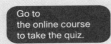

Quiz

Take the chapter quiz to check your knowledge.

Your Chapter Notes

CHAPTER 5

Creating the Network Design

Introduction

Refer to **Figure** in online course

5.1 Analyzing the Requirements

5.1.1 Analyzing Business Goals & Technical Requirements

Refer to **Figure** in online course

The design of the stadium network upgrade begins only after all of the requirements are gathered and the existing network is analyzed.

First, the network designer considers the prioritized business goals. Earlier in the PPDIOO process, the designer created the Design Requirements document that lists the business goals as well as the technical requirements that support them. It is critical to the success of the project that all business goals are addressed with the new design.

Determining how to design a network to meet business goals is a multistep process. The designer usually follows these steps:

Step 1: List the business goals that must be met by the new design.

Step 2: Determine what changes or additions are necessary for the business to meet its goals.

Step 3: Decide what technical requirements are necessary to implement each change.

Step 4: Determine how the design can address each of the technical requirements.

Step 5: Decide which design elements must be present in the final design.

By following these steps for each of the business goals, the designer determines what must be included in the network design.

Dealing with Constraints

Refer to **Figure** in online course

The Design Requirements document includes a list of constraints. Usually, when constraints affect the design, compromises must be made. The network designer explores all possible alternatives and selects the best ones to include in the design.

Making Trade-offs

A trade-off is an exchange of one benefit or advantage for another benefit that is determined to be more desirable. Network design constraints often force trade-offs between the ideal design and a design that is realistically achievable. Trade-offs between the benefits of an ideal solution and the reality of cost or time constraints are common. It is the job of the designer to minimize the effects of these trade-offs on the main goals of scalability, availability, security, and manageability.

An example of a trade-off in the stadium network design is a budget limitation that prevents a connection to a secondary Internet service provider (ISP). Because of this limitation, an alternative strategy must be designed to meet the availability requirements for the e-commerce servers. The designer recommends that additional redundant servers be *co-located* at the ISP site, to provide the needed availability in the event of a loss of connectivity to the ISP.

Whenever a trade-off is made during the design phase, the designer must ensure that the customer is informed and agrees to the compromise.

Full-page Activity: MCMA

Identify network design elements that may be affected by the design constraints.

Lab Activity

Analyze how the constraints imposed on the FilmCompany network affect the design process.

5.1.2 Requirements for Scalability

The stadium management anticipates significant growth in certain areas of the network. They do not expect the number of wired connections to increase rapidly. The stadium management plans to add at least two new remote office sites. This expansion increases the number of users by 50 percent, to approximately 750 users.

The scalability requirements received from the stadium management are significant:

- 50 percent increase in the number of total users (LAN and WAN)

- 75 percent increase in the number of wireless users

- 75 percent increase in the number of online transactions serviced by the stadium e-commerce servers

- 100 percent increase in the number of remote sites

- Addition of IP phones, and the incorporation of the video network, adding 350 end devices

The network designer believes the stadium management is significantly underestimating the need for wireless support. The stadium management is estimating only a 75 percent increase over the 40 currently connected wireless devices. The designer anticipates that considerably more devices are needed in the initial design to support the requested coverage areas. Additionally, the designer always recommends allowing for 20 percent growth. The designer makes a note to discuss this issue immediately with the stadium management.

To support this rapid growth, the network designer develops a strategy to enable the network to scale effectively and easily. Included in the strategy are the following recommendations:

- Design Access Layer modules that can be added as necessary without affecting the design of the Distribution and Core Layers.

- Use expandable, modular equipment or *clustered* devices that can be easily upgraded to increase capabilities.

- Choose routers or multilayer switches to limit broadcasts and filter other undesirable traffic from the network.

- Plan to use multiple links between equipment, using either *EtherChannel* or equal cost load balancing, to increase bandwidth.

- Create an IP address strategy that is hierarchical and that supports summarization.

- When possible, keep VLANs local to the wiring closet.

Refer to
Interactive Graphic
in online course.

Activity

Based on the number of planned APs, and an estimate of 20 data devices per AP, approximately how many wireless devices can the proposed stadium network support?

Refer to
Lab Activity
for this chapter

Lab Activity

Identify the design strategies that meet the scalability requirements of the FilmCompany network.

Refer to
Figure
in online course

5.1.3 Requirements for Availability

On the stadium network, the planned e-commerce, security, and IP telephony systems rely on the underlying network being available 24 hours a day, 7 days a week.

Incomplete website transactions can cause the stadium management to lose revenue. If the security monitoring becomes unavailable, the safety of the stadium customers can be endangered. In the event that the telephone system is down, vital communications are lost.

The network designer must develop a strategy for availability that provides the maximum protection from failure and that is not too expensive to implement. To provide the nearly 100 percent up-time requirement of the network applications, the designer must implement high availability and redundancy characteristics in the new design.

Refer to
Figure
in online course

Availability for E-Commerce

An unreliable website can quickly become a support problem and even discourage customers from making transactions. To ensure reliability for e-commerce, use the following recommended practices:

- Dual connect the servers on two different Access Layer switches.

- Provide redundant connections at the Distribution Layer.

- Provide secondary DNS servers co-located at the ISP.

- Include additional monitoring locally and through the Internet for devices in the critical path.

- Where possible, include redundant modules and power supplies in critical pieces of equipment.

- Provide UPS and generator power backup.

- Choose a routing protocol strategy that ensures fast convergence and reliable operation.

- Investigate options to provide an additional Internet service provider (ISP) or redundant connectivity to the single ISP.

Refer to
Figure
in online course

The Security Monitoring System

The servers that maintain the video files and the security management software have the same availability requirements as the e-commerce servers. The following additional measures are needed for the cameras and surveillance equipment:

- Redundant cameras in critical areas that are connected to separate switches to limit the affect of a failure

■ Power over Ethernet (PoE) to the cameras, with UPS and/or generator backup

The IP Telephone System

Although the installation of the new IP telephone system is outside the scope of this network design project, it is still necessary for the network designer to consider the availability requirements in the design. The designer focuses on the following requirements for providing redundancy and high availability on the Access Layer switches:

■ Implement Layer 3 connectivity between the Access Layer and Distribution Layer devices when possible.

■ Provide redundant power and UPS backup.

■ Create redundant paths from the Access Layer to the Core Layer.

■ Reduce the size of failure domains.

■ When possible, select equipment that can support redundant components.

■ Use a fast, converging routing protocol, such as EIGRP.

Refer to **Interactive Graphic** in online course.

Activity

Describe how various availability strategies improve the reliability of the network and limit the effects of failures.

Refer to **Lab Activity** for this chapter

Lab Activity

Identify the availability strategies that meet the design requirements of the FilmCompany network.

5.1.4 Requirements for Network Performance

Refer to **Figure** in online course

Converged networks, such as the network being designed for the stadium, carry a combination of data, voice, and video traffic. Each type of traffic has unique service requirements.

Characteristic features of applications on a typical converged network include:

■ Packets of various sizes

■ Distinct sets of protocols

■ Different tolerances to *delay* and *jitter*

Sometimes the service requirements of one application conflict with the service requirements of another, resulting in performance problems. When this situation occurs, frustrated users call the help desk to report that their application is slow.

Even skilled, experienced IT professionals struggle to maintain high application performance. Deploying new applications and services without disrupting existing ones is difficult.

On the new stadium network, three applications have specific performance requirements that must be addressed:

■ Transaction-Processing

■ Video Distribution and Monitoring

■ IP Telephone Voice Quality

Refer to **Figure** in online course

The network designer creates a list of the design goals and considerations that could affect the performance of these high-priority applications.

Goal: Improve transaction-processing time to less than 3 seconds.

- Reduce the *network diameter*.

- Restrict unwanted traffic and broadcasts.

- Provide high-bandwidth paths to key servers.

- Recommend additional high-speed storage or content servers.

Goal: Provide high-quality voice and streaming video.

- Design VLAN and traffic classification strategy.

- Keep the paths from server to end-points short.

- Reduce the number of times traffic is filtered or processed.

- Increase WAN site bandwidth and improve connectivity.

- Determine QoS strategy and traffic priorities.

- Identify areas where bottlenecks might occur and deploy a QoS strategy.

5.1.5 Requirements for Security

Refer to
Figure
in online course

Security is the one area of network design where trade-offs should not be made. Although it may be necessary to find lower cost or less streamlined ways to provide a secure network, it is never acceptable to disregard security in order to add other network capabilities.

A network risk assessment identifies the areas where a network is most vulnerable. Networks that contain highly confidential or critical information often have unique security considerations. Organizations do risk assessments as part of their overall business continuity and disaster recovery planning.

Most networks benefit from standard recommended practices when it comes to deploying security. Recommended security practices include:

- Use firewalls to separate all levels of the secured corporate network from other unsecured networks, such as the Internet. Configure firewalls to monitor and control the traffic, based on a written security policy.

- Create secured communications by using VPNs to encrypt information before it is sent through third party or unprotected networks.

- Prevent network intrusions and attacks by deploying *intrusion prevention system*s. These systems scan the network for harmful or malicious behavior and alert network managers.

- Control Internet threats by employing defenses to protect content and users from viruses, spyware, and spam.

- Manage endpoint security to protect the network by verifying the identity of each user before granting access.

- Ensure that physical security measures are in place to prevent unauthorized access to network devices and facilities.

- Secure wireless APs and deploy wireless management solutions.

Refer to
Lab Activity
for this chapter

Lab Activity

Using the FilmCompany requirements, research different security options and make a recommendation.

5.1.6 Making Network Design Tradeoffs

Refer to
Figure
in online course

After the network designer lists all the elements that need to be present in the stadium upgrade design, some hard decisions must be made. Unfortunately, few networks can be designed without considering:

- The cost of the network
- The difficulty of implementation
- The future support requirements

The StadiumCompany has placed some constraints on the network upgrade that require the designer to evaluate different design options. It may be necessary to make trade-offs in some areas to accommodate these constraints.

The primary business goal of the StadiumCompany is to improve the atmosphere and safety for the thousands of people who attend stadium events. Network improvements that directly affect how the network supports this goal must be a top priority for the designer when making design trade-offs.

Supporting the business goals may lead to decisions that eliminate or complicate other desirable or necessary improvements. For example, adding wireless access to improve the customer experience in the luxury boxes and restaurant may decrease server security unless the guest access is isolated from the internal network.

Refer to
Interactive Graphic
in online course.

Activity

Evaluate potential trade-offs based on the prioritized business goals.

5.2 Selecting the Appropriate LAN Topology

5.2.1 Designing an Access Layer Topology

Refer to
Figure
in online course

The network designer is ready to begin the design of the stadium LAN upgrade. The existing LAN is a flat network topology with no redundant links and very little security. This design does not meet the requirements of stadium management.

Access Layer Requirements

The designer creates the following list of Access Layer network requirements for the new network:

- Provide connectivity for existing network devices and add wireless access and IP telephones.
- Create VLANs to separate voice, security surveillance monitoring, wireless access, and normal data devices.
- Restrict VLANs to wiring closets, with the exception of the wireless VLAN, to support future roaming requirements.
- Provide redundant links to the Distribution Layer network.
- Use the 16 existing 2960 switches where possible.

- Provide Power over Ethernet (PoE) to IP phones and wireless access points, if possible.

- Provide QoS classification and marking capabilities.

Refer to
Figure
in online course

An increase in the number of hosts does not always necessitate an equal increase in the number of devices and ports. For example, IP phones and other devices include an embedded switch that permits a PC to be plugged directly into the phone. This switch reduces the number of ports needed in the wiring closet to connect the additional devices. Assuming that over 50 percent of the IP phones also connect PC devices, adding more data connections may not require the addition of a new switch to the wiring closet.

IP Phones have three ports:

- Port 1 is an external port that connects to the switch or another VoIP device.

- Port 2 is an internal 10/100 interface that carries the IP phone traffic.

- Port 3 is an external access port that connects to a PC or another device.

Refer to
Figure
in online course

The 16 existing 2960 switches are to be used in the Access Layer to provide end-user connectivity. The network designer must ensure that the 2960 switch is suitable for the new network.

2960 Switch Capabilities

These switches are *fixed configuration* 10/100 Ethernet switches with two 10/100/1000 uplink ports. The 2960 can support most of the following requirements of the Access Layer network:

- **Scalability** - The 2960 supports *Cisco switch clustering*; therefore, new switches can easily be added to support additional connectivity.

- **Availability** - The 2960 supports redundant power supplies. Redundant switch management is available when the switches are configured in a cluster. Two switches can be configured as the command switches. If one fails, the rest of the cluster can still function. Classification and marking capabilities are also available in this model.

- **Security** - Port security and other switch security options are available.

- **Manageability** - The switches support Simple Network Management Protocol (*SNMP*). They can be managed *in-band* and *out-of-band*. The 2960 supports the standard Cisco IOS software command set, as well as Cisco Network Assistant GUI configuration and management tools.

Refer to
Figure
in online course

Limitations of the Existing Equipment

The 2960 switch has certain limitations in the new network design. The current 2960 switches in the stadium network need additional transceivers to support the fiber uplinks. Because only two fiber connections are available to each wiring closet, multiple 2960 switches must be clustered to share the uplinks. The 2960 is a Layer 2 switch; therefore, the network designer is limited to providing Layer 2 functionality at the Access Layer.

Power Requirements

Although the 2960 switch does not support PoE, it does support voice VLAN capability. It may be necessary to use powered patch panels to provide power to the IP phones until the switches are replaced in the future.

UPS units provide backup power for the switches and the powered patch panels. The designer recommends the purchase of a generator to provide power to critical areas of the Access Layer.

The designer does not specify how the wireless network is supported in the Access Layer. There are other factors, like roaming capability, that affect the wireless network design. The designer knows that the wireless design is not yet complete.

5.2.2 Designing Distribution Layer Topology

Refer to **Figure** in online course

The Distribution Layer of the stadium network is responsible for routing traffic between VLANs and for filtering unwanted traffic.

Distribution Layer Requirements

The network designer creates the following list of Distribution Layer requirements for the new network:

- Provide redundant components and links to minimize the effect of a failure.
- Support high-density routing. Each of the 16 wiring closets in the stadium may eventually have more than one uplink to the Distribution Layer switches.
- Provide traffic filtering capabilities.
- Implement QoS mechanisms.
- Provide high-bandwidth connectivity.
- Implement a fast-converging routing protocol.
- Aggregate traffic and perform route summarization.

Multilayer switches are an appropriate choice for meeting these requirements. They provide high port density and support the necessary routing capabilities. The Distribution Layer design includes connectivity for the LAN users, server farm, and enterprise edge distribution. Six multilayer switches need to be purchased to provide the required support.

Refer to **Figure** in online course

Design Constraints

The limited amount of fiber connectivity to the wiring closets is the only design constraint that limits the Distribution Layer. The two fiber pairs that connect the wiring closets limit the number of switches that can be redundantly connected to the Distribution Layer equipment. Because all of the fiber terminates in a central location, much of the Distribution Layer equipment must be installed in the new data center.

Multilayer Switch Capabilities

Using Multilayer switches at the Distribution Layer meets the stadium design technical requirements:

- *Scalability* - The modular multilayer switches support additional fiber and copper ports. Using routing at the Distribution Layer avoids many Layer 2 Spanning Tree Protocol (*STP*) reconfiguration issues. New switch blocks can be added without affecting the existing topology.
- *Availability* - The midrange multilayer switches support redundant power supplies and fans. More importantly, they support redundant management modules and fast failover technology. If one management module fails, the secondary module takes over, with no perceptible loss of connectivity. The Layer 3 switched design makes the best use of network links by efficient load balancing of the routed traffic. Routing protocols can be configured to converge as fast as STP or faster. Route summarization can occur at the Distribution Layer, reducing the impact of an Access Layer device or link failure on the Core Layer routing.

- *Security* - Access-list filtering, port security, and firewall feature sets are available on the multilayer switch Cisco IOS. Additional security features prevent unauthorized or unwanted network traffic.

- *Manageability* - The switches support SNMP. They can be managed both in-band and out-of-band.

Refer to **Packet Tracer Activity** for this chapter

Packet Tracer Activity

Plan the interconnection of an Access Layer switch block with redundant connections to two Distribution Layer switches.

5.2.3 Designing Core Layer Topology

Refer to **Figure** in online course

The Core Layer of the stadium LAN must provide high-speed connectivity and high availability. Both the local and remote stadium networks depend on the Core switches for connectivity.

Core Layer Requirements

Design requirements for the Core Layer network include:

- High-speed connectivity to the Distribution Layer switches

- 24 X 7 availability

- Routed interconnections between Core devices

- High-speed redundant links between Core switches and between the Core and Distribution Layer devices

The Core Layer design requires high-speed, lower-density, multilayer switching. In the new design, the Core Layer network for the stadium can be implemented on two powerful multilayer switches.

The Core Layer is reserved for high-speed traffic switching; therefore, little or no packet filtering is done at this layer.

In a small business environment, the Distribution and the Core Layers are frequently combined. This may be referred to as a collapsed Core or a collapsed backbone.

Refer to **Figure** in online course

High Availability

The top priority at the Core Layer of the network is high availability. The network designer needs to consider any measures that can be taken to improve reliability and uptime.

Redundant links between the Core Layer and the Distribution Layer should be established. Installing redundant components and taking additional measures to provide redundant air conditioning, power, and services to the Core Layer devices should be implemented wherever possible.

Using a Layer 3 routing protocol such as EIGRP or OSPF at the Core Layer can decrease the time it takes to recover from a link failure. Routed connections between the Core Layer switches can provide equal cost load balancing as well as rapid recovery.

Speed

The next priority at the Core Layer is speed. Almost all of the stadium network traffic must travel through the Core Layer devices. High-speed interfaces, fiber connectivity, and technologies such as *EtherChannel* can provide enough bandwidth to support the traffic level and let the network grow in the future.

Lab Activity

Work through the FilmCompany case study to produce the recommended network design for the Core Layer.

5.2.4 Creating the Logical Network Design for the LAN

Creating the Logical LAN Diagram

The final step in the preliminary LAN network design is to create the logical diagram for the new stadium network. This diagram shows how all of the various layers and devices interconnect.

In the new stadium LAN, each of the 16 wiring closets contains at least one 2960 switch. Because there are three distinct modules in the stadium network, six Distribution Layer switches aggregate and route traffic between the Access Layer and the Core Layer.

The Core Layer consists of two high-end multilayer switches with redundancy. They are connected to the Distribution Layer and to each other with gigabit links.

The network designer makes notes on the network diagram to indicate where the servers and IP services are located. After completing the wired campus LAN design, the designer then plans the portion of the network that supports remote connectivity into the stadium LAN.

Lab Activity

Create a diagram of the new FilmCompany LAN.

5.3 Designing the WAN and Remote Worker Support

5.3.1 Determining Connectivity for Remote Sites

At the enterprise edge, the stadium network connects to the Internet via DSL provided by a local ISP. ISP-managed routers are located at the stadium connected to the EdgeRouter of the StadiumCompany.

Extending Services to Remote Locations

The two existing remote locations, a ticketing office located in the downtown area and a souvenir shop in a local shopping mall, use the same ISP provider as the main stadium site. The ISP also provides a managed VPN service to them. These connections provide the remote sites with access to the databases located on servers in the stadium management offices.

One of the high-priority goals of the new stadium network is to extend the voice and video network to the remote locations. There are two additional remote connections planned:

- A film production company, hired to provide video during and after events, needs to connect to the stadium network to exchange files.

- A sports team that currently leases space in the stadium is expanding to a remote office location. The team needs access to the same network resources that it uses on the stadium LAN.

The ISP does not support QoS or SLAs. The network designer recommends that the stadium install a separate WAN to provide the QoS needed for the enterprise applications.

Adding New WAN Connections

The network designer realizes that dedicated WAN connections are required to meet these new goals. A RFQ is sent to the Telecommunications Service Providers (*TSPs*) in the area to determine the cost and availability of WAN services.

Because the stadium is located outside the city limits, the choices for WAN connectivity are limited to *point-to-point T1* and *Frame Relay*. These services are available to both the stadium and the remote locations through a local TSP.

Although the point-to-point T1 service offers the most control over the quality of service available to the WAN sites, the Frame Relay service is less expensive. The network designer recommends that the stadium use Frame Relay to connect to the remote sites until a *Metro Ethernet* or other high-speed service becomes available in the area.

Refer to **Figure** in online course

An advantage of using a Frame Relay connection over point-to-point T1 connections is that a single physical connection to the TSP can provide connectivity from the stadium to multiple remote site locations.

Frame Relay Connection Types

Frame Relay networks transfer data using one of these two connection types:

- **switched virtual circuits** (*SVCs*) are temporary connections created for each data transfer and then terminated when the data transfer is complete.

- **permanent virtual circuits** (*PVCs*) are permanent connections. This type of connection is to be provided between the stadium network and the remote WAN sites.

After discussions with stadium management, the NetworkingCompany staff decides to install a Frame Relay connection from the stadium to the souvenir shop as a pilot to test the dedicated WAN connectivity. A *pilot installation* is a small implementation of a new network technology used to test how well the technology meets the design goals.

5.3.2 Defining Traffic Patterns and Application Support

Refer to **Figure** in online course

Network Services for Remote Sites

When determining the physical method for connecting the remote sites to the main stadium network, the network designer must also analyze how workers at the remote sites expect to use the network services. The remote sites have some applications in common and some requirements that are unique. Services needed by the remote sites include:

- Access to the e-commerce and database services

- IP telephony

- Video surveillance and monitoring

In addition, the new remote team office requires access to the team payroll and accounting server located at the stadium.

The FilmCompany employees need to be able to remotely monitor the video screens throughout the stadium and transfer video files to the stadium web servers.

The designer makes a chart of the traffic flows from each WAN connection through the network to the various service locations. This chart provides the designer with information to create firewall rules and ACL filters. These rules and filters ensure that workers at each remote site are able to access the services required.

Refer to **Packet Tracer Activity** for this chapter

Packet Tracer Activity

Using a preconfigured Frame Relay network, examine the connections to the two WAN sites.

5.3.3 Designing VPN End-Point Connectivity Options

Refer to **Figure** in online course

Backing up the Frame Relay Link

The ticket sales office and the souvenir shop connect back to the stadium network using site-to-site VPNs through the Internet. The routers at the stadium and remote sites that provide end-points for each VPN are owned and managed by the ISP. The network designer plans to use these VPN connections as a backup to the Frame Relay dedicated connections, in the event that the Frame Relay link fails. The designer recommends a backup link from each of the two new sites as well. A second edge router at the main site is planned for redundancy.

Supporting Remote Workers

The stadium management would also like to support remote workers who occasionally work from home or from other remote sites. The sports team personnel, for example, need to be able to access the team server securely when traveling. Client VPN access can be provided through the same ISP-managed service. The designer recommends that the stadium management investigate this option. They agree to contact the ISP to discuss the upgrade.

5.3.4 Creating the Logical Network Design for the WAN

Refer to **Figure** in online course

Routing and IP Addressing

In the existing network, the WAN sites use only the VPN to connect back to the stadium. Simple static routes are sufficient to ensure connectivity. DHCP addressing is provided to the remote site LANs by the ISP-managed services router.

Providing both VPN and dedicated WAN connections to each site requires that the network designer carefully choose the IP address ranges that are used for each site. It may be necessary to change the address ranges for the remote sites.

The addition of the new WAN connection to each of the sites increases the number of possible paths to the stadium network from one to two. As a result, static routing may not be the best method used to ensure connectivity to the services on the stadium LAN. It may be necessary to use a dynamic routing protocol to enable the remote LANs to maintain connectivity in the event of a Frame Relay link failure. The network designer makes a note of this, so that it is considered when the stadium routing protocol implementation is designed.

Refer to **Packet Tracer Activity** for this chapter

Packet Tracer Activity

Using preconfigured routers to illustrate a remote site connection back into the stadium network, observe what happens using static routing and then dynamic routing.

5.4 Designing Wireless Networks

5.4.1 Designing Coverage Options and Mobility

Refer to **Figure** in online course

Adding Wireless Network Coverage

A primary goal of the new design is to add wireless network coverage to the network.

In response to requests from the local media, the stadium management added an inexpensive wireless AP to provide wireless Internet in the press box. Some employees also purchased wireless access routers, providing low-grade wireless coverage in the team offices. These types of devices are not robust enough for an enterprise LAN wireless implementation.

Wireless Network Coverage

To meet the goals for the new stadium network design, wireless coverage is necessary in four identified areas:

- Press box

- Team lounge areas

- Stadium restaurant

- Luxury suites located around the stadium

The two existing wireless APs need to be replaced with more manageable devices. Some areas require guest wireless access. The team areas also require secured access to the team payroll and accounting servers.

The stadium management expects the demand for wireless access to grow rapidly. They anticipate wireless IP phone support to be required within the next two years. Supporting the IP phones requires wireless roaming capabilities and QoS mechanisms to be present in the wireless network.

Unified Wireless and Wired Solutions

Refer to **Figure** in online course

Integration of the new wireless network with the wired stadium LAN simplifies management and makes use of the security and redundancy of the Ethernet infrastructure.

Standalone APs connected to the Ethernet switches in the wiring closet can provide the necessary wireless coverage to the four previously identified areas in the stadium. Limited wireless roaming can be supported by creating wireless VLANs that span the network and wireless coverage areas that overlap.

Although this solution meets the current stadium network goals, the network designer recommends that the stadium purchase Lightweight Access Points *LAPs* and *wireless LAN controllers* to support the wireless requirements. LAPs are not standalone devices; they rely on the wireless controller for configuration and security information.

Unified wireless network solutions that include wireless control system software offer advanced features, such as centralized management and multiple service levels for different user and client types. These systems allow different levels of QoS and security for different types of wireless use.

Adding the wireless controller and management software to the network also simplifies the deployment of wireless roaming features and wireless IP phones. This configuration eliminates the need to create a single end-to-end VLAN for wireless roaming.

Refer to **Figure** in online course

The wireless solution proposed by the network designer meets the following requirements for the stadium network upgrade:

- *Scalability* - New LAPs can be added easily and managed centrally.

- *Availability* - APs can automatically increase their signal strength if one AP fails.

- *Security* - Enterprise-wide security policies apply to all layers of a wireless network, from the radio layer through the MAC Layer and into the Network Layer. This solution makes it easier to provide uniformly enforced security, QoS, and user policies. These policies address the specific capabilities of different classes of devices, such as handheld scanners, PDAs, and notebook computers. Security policies also provide discovery and mitigation of DoS attacks, and detection and denial of rogue APs. These functions occur across an entire managed WLAN.

- *Manageability* - The solution provides dynamic, system-wide RF management, including features that aid smooth wireless operations, such as *dynamic channel assignment*, *transmit power control*, and load balancing. The single graphical interface for enterprise-wide policies includes VLANs, security, and QoS.

Refer to
Interactive Graphic
in online course.

Full Screen Activity

Refer to
Figure
in online course

5.4.2 Locating Wireless APs

The results of the stadium wireless site survey indicate that the restaurant requires at least two APs to provide high-quality wireless coverage.

The network designer determines that to contain the wireless signal within the restaurant, it is best to mount directional APs against the two outside walls.

The site survey did not uncover any issues that would cause wireless interference within the eating areas. However, the kitchen area microwave oven may cause interference near the bar. Depending on the APs selected, a second survey may be necessary to ensure that the coverage is adequate.

Each of the 20 luxury suites located around the stadium requires a single, ceiling-mounted, low-power AP in the center of room.

The press box currently has a single standalone AP that does not have adequate coverage. Two new lightweight APs are recommended.

Refer to
Lab Activity
for this chapter

Lab Activity

Using the floor plan of the FilmCompany offices, with the results of the wireless survey indicated, select the correct APs and antennas for the installation.

5.4.3 Redundancy and Resiliency in a Wireless Network

Availability Considerations

Refer to
Figure
in online course

The availability of a wireless connection is dependent on the following factors:

- Location of the AP

- Signal strength of the AP

- Number of users sharing the AP connectivity

Wireless networks using standalone APs usually have the APs configured and deployed with the channel and power statically set. The channel and power settings are determined by the network designer. Once they are configured, these settings do not take into account the variability of wireless signals through the air. Site surveys record coverage at a specific point in time. It is difficult for the designer to anticipate reconfiguration of offices and the introduction of new sources of interference.

Dynamic Reconfiguration

In contrast to the autonomous APs, wireless LAN controllers automatically determine the signal strength that exists between lightweight APs within the same network. These controllers can use this information to create a dynamic, optimal RF topology for the network.

When a Cisco LAP boots, it immediately looks for a wireless LAN controller within the network. When it detects a wireless LAN controller, the AP sends out encrypted neighbor messages that include the MAC address and signal strength of any neighboring APs. In a single wireless LAN controller network, the controller tunes each AP channel for optimal signal strength, coverage, and capacity.

Refer to
Figure
in online course

Centralization Load Balances Users

Through encrypted over-the-air messages, Cisco wireless LAN controllers detect the entire network. These controllers also detect signal strength between APs. When a client looks for an AP to connect to, a probe is sent to the controller from each AP that hears the request from the client. The controller determines which AP responds to the request from the client, taking into account the signal strength of the client and signal-to-noise ratio.

For example, an adjacent AP may provide an equivalent service but at a lower signal strength. The controller determines which AP should respond to the probe from the client, based on its signal strength, or Receiver Signal Strength Indicator (*RSSI*).

These measures improve the availability of wireless services within the WLAN. Wireless controllers centrally located in the data center benefit from the high availability and redundant connections contained in the wired LAN.

5.4.4 Creating the Logical Network Design for the WLAN

Refer to
Figure
in online course

IP Addressing in a WLAN

The network designer must also consider the IP addressing structure when planning wireless roaming in a WLAN. In the case of standalone APs, a single VLAN is created and extended to all of the wiring closets to connect the APs in the same Layer 3 IP network. However, if a large number of wireless users connect to the network, broadcasts become a problem. The network is no longer scalable.

Layer 3 Roaming

When using the wireless controllers and lightweight APs, Layer 3 roaming can be introduced into a network. It is not necessary to extend VLANs to all of the APs in the network to keep a flat wireless subnet.

With the wireless controller, the lightweight APs are installed in the normal subnet infrastructure and are given an IP address that is local to the subnet to which they are deployed. All traffic that comes from wireless clients is placed into a packet that is tunneled through the underlying network to the wireless LAN controller.

Client devices receive their IP addresses from the controller, not the subnet in the area of a building where they reside. The underlying IP infrastructure is hidden from the client. The controller manages all roaming and tunneling, so that clients can keep the same IP address as they roam.

Refer to
Interactive Graphic
in online course.

Activity

Given a diagram of a network including a wireless controller and APs, answer questions about the IP addressing.

5.5 Incorporating Security

5.5.1 Placing Security Functions and Appliances

Refer to
Figure
in online course

Threats to networks can come in many different forms, and from both internal and external sources. Simply placing a firewall at the enterprise edge does not ensure network security. The network designer must identify which data and communications are at risk and what the potential sources of attacks are. Security services then need to be placed at appropriate points throughout the network design to prevent likely attacks.

The e-commerce servers on the stadium network contain customer information that may include credit card and banking details. Users access these servers from within the stadium network and through the Internet.

The stadium management and team administrative servers contain personnel and payroll information. These servers, and the infrastructure that transports the data they contain, must be secured adequately to protect this information from unauthorized use.

Security measures relating to the stadium wireless network need to be considered as well.

Refer to **Figure** in online course

Security services help protect the devices and the network from intrusion, tampering, altering of data, and disruption of services through Denial of Service (*DoS*) attacks. The primary categories of security services include:

- Infrastructure protection
- Secure connectivity
- Threat detection, defense, and mitigation

Infrastructure Protection

Network security begins with securing the network devices themselves. This involves securing Cisco IOS software-based routers, switches, and appliances from direct as well as indirect attacks. This protection helps to ensure availability of the network for data transport.

Secure Connectivity

It is critical to prevent unauthorized users from accessing the network. This can be done by ensuring that the physical network is secure, and by requiring authentication to gain access to wireless services. Stadium employees and guests should be assigned to different SSIDs and WLANs. Securing the data while it is in transit can be done using VPNs or data encryption.

Threat Detection, Defense, and Mitigation

Firewalls, IDS, IPS and ACLs provide protection from threats and attackers. ACLs and firewall rules filter traffic to permit only desirable traffic through the network.

Refer to **Figure** in online course

Implementing Security Services

Security services are not effective if they are not implemented at the correct locations throughout the network. Firewalls and filters placed at the enterprise edge do not protect servers from attacks from within the LAN. The network designer analyzes the traffic flow diagrams that were created earlier that show:

- Resources that are accessed by internal users
- Resources that are accessed by external users
- Paths that this access takes through the network

This information helps the designer place the security services in the appropriate places to enforce the stadium security policies.

Using Integrated Services

Wherever possible, the network designer uses integrated services, such as IOS-based firewall features and IDS modules to eliminate the need for additional security devices. In a larger network, it is necessary to use separate devices because the additional processing can cause routers and switches to become overloaded.

Refer to
Interactive Graphic
in online course.

Full Screen Activity

Determine the appropriate place to provide the security service.

5.5.2 Implementing Access Control Lists and Filtering

Refer to
Figure
in online course

The network designer works with the stadium IT staff to define the *firewall rule set*s to be implemented in the stadium network upgrade.

Examples of firewall rule sets include these statements:

- *Deny all inbound traffic with network addresses matching internal-registered IP addresses* - Inbound traffic should not originate from network addresses matching internal addresses.

- *Deny all inbound traffic to server external addresses* - This rule includes denying server translated addresses, with the exception of permitted ports.

- *Deny all inbound ICMP echo request traffic* - This rule prevents internal network hosts from receiving ping requests generated from outside the trusted network.

- *Deny all inbound Microsoft Domain Local Broadcasts, Active Directory, and SQL server ports* - Microsoft domain traffic should be carried over VPN connections.

- *Allow DNS (UDP 53) to DNS server* - Permit external DNS lookups.

- Allow web traffic (TCP 80/443) from any external address to the web server address range.

- *Allow traffic (TCP 21) to FTP server address ranges* - If FTP services are provided to external users, this rule permits access to the FTP server. As a reminder, when using FTP services, user account and password information is transmitted in clear text. Use of passive FTP (PASV) negotiates a random data port versus the use of TCP port 20.

- *Allow traffic (TCP 25) to SMTP server* - Permit external SMTP users and servers access to internal SMTP mail server.

- *Allow traffic (TCP 143) to internal IMAP server* - Permit external IMAP clients access to internal IMAP server.

Refer to
Figure
in online course

The security policies of the stadium management dictate user and group permissions to resources. The designer also complies with the recommended practices defined by the server operating system vendors. These practices help to identify and filter traffic that is known to be malicious.

When designing firewall rule sets and ACLs, the general policy is to deny all traffic that is either not specifically authorized or is not in response to a permitted inquiry.

Rule Sets and Access Control Lists

Firewall rule sets are used to create the ACL statements that are implemented on the routers and firewall appliances. Each firewall rule set may require more than one ACL statement and may require both inbound and outbound placement.

5.5.3 Updating the Logical Network Design Documentation

Refer to
Figure
in online course

The design documentation includes all firewall rule sets and ACLs and defines where they are implemented. Rule set statements become part of the stadium management security policy documentation.

Documenting the firewall rule sets and the ACL placement offers these benefits:

- Provides evidence that the security policy is implemented on the network
- Ensures that when changes are necessary, all instances of a permit or deny condition are known and evaluated
- Assists in troubleshooting problems with access to applications or segments of the network

Refer to **Packet Tracer Activity** for this chapter

Packet Tracer Activity

Using the stadium network enterprise edge diagram, implement ACLs to match a defined rule set.

Refer to **Lab Activity** for this chapter

Lab Activity

Given a security policy for the FilmCompany, create a firewall rule set and implement the ACLs to enforce the rule set.

Summary

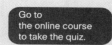

Quiz

Take the chapter quiz to check your knowledge.

Your Chapter Notes

CHAPTER 6

Using IP Addressing in the Network Design

Introduction

Refer to Figure in online course

6.1 Creating an Appropriate IP Addressing Design

6.1.1 Using Hierarchical Routing and Addressing Schemes

The IP Addressing Scheme

Refer to Figure in online course

In the existing IP addressing scheme for the stadium network, the network administrator chose the private IP network address of 192.168.2.0/23. Two additional subnets, 192.168.4.0/24 and 192.168.5.0/24, were used for addressing the two remote locations. The administrator assigned unique client IP addresses, using DHCP and static addresses, to each of the various network devices.

The current addressing scheme used for the stadium is not adequate because it cannot support the planned expansion of the network. In addition, the two wireless APs are assigning IP addresses that overlap with the existing StadiumCompany addresses.

The new design needs to use an IP addressing scheme that ensures that each network device is assigned a unique IP address.

Refer to Figure in online course

If the same IP address is assigned to more than one device on a network, an IP conflict occurs. An IP conflict on the network means that packets are not reliably delivered to the devices with the same IP address.

With proper network planning, a new IP addressing scheme can support hierarchical routing and provide an efficient Layer 3 structure. The allocation of IP addresses must be planned and documented to:

- Prevent duplication of addresses
- Provide and control access
- Monitor security and performance
- Support a modular design
- Support a scalable solution that uses route aggregation

With a hierarchal IP addressing design, the stadium network is easier to support.

Using a Hierarchal IP Addressing Scheme

Refer to Figure in online course

A flat IP addressing scheme does not meet the stadium network requirements for scalability.

A network with the correct allocation and deployment of IP address blocks has the following characteristics:

- Routing stability
- Service availability
- Network scalability
- Network modularity

Using a hierarchical IP addressing scheme for the stadium network makes it easier to increase the size of the network. A larger network can accommodate more users, ticketing kiosks, remote offices, and souvenir shops.

A properly designed hierarchical IP addressing scheme also makes it easier to perform *route summarization*.

Refer to **Packet Tracer Activity** for this chapter

Packet Tracer Activity

Design and address a topology.

6.1.2 Classful Subnets and Summarization

Refer to **Figure** in online course

To support summarization, a network must be designed to have contiguous subnets. If a network is contiguous, all the subnets of the network are adjacent to all other subnets of the same network.

A *discontiguous network* has non-adjacent subnets, or subnets that are separated from other subnets of the same network by other networks.

Poorly planned IP addressing can result in a discontiguous network. Discontiguous networks can cause routing issues, because there is more than one summary route entry in the routing table used to reach the subnets of a network. Routing protocols may not properly route traffic unless manually configured because some routing protocols automatically summarize routes by default.

Disabling Automatic Summarization

Usually, automatic summarization is desirable. However, in the case of discontiguous subnets, the following command must be entered for both Routing Information Protocol version 2 (*RIPv2*) and EIGRP to disable automatic summarization:

```
Router(config-router)#no auto-summary
```

Refer to **Packet Tracer Activity** for this chapter

Packet Tracer Activity

Resolve issues with a discontiguous network.

6.1.3 Using VLSM when Designing IP Addressing

Refer to **Figure** in online course

Stadium management and the network designer believe that the stadium network will grow significantly over the next two years. To meet the scalability requirement, the designer proposes using a hierarchical IP addressing scheme as well as a classless routing protocol.

Variable Length Subnet Mask (*VLSM*)

The network designer uses VLSM to create the subnet scheme for the proposed network. Using VLSM eliminates the requirement that all subnets of the same parent network have the same number of host addresses and the same prefix length. VLSM affords more efficient use of IP address space. VLSM also enables routers to summarize routes on boundaries that are not the same as the classed boundaries.

Classless InterDomain Routing (*CIDR*)

When VLSM is used in the IP addressing scheme, the designer must use a routing protocol that supports CIDR.

Classful routing protocols do not send subnet mask or prefix length information in routing updates. These protocols depend on the default subnet masks to determine the network portion of the IP addresses.

Classless routing protocols send the prefix length along with the route information in routing updates. These protocols enable routers to determine the network portion of the address without using the default masks.

Refer to Packet Tracer Activity for this chapter

Packet Tracer Activity

Apply VLSM to a hierarchical routing scheme.

6.1.4 Using CIDR Routing and Summarization

Refer to Figure in online course

CIDR and Summarization

The hierarchal network design of the stadium is intended to make route summarization easier and to reduce routing protocol processing. Route summarization is also known as route aggregation. It is the process of advertising a set of contiguous addresses as a single entry with a shorter, less specific subnet mask or prefix.

Because CIDR ignores the limitation of classful boundaries, it enables summarization with VLSMs that are shorter than the default classful mask. A network address with a prefix length shorter than the default classed prefix length is referred to as a *supernet*. An example of a supernet address is 172.16.0.0/14. The default prefix for the Class B 172.16.0.0 address is 16 bits. Using a /14 prefix, four contiguous Class B addresses can be summarized into one routing table entry.

This type of summarization helps reduce the number of entries in routing updates and lowers the number of entries in local routing tables. The result is faster routing table lookups.

Refer to Figure in online course

Prefix Addresses and Summarization

Classless routing protocols carry the prefix length and subnet mask with the 32-bit address in routing updates.

A complex hierarchy of variable-sized networks and subnetworks can be summarized at various points using a *prefix address*. For example, a summary route can contain a 14-bit prefix that is common to all the addresses reachable through a router. The prefix :

172.16.0.0/14 or

10101100.00010000.00000000.00000000

with a subnet mask of:

11111111.11111100.00000000.00000000

summarizes the 172.16.0.0 /16, 172.17.0.0 /16, 172.18.0.0 /16, and 172.19.0.0 /16 subnets into an aggregate address.

Route summarization reduces the burden on upstream routers.

For summarization to work properly, addresses must be carefully assigned in a hierarchical fashion so that summarized addresses share the same high-order bits.

Refer to
Lab Activity
for this chapter

Lab Activity

Use CIDR notation to ensure route summarization within a topology that is using OSPF or EIGRP.

6.2 Creating the IP Address and Naming Scheme

6.2.1 Designing the Logical LAN IP Address Scheme

Refer to
Figure
in online course

For the network designer, some decisions about IP addressing for the stadium network are easy - for example, using a private address range for the LAN rather than a public address range. Other decisions require more careful planning.

When creating an IP addressing scheme, the designer follows these steps:

Step 1: Plan the entire addressing scheme before assigning any addresses.

Step 2: Allow for significant growth.

Step 3: Begin with the Core network summary addresses and work out to the edge.

Step 4: Identify which machines and devices require statically assigned addresses.

Step 5: Determine where and how dynamic addressing is implemented.

These considerations apply whether or not the designer is using public or private addressing.

Refer to
Figure
in online course

Network address design is determined by several criteria:

- The number of hosts and networking devices that are currently supported on the network
- How much growth is anticipated
- The number of hosts that must be reachable from networks that are not part of the local LAN or Intranet
- The physical layout of the network
- The routing and security policies that are in place

In the current stadium network, there are not many hosts. Approximately 500 hosts are attached to the wired network and a small number of hosts connect wirelessly. Based on the anticipated growth of the StadiumCompany, the network designer estimates at least 2000 end user devices within two years. This number includes printers, scanners, APs, wireless devices, IP phones, and cameras on the network that need individual IP addresses. To provide room for this growth, the designer decides to use a private Class B IP address block.

Refer to
Figure
in online course

Reachability of Hosts

Some hosts in the network must be reachable from networks that are not part of the local LAN or Intranet. To be accessible from the Internet, servers and services must be assigned a publicly registered IP address. There needs to be sufficient public addresses to use with NAT. At the stadium, the two team servers and the web and e-commerce servers offer services that must be accessible from the Internet. The network designer concludes that the existing /27 subnet block of 30 public addresses from the Internet Service Provider is appropriate.

Physical Layout of the Network

At the stadium, 16 separate wiring closets are available to support the geographic distribution of end user devices. It is a good policy to restrict the IP subnets to the individual physical wiring closet locations. Separate network addresses are needed for each redundant connection between the routers, Layer 3 switches, and the WAN.

Security and Routing Policies

Sometimes additional IP networks are needed to separate traffic for security or filtering purposes. In these cases, separate IP subnets are usually created. Wireless and IP telephones require separate IP networks.

The choice of a routing protocol affects how a network is addressed. Some routing protocols do not support classless IP addressing. The default summarization implemented in the routing protocol is also a consideration. The designer notes that the planned Class B addressing scheme requires a classless routing protocol.

Refer to Lab Activity for this chapter

Lab Activity

Determine an appropriate IP addressing strategy for the FilmCompany network.

6.2.2 Determining the Addressing Blocks

Refer to Figure in online course

The network designer determines the number of IP networks or subnets required, based on the IP addressing strategy for the stadium.

The designer counts the number of subnets and notes the current and projected number of users or devices on each network.

Each wiring closet has a minimum of four subnets:

- Data
- IP Voice
- Video surveillance and game video
- Network management services

In some areas, more than four subnets are necessary to separate traffic. VLANs are used on the switches to support each separate subnet.

For each location within the network, the designer records the following information:

- Location and description
- VLAN or network type
- Number of networks and hosts

Location and Description

The designer identifies each location by documenting the wiring closet or data center room number and a description of the area of the stadium to which the wiring closet connects.

VLAN or Network Type

Documenting the type of VLAN or network enables the designer to accurately estimate the potential growth in the number of hosts. A data VLAN may increase in size more than a VLAN supporting IP telephones. A point-to-point Layer 3 network usually does not expand beyond the two original host addresses.

Refer to
Lab Activity
for this chapter

Number of Networks and Hosts per Network

Next, the designer counts and lists the number of networks and the number of hosts per network that exist in the new design. This count represents the current address requirements. The designer can then estimate the growth in each area to determine the size of the IP network or subnet.

The wireless network requirements are specified separately. Adding wirelessly connected devices increases the number of IP addresses needed without adding any new switches or ports.

Lab Activity

Determine the number of networks and number of hosts in a section of the FilmCompany network.

6.2.3 Designating the Routing Strategy

The network designer needs to select a routing protocol that meets these stadium requirements:

Refer to
Figure
in online course

- Classless routing operation that supports VLSM

- Small and infrequent routing table updates to reduce traffic

- Fast convergence in the event of a failure

The stadium has the constraint that the existing networking staff must be able to support the resulting network. Therefore, the routing protocol must be easy to troubleshoot and reconfigure in the event of a failure.

Two members of the network staff have experience using EIGRP. Because EIGRP meets all of the stadium requirements, the network designer selects EIGRP instead of OSPF and RIPv2.

EIGRP is a Cisco proprietary routing protocol. All of the stadium devices participating in dynamic routing must be Cisco devices.

EIGRP Load Balancing

Refer to
Figure
in online course

In the design of the stadium network, redundant and backup links are necessary to meet the availability requirements. EIGRP is a good choice because it can support load balancing over these additional links. By default, EIGRP installs up to four equal cost paths to the same destination in the routing table. To control the number of routes EIGRP installs, the `maximum-paths` command is used. Acceptable values for the `maximum-paths` command are between 1 and 6. If a value of 1 is configured, it disables load balancing, since only 1 route can be installed in the routing table for a specific destination.

Unequal Cost Load Balancing

There are times, such as during ticketing for popular events, that it may be necessary to use backup links for load balancing the heavy traffic. Because the backup links do not always have the same routing cost as the primary links, traffic is not load balanced across the backup links by default. A router in an EIGRP network can be configured to use unequal cost load balancing by using the `variance` command.

A variance is a value that EIGRP uses to determine whether or not to install a specific route in the route table to be available for load balancing. The formula EIGRP uses to set the range of acceptable route costs is *variance times metric*. Use the `variance` command followed by a value between 1 and 128. An example of the command is:

```
Router(config-router)# variance 2
```
Splitting traffic in this way prevents a single path from being overburdened by heavy traffic when alternate paths are available.

Refer to
Figure
in online course

Authentication

In the stadium network, there are vendors and remote sites that participate in the network routing. It is important to know that routing updates are coming from routers that are trusted. Routing protocols can be configured to only accept updates from trusted devices by using neighbor authentication. When neighbor authentication is configured on a router, the router authenticates the source of each routing update packet that it receives.

There are two types of neighbor authentication: plain text authentication and Message Digest Algorithm Version 5 (*MD5*) authentication. Using MD5 authentication is a recommended security practice, because the key or password cannot be intercepted and read in transit.

Key Management

In MD5 authentication, each participating neighbor router is configured to share an authenticating key. RIPv2 and EIGRP routing protocols offer the additional function of managing keys by using key chains. A series of keys can be configured and the Cisco IOS software rotates through each of the keys. This decreases the likelihood that keys will be compromised.

Every key definition must specify the time interval when the key is active (its "lifetime"). Then, during a given key's lifetime, routing update packets are sent with the activated key. It is recommended that for a given set of keys, key activation times overlap to avoid any period of time for which no key is active. If a time period occurs during which no key is active, neighbor authentication cannot occur, and therefore routing updates will fail.

To set the time period during which an authentication key on a key chain is valid to be sent, use the **send-lifetime** command. The **accept-lifetime** command sets the time during which the router will accept updates with the key. The default value for both commands is forever.

> Refer to **Packet Tracer Activity** for this chapter

Packet Tracer Activity

Configure a multirouter EIGRP network.

6.2.4 Plan for Summarization and Route Distribution

> Refer to **Figure** in online course

In a hierarchical design, route summarization occurs at the Layer 3 devices that act as gateways for multiple contiguous IP networks. These summary routes are then advertised toward the Core Layer of the network. The summarization in the stadium LAN occurs at the Distribution Layer routers and Layer 3 switches.

EIGRP enables classless summarization with masks that are different from the default classful mask. This type of summarization helps reduce the number of entries in routing updates and lowers the number of entries in local routing tables. Summarization reduces the amount of bandwidth used by routing updates and results in faster routing table lookups.

EIGRP includes an automatic route summarization feature. However, this automatic summarization occurs only at the default classful network boundary. This feature is not appropriate for the stadium network design. To be able to summarize the subnets of the proposed Class B addressing scheme, the automatic route summarization in EIGRP must be disabled.

> Refer to **Figure** in online course

When auto summarization is disabled, manual summarization must be configured.

The network designer determines a summary route by following these steps:

Step 1: Convert the addresses of the networks into binary format.

Step 2: Find the subnet mask to be used for the summary route.

Step 3: Determine the network address of the summary route.

When using summary routes, the designer must be sure that the routes do not overlap with other summary or individual routes.

When the route is determined, the designer manually configures this information on the router.

Refer to
Interactive Graphic
in online course.

Full Screen **Activity**

Match the summary routes to the networks they advertise.

6.2.5 Designing the Addressing Scheme

Refer to
Figure
in online course

IP Address Blocks

Based on the information contained in the IP Network Requirements charts, the network designer determines the size of the IP address blocks that are needed for each area of the network. The designer groups areas that have similar requirements, to reduce the number of different subnet masks that must be supported.

If all the devices needed registered public IP addresses, grouping would be wasteful. However, when using private IP addresses, grouping areas is a good practice. By reducing the number of subnet combinations, the designer simplifies the configurations. This makes it easier for the existing stadium network staff to support and troubleshoot. The designer decides to support 4 subnet masks: /19, /22, /24, and /30.

Assigning Address Blocks

The designer follows a step-by-step process to allocate the subnets, beginning with the largest block and working to the smallest.

The network designer reserves the subnet 0 and the subnet containing the all-1s address for special consideration. In certain more complex network situations, these subnets may require unique configuration. Although the stadium network does not currently have any condition that might cause these networks to be unstable, the designer cannot predict what situations might arise. The IP network scheme that the designer is using has more than enough usable addresses; therefore, using these subnets is not necessary.

Refer to
Figure
in online course

Using Subnet 0 and the All-1s Subnet

Even though it is not a recommended practice, the use of subnet 0 and the all-1s subnet is explicitly allowed since Cisco IOS Software Release 12.0. In previous releases, subnet 0 could be used by entering the **ip subnet-zero** global configuration command.

The RFC 1878 states that the practice of excluding all-0s and all-1s subnets is obsolete. Modern software is capable of using all definable networks.

Today, the use of subnet 0 and the all-1s subnet is generally accepted and most vendors support their use. However, on certain networks, particularly networks using legacy software, the use of subnet 0 and the all-1s subnet can still lead to problems.

Refer to **Packet
Tracer Activity**
for this chapter

Packet Tracer Activity

Assign the addresses within one section of the stadium network.

Refer to
Lab Activity
for this chapter

Lab Activity:

Create an address allocation spreadsheet for the FilmCompany network.

6.2.6 Designing a Naming Scheme

Refer to
Figure
in online course

Network device names are often assigned arbitrarily. Little thought is given to their scheme or what information they contain. A good network naming scheme makes the network easier to manage and easier for users to navigate.

There are two primary types of network names to assign:

- *Internal Device Names* - These names can only be seen by administrators. Router and switch names are examples of internal devices.

- *External Names* - These names can be viewed by users on the network. The Windows device name that can be viewed in network neighborhood is an example. DNS names are also external names.

Naming Guidelines

Common sense often dictates a naming scheme. A good naming scheme follows these guidelines:

- Keep the names as short as possible; fewer than twelve characters is recommended.

- Indicate the device type, purpose, and location with codes, rather than words or abbreviations.

- Maintain a consistent scheme. This makes it easier to sort and report on the devices, and to set up management systems.

- Document the names in the IT department files and on the network maps.

- Avoid names that make it easy to find protected resources.

Hackers can sometimes get enough information from just the network names to find targets and exploit known vulnerabilities. A compromise can be made for external DNS names that must be easy to remember and use.

Refer to Lab Activity for this chapter

Lab Activity:

Diagram the new FilmCompany network, including devices, device names, and IP addressing.

6.3 Describing IPv4 and IPv6

6.3.1 Contrasting IPv4 and IPv6 Addressing

Refer to Figure in online course

The IPv4 address space provides approximately 4.3 billion addresses. Of that address space, approximately 3.7 billion addresses are actually assignable. The other addresses are reserved for special purposes such as *multicast*, private address space, loopback testing, and research. There are few IPv4 address ranges available for assignment. Some ISPs are beginning to pass out IPv6 address assignments.

An IPv6 address is a 128-bit binary value, which can be displayed as 32 *hexadecimal* digits. It provides 3.4 X 10^38 IP addresses.

Refer to Figure in online course

IPv6 offers powerful enhancements to IPv4. The enhancements include:

- Mobility and security

- Simpler header

- Address formatting

Mobility and Security

Mobility enables people with mobile network devices to move around in networks. *Mobile IP* is an IETF standard that is available for both IPv4 and IPv6. This standard enables mobile devices to move without breaks in established network connections. IPv4 does not support this kind of mobility. Mobility is an IPv6 feature.

IPSec is the IETF standard for IP network security. It is available for both IPv4 and IPv6. The IP network security functions are essentially identical in both environments. IPSec is more tightly integrated in IPv6 and can be enabled on every IPv6 node.

Simpler Header

The header used for IPv6 increases routing efficiency by reducing the number of entries in the routing tables.

No broadcasts are associated with IPv6. With IPv4, the broadcasts created generate a high level of traffic within the network. This traffic creates an event known as a broadcast storm and the entire network ceases to function. IPv6 replaces broadcasts with multicasts and anycasts.

Refer to
Figure
in online course

Address Formatting

Colons separate entries in a series of eight 16-bit hexadecimal fields that represent IPv6 addresses. The hexadecimal digits A, B, C, D, E, and F represented in IPv6 addresses are not case-sensitive.

Unlike IPv4, the IPv6 address string format is not fixed. The following guidelines are used for IPv6 address string notations:

- The leading 0s in a field are optional: 09C0 equals 9C0 and 0000 equals 0.

- One or more groups of 0s can be omitted and replaced with "::". Only one "::" is allowed in an address.

- An unspecified address is written as "::" because it contains only 0s.

Using the "::" notation greatly reduces the size of most addresses. For example, FF01:0:0:0:0:0:0:1 becomes FF01::1. This formatting is in contrast to the 32-bit dotted decimal notation of IPv4. The primary type of IPv6 address is called *unicast*.

Unicast sends packets to one specific device with one specific address. Multicast sends a packet to every member of a group. Anycast addresses send a packet to any one member of the group of devices that has an anycast address assigned. For efficiency, a packet that is sent to an anycast address is delivered to the closest interface. For that reason, anycast can also be thought of as a one-to-nearest type of address.

Refer to
Figure
in online course

The basic types of IPv6 unicast addresses are:

- Global

- Reserved (private, loopback, unspecified)

Global Unicast Addresses

The IPv6 host is the equivalent of a registered IPv4 host address. Registered IPv6 host addresses are referred to as global unicast addresses. The global unicast address block is structured to enable the aggregation of *routing prefix*es. This aggregation reduces the number of entries in the routing table. Global unicast addresses are aggregated upward through organizations and eventually to the ISPs.

Reserved Addresses

The IETF reserves a portion of the IPv6 address space for various uses. In contrast to IPv4, IPv6 supports significantly more reserved addresses. The IPv6 reserves 1/256th of the total IPv6 address space. Some of the other types of IPv6 addresses come from this block, such as private and loopback addresses.

Like IPv4, a block of IPv6 addresses is set aside for private addresses. Private addresses have a first octet value of FE in hexadecimal notation. The next hexadecimal digit is a value from 8 to F.

6.3.2 Migrating from IPv4 to IPv6

Refer to
Figure
in online course

Transition Richness

There are several ways to integrate an IPv6 structure into an existing IPv4 network. The transition from IPv4 to IPv6 does not have to be done all at once. The three most common transition methods are:

- Dual stack
- Tunneling
- Proxying and translation

In the dual stack transition method, both IPv4 and IPv6 configurations are implemented on a network device. Both protocol stacks run on the same device. This method enables IPv4 and IPv6 to coexist.

Tunneling is a technique that is becoming more prominent as the adoption of IPv6 grows. Tunneling is the encapsulation of one protocol packet within another protocol. For example, an IPv6 packet can be encapsulated within an IPv4 protocol. There are a variety of IPv6 over IPv4 tunneling methods. Some methods require manual configuration and others are more automatic.

Cisco IOS Releases 12.3(2)T and later, include Network Address Translation-Protocol Translation (*NAT-PT*) between IPv6 and IPv4. This translation allows direct communication between hosts that use different versions of the IP protocol.

A total global migration from IPv4 to IPv6 may not happen in the near future. However, it has already been integrated in parts of the world that have nearly depleted their IPv4 addresses.

6.3.3 Implementing IPv6 on a Cisco Device

Refer to
Figure
in online course

By default, IPv6 traffic forwarding is disabled on a Cisco router. To activate IPv6 on a router, follow these two basic steps:

Step 1: Activate IPv6 traffic forwarding with the global configuration command **ipv6 unicast-routing**.

Step 2: Configure interfaces to support IPv6.

Interface identifiers in IPv6 addresses are used to identify interfaces on a link. They can be thought of as the host portion of an IPv6 address. Interface identifiers have to be unique, are always 64 bits, and can be dynamically derived from Layer 2 media and encapsulation.

The IPv6 address command can configure a global IPv6 address. The entire 128-bit IPv6 address can be specified using the **ipv6 address** *ipv6-address/prefix-length* command:

```
RouterX(config-if)# ipv6 address 2001:DB8:2222:7272::72/64
```

Another option is to configure the *EUI-64* identifier for the network portion of the address. The host identifier is the host portion of the address in the EUI-64 format on an Ethernet network and is the MAC address of the device. The EUI-64 method uses the **ipv6 address** *ipv6-prefix/prefix-length* **eui-64** command:

```
RouterX(config-if)# ipv6 address 2001:DB8:c18:1::/64 eui-64
```

Refer to
Figure
in online course

If it is necessary to configure a router to locally resolve host names to IPv6 addresses, use the **ipv6 host** *name ipv6addr* command.

To specify an external DNS server to resolve IPv6 addresses, use the **ip name-server** *address* command.

Configuring name resolution on a router is done for the convenience of a technician who uses the router to access other devices on the network by name. It does not affect the operation of the router and does not advertise this DNS server name to DHCP clients.

Refer to
Figure
in online course

Configuring and Verifying RIPng for IPv6

The syntax used to configure RIPng for IPv6 is similar to IPv4, but there are important differences. IPv4 uses the **network** command to identify which interfaces are included in the routing update. IPv6 uses the command **ipv6 rip** *tag* **enable** in interface configuration mode to enable RIPng on an interface.

The *tag* parameter that is used for the **ipv6 rip enable** command must match the *tag* parameter in the **ipv6 router rip** command.

To verify the configuration of RIP use the **show ipv6 rip** command or **show ipv6 route rip** command. Enabling RIP on an interface automatically creates a router rip process as needed.

Refer to
Figure
in online course

RIPng for IPv6 Configuration

Configuring routers that are directly connected enables the use of the **ipv6 rip** *name* **enable** command.

For example, if two routers are connected on a network, both routers use the tag *RT0* to identify the RIPng process. RIPng is enabled on the Ethernet interface of the routers using the **ipv6 rip RT0 enable** command.

Refer to
Interactive Graphic
in online course.

Full Screen Activity

Summary

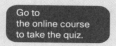

Quiz

Take the chapter quiz to check your knowledge.

Your Chapter Notes

CHAPTER 7

Prototyping the Campus Network

Introduction

Refer to
Figure
in online course

7.1 Building a Prototype to Validate a Design

7.1.1 Purpose of a Prototype

Refer to
Figure
in online course

Prototypes and Pilots

It is a recommended practice to test any new design before design approval and implementation. Testing provides a *proof-of-concept* for the design. The testing phase provides an opportunity to identify parts of the design that do not operate appropriately and redesign them.

The proposed stadium network has many design changes. Therefore, the NetworkingCompany designer tests the function of critical areas of the design before creating the final proposal.

There are two common methods used to test a network design:

- *Building a prototype network -* A prototype network consists of only the portion of the network necessary to test a particular function or capability. Prototype networks are separate from the existing network.

- *Installing a pilot network -* A pilot is a test of new functionality or capability using a portion of the existing network.

Both methods test the functions of the design that affect the network's ability to meet the high-priority business goals.

Refer to
Figure
in online course

Choosing a Pilot or Prototype

The decision to create a prototype or a pilot depends on the following factors:

- The type of testing required
- The potential disruption from a pilot on the existing network

Prototypes are usually easy to configure and control because no active network users are affected. In prototype networks, it is easy to take a device offline, make hardware or configuration changes, and redo the test under different conditions. In a pilot, this type of activity can cause major disruptions in the network.

When to Create a Pilot?

Many functions of the proposed network can be tested using prototypes. However, using a pilot is a good option in the following circumstances:

- *When the prototype is not big enough to test functionality* - Testing the operation of a routing protocol in a network with one hundred routers may not be feasible in a prototype.

- *When the performance of the network is dependent on the operation of a specific device or third-party technology* - An example is an expensive video scoreboard or a third-party provided WAN link.

The only major design change that requires a pilot is the installation of the Frame Relay connection to the remote sites. A pilot is a good choice to test this connection because it tests the actual connection quality as well as the device configuration and functionality.

Full Screen **Activity**

Refer to Interactive Graphic in online course.

Look at the network scenarios and decide if a prototype or a pilot is most appropriate. Click in the Prototype or Pilot column for each of the scenarios and then click Check.

7.1.2 Creating a Test Plan

Building a prototype to test a network design requires a significant amount of planning. The network designer creates a test plan before beginning the process, to ensure that the goals of the test are clear and measurable. A test plan is a document containing several sections.

7.1.3 Verifying the Design Meets Goals and Requirements

Benefits of Prototyping

Refer to Figure in online course

Testing the design with a prototype network plays an important role. It demonstrates to both the customer and the network designer that the network design meets the business goals and technical requirements. It creates an opportunity to compare different design options to see which one performs best.

Before beginning tests to verify specific design functionality, the NetworkingCompany staff builds and verifies the prototype network in the test plan. The designer then works with the Networking-Company staff to set up and perform the test plan. They discuss the methods for measuring the prototype network functions under different conditions.

Refer to Figure in online course

Basic Connectivity

After connecting all the equipment, the staff tests the prototype network to ensure that it provides basic connectivity. Basic connectivity is achieved when the network is operational and devices are sending and receiving data. Verifying basic connectivity is usually not part of the formal test plan. However, performing this verification ensures that the designer has a functioning network before performing further testing.

Methods used to verify basic connectivity include:

- Visually inspecting LED indicators on NICs and networking devices.

- Using console connections to devices to verify the status of the interfaces.

- Using **show** commands to provide information about devices with a direct connection. Router **show** commands commonly used to see locally attached devices include **show cdp neighbors** and **show ip arp**.

Refer to
Figure
in online course

Functionality Testing

When the prototype configuration is complete, the functionality testing can begin. The business goals determine the types of tests that are run on the network. The network designer aligns each business goal with the technical requirements. Doing this helps to determine the best method to demonstrate the network capabilities.

Choosing a Testing Method

The primary goals of the stadium management are to improve the customer experience and to ensure customer safety when attending an event at the stadium.

One of the technical requirements supporting these goals is the integration of the security camera surveillance video network into the stadium LAN.

To demonstrate this functionality, it must be possible to view the surveillance video from a PC located on a different segment of the network. The prototype must show that only the authorized stations can view it. The designer lists what must occur to accomplish this goal:

- Create Access Layer VLANs to isolate the surveillance video from the rest of the network traffic.

- Implement an IP address structure that supports the video network VLANs.

- Trunk the VLANs to the Distribution Layer devices.

- Feed the video streams to the video surveillance server.

- Configure ACLs so that the security video can be viewed from other areas of the stadium by authorized personnel, but not by guest users.

- Implement an authentication mechanism on the video surveillance server to ensure that only the authorized users have access to the security videos.

The designer creates a checklist to ensure that the network setup and configuration are correct. Each of the elements has to function correctly or the end-to-end performance test fails.

7.1.4 Validating LAN Technologies and Devices

Refer to
Figure
in online course

There are common tools available for analyzing the performance of the prototype network.

Cisco IOS Commands

Many aspects of the network operation and performance are observable using Cisco IOS software `show` and `debug` commands. The `show` commands display the current state of interfaces, protocols, routing tables, CPU and memory utilization, and many other variables. The `debug` commands enable the network designer and the NetworkingCompany staff to view the processing of information in real time. Software logging functions save and display valuable information for later analysis.

IP Utilities and Tools

Two of the best-known network connectivity and reachability testing commands are `ping` and `traceroute`. Many other utilities and tools can assist in determining the functionality of a network. For example, on a Windows PC, `netstat`, `nslookup`, `arp`, and `telnet` can test connectivity and display information from the PC.

Protocol Analyzers

In a prototype, protocol analyzers verify that packets and frames contain the correct information. Protocol analyzers help detect the presence of certain traffic types, such as broadcast and ARP, that are difficult to identify without examining data at the packet or frame level.

Refer to **Figure** in online course

Sometimes it is necessary to test network functionality in an environment that cannot be duplicated by the prototype network. In this case, the network designer can use a network simulation tool.

Network Simulation Tools

Software tools can test concepts in a simulated environment, similar to the Networking Academy Packet Tracer tool licensed for use in this course. Network topologies and configurations can be created or modified quickly. Simulations can test networks that are too large to build as prototypes.

The same IOS, IP tools, and utilities that are used in the actual prototype network can be used to test the simulated network.

The designer and the NetworkingCompany staff determine the appropriate tools to use for each test to demonstrate the network functionality. For example, `traceroute` is a very useful tool for showing the route path that a packet takes through a network. However, it is not a good tool for demonstrating the configuration for route summarization.

Refer to **Packet Tracer Activity** for this chapter

Packet Tracer Activity

Use different Cisco IOS software and Windows commands. Determine whether those commands provide the information necessary to test network functionality. This activity is based on a preconfigured prototype network.

Refer to **Interactive Graphic** in online course.

Full Screen **Activity**

Match the test tool to the type of information that it provides.

Note: A tool may be dragged to more than one box. More than one tool may be dragged to a single box.

7.1.5 Test the Redundancy and Resiliency of the Network

Refer to **Figure** in online course

Overcoming Device and Link Failures

When a business adds applications that need high availability, the network designer adds redundancy to the network. Sometimes this redundancy is added without considering what occurs in an actual network failure. It is important to test how redundant links function during a failure situation. Tests should measure how long a network takes to stabilize after the redundant link becomes active.

Redundant Links

Prototype designs use various types of redundant links to test network availability. Redundant links can be used for failover and sometimes, for load balancing during normal operation.

Load Balancing

Not all types of redundant links support load balancing. Because of STP operation, simple redundant links between Layer 2 switches cannot be used for load balancing. Equal cost routed links, and Layer 2 and Layer 3 links configured as part of an EtherChannel, can be used to load balance traffic during normal operation. They can also forward traffic in the event of a link failure.

The stadium network has two types of redundant links between devices: Layer 2 uplinks and equal cost Layer 3 links.

To test the two types of links, the designer and the NetworkingCompany staff introduce link failures into the topology. By observing the amount of disruption in network service, they can determine how long it takes for the network to resume normal functionality.

7.1.6 Identify Risks or Weaknesses in the Design

Refer to
Figure
in online course

Prototypes and simulations can be used to identify risks and weaknesses inherent in the network design. A weakness is a limitation or a flaw in the design. Risks are adverse affects that might occur as a result of the weakness. Risks increase when there are areas in the network that are not optimally designed. These limitations may be due to equipment restrictions or previously identified constraints.

Some possible design weaknesses and their associated risks include:

- *Single points of failure* - In areas where there is either limited or no redundancy to provide connectivity, there is a risk that a single device or link failure can impact the entire area.

- *Large failure domains* - If a single point of failure such as a non-redundant Internet connection, can adversely affect a large portion of the network, the risk that such a failure will have a major impact on the business increases.

- *Possible bottlenecks* - Some areas may be vulnerable to congestion if traffic volumes increase, creating a risk that response time will seriously degrade.

- *Limited scalability* - Areas or devices can present scalability problems if the network grows faster than anticipated. The lack of scalability can require a network redesign or costly upgrade.

- *Existing staff capabilities* - Prototypes sometimes indicate that the network configurations are too complex for the existing staff to support and troubleshoot. In cases like this, a risk exists until staff receives the appropriate training or a new support strategy is in place.

Weaknesses identified by the network designer and NetworkingCompany staff during the prototype testing phase must be communicated to the customer. It is also important to include what risks might be associated with the identified weaknesses. Communicating the risks enables the customer to anticipate what might occur in the future, and to make contingency plans regarding how to handle these situations if they do arise.

Refer to
Lab Activity
for this chapter

Lab Activity

Analyze a sample test plan and perform a test.

7.2 Prototyping the LAN

7.2.1 Identify Goals and Requirements Met by LAN Design

Refer to
Figure
in online course

Testing the New Design

A high-priority business goal of the stadium management is to reduce costs by implementing a converged network to support data traffic, IP telephony, and video surveillance. As a result, the new design incorporates significant changes to the stadium LAN. The network designer must decide how to test the various elements of the design to ensure that the goals of the network upgrade are met. The designer decides to test the design using a prototype network.

What Needs to Be Tested?

The designer must first decide which network functions need to be included in the prototype test. Because the goal is to create a network that supports data traffic, IP telephony, and video surveillance, it is necessary to test the elements of the design that directly impact that goal.

In the stadium network, these elements are:

- Conversion from a flat network to a modular three-layer hierarchy
- Creation of separate VLANs and IP subnets to support the different types of traffic and classes of users
- Implementation of redundant topology
- Configuration of ACLs to ensure that only authorized personnel have access to the stadium resources

7.2.2 Creating the Test Plan

Refer to **Figure** in online course

After deciding which business goals and technical requirements can be tested using a prototype of the network, the network designer creates the test plan.

The Test Plan

The designer needs to demonstrate functionality of the converged network combining data, IP telephony, and video surveillance traffic. To do this, the designer must decide:

- What types of tests to run
- How much of the network must be built to perform the tests
- How to determine the success or failure of the test

The designer lists the test outcomes that indicate that the goal of a converged network can be met. The main focus of the test is to show how the new network serves the main business goal. The NetworkingCompany staff tests the individual technical requirements to determine if the network design addresses each goal. They repeat this process for each of the high-priority goals.

Refer to **Figure** in online course

Testing Using a Sample Topology

The network designer creates a prototype test topology for the stadium that is large enough to demonstrate the operation of the planned network.

Simulating a Three-Layer Hierarchy

For the purpose of the prototype, the three-layer hierarchy can be simulated using two Layer 2 devices and four Layer 3 devices. The designer chooses Layer 2 switches to simulate the Access Layer and uses Layer 3 switches or routers to simulate the Distribution and Core Layers. The designer lists all of the devices, and possible substitutions, on the test plan.

To ensure that the prototype network is built correctly, the designer makes a checklist for the NetworkingCompany staff to follow. The checklist includes all of the functions that need to be working when the testing begins. It includes any planned changes to the configurations that have to occur during the actual testing.

Refer to **Packet Tracer Activity** for this chapter

Packet Tracer Activity

Perform the Basic Connectivity Test on a prototype network. Create a success criteria checklist.

The following document should be downloaded to perform the Packet Tracer activity:

1. Stadium Prototype Test Plan

Refer to **Lab Activity** for this chapter

Lab Activity

Using the FilmCompany network design, create a test plan.

The following document should be downloaded to perform this lab activity:

1. LAN Design Test Plan

7.2.3 Validating the Choice of Devices and Topologies

Refer to **Figure** in online course

The existing stadium network is a flat, switched network, with no routing or filtering. The network designer proposes incorporating hierarchical Layer 3 services in addition to Layer 2 switching. The proposed design includes Distribution and Core Layers in the network. The designer recommends these changes to support the scalability and availability requirements.

Routed Versus Flat Topologies

The designer wants to demonstrate the differences between flat and hierarchical topologies when link failures occur. This demonstration illustrates why the routed hierarchical topology is a better choice.

The modular hierarchal design proposed for the new network permits Access Layer modules to be added without affecting existing users. A large prototype would have to be built to demonstrate this properly. Because this is not practical, the designer decides to use a simulation tool instead of a prototype to illustrate this potential benefit. The simulation tool helps validate the choice of a routed hierarchical topology.

The designer creates a test plan for the simulation identical to one that would have been written for a prototype network.

Refer to **Packet Tracer Activity** for this chapter

Packet Tracer Activity

Following a test plan, compare the way switched and routed hierarchical networks stabilize after a major link failure.

The following documents should be downloaded to perform the Packet Tracer activity:

1. Stadium Redundancy Test Plan

2. Installation Checklist

7.2.4 Validating the Choice of Routing Protocol

Refer to **Figure** in online course

Testing the Routing Protocol

The hierarchical design of the proposed stadium network includes EIGRP as the dynamic routing protocol. The network designer recommends that the EIGRP dynamic routing protocol be configured because it is easy to use and scales well. EIGRP is a proprietary protocol; it cannot be configured on non-Cisco devices.

To demonstrate how well a routing protocol converges in the event of a link failure is difficult to do with a prototype network, and is risky to attempt in a pilot network. In a pilot, a single routing protocol misconfiguration can disrupt the entire network. Because of this risk, the designer decides to use the simulator for the routing protocol tests.

The designer wants to compare the use of static routes for the redundant links to the use of the EIGRP routing protocol. The test plan outlines a test of static routes first, then the configuration of EIGRP, so that a comparison can be made.

Refer to **Packet Tracer Activity** for this chapter

Packet Tracer Activity

Following a test plan, build and test a multirouter network with redundant links.

The following documents should be downloaded to perform the Packet Tracer activity:

1. Stadium Routing Protocol Test Plan

7.2.5 Validating the IP Addressing Scheme

Refer to
Figure
in online course

The IP addressing scheme proposed for use in the stadium network can be tested using the prototype network. The network designer recommends a simulation tool to test the IP addressing scheme. Using the simulation tool, the designer can determine if the addressing structure enables summarization and can support the necessary scalability.

The designer configures the simulated network with the same number of networking devices as the planned network. The designer then validates the placement of the various subnets and the configuration of the route summarization.

Refer to **Packet Tracer Activity** for this chapter

Packet Tracer Activity

Apply an IP addressing scheme to a Distribution Layer module of the stadium LAN.

The following document should be downloaded to perform the Packet Tracer activity:

1. Stadium IP Address Test Plan

Refer to
Lab Activity
for this chapter

Lab Activity

Build the FilmCompany prototype network. Perform the tests according to the test plan created earlier in this chapter.

Analyze the results to determine success or failure. Complete the Actual Results section of the test plan.

7.2.6 Identify Risks and Weaknesses

Refer to
Figure
in online course

Recording Risks and Weaknesses

In the Conclusion section of the test plan, the network designer and the NetworkingCompany staff record their observations and opinions about the results of the testing. An important part of this section is the analysis of risks and weaknesses in the design. In the case of the proposed stadium network, there are a few risks that must be stated. Documenting these risks helps the stadium management make informed decisions about implementing the design.

The risks and weaknesses include:

- *No redundancy at the Access Layer of the network -* Most end user devices attach to a single access switch. This is a single point of failure for the end devices. Due to the higher risk of server loss, the servers in the data center are connected with dual NICs to separate access switches.

- *Single ISP for Internet connectivity -* If the ISP connection fails, or if there is a problem at the ISP, all Internet connectivity to the stadium network is lost.

- *Limited bandwidth to the WAN and Internet -* When the requirements for WAN and Internet connectivity increase, bandwidth limitations can cause a bottleneck and reduce application performance.

- *Limited fiber connectivity from the wiring closets -* Because of this constraint, the number of redundant links from the Access Layer devices is limited to two. Therefore, multiple switches in a wiring closet must share the uplinks.

Refer to
Lab Activity
for this chapter

Lab Activity

Analyze the results of the prototype tests to determine the level of risk in the FilmCompany network.

Complete the Conclusions section of the test plan.

7.3 Prototyping the Server Farm

7.3.1 Identifying Server Farm Goals and Requirements

Refer to
Figure
in online course

One of the business goals of the stadium network is to provide better customer service. This goal can be achieved by improving access to the website for viewing schedules, purchasing and printing tickets, and purchasing merchandise.

The proposed design recommends relocating the web server, DNS server, and database server to a server farm located in a new data center.

Server Relocation for the Stadium Network

Relocating the servers from the stadium management offices to a new data center is a major change in the way the traffic flows in the stadium network. It is a critical piece of the proposed design. The requirements for nearly 100 percent uptime and availability can be better accomplished if the servers are located in a central data center. The data center design is a network module that can be tested in a prototype.

7.3.2 Creating the Test Plan

What Needs to Be Tested?

Refer to
Figure
in online course

In the proposed network design for the stadium, the following elements directly impact the server farm:

- Creation of modular server farm topology

- Implementation of redundant links for server connectivity

- Location of redundant Layer 2 switches for server connectivity

- Use of a per-VLAN rapid spanning tree to shorten the time for redundant switched links to become active after a failure

- Configuration of a flexible IP addressing structure

- Configuration of EIGRP in the data center Core and Distribution Layers

- Configuration of strict traffic filtering policies to prevent unauthorized access

The network designer decides to build a prototype network. Because the designer does not have multilayer switches available, routers are used to perform the Layer 3 function. The prototype network topology consists of five Layer 2 switches, five Layer 3 devices, and a number of PCs emulating servers running various applications. Using this topology, the NetworkingCompany staff can demonstrate that the business goals and technical requirements can be met with the proposed design.

Refer to
Figure
in online course

The NetworkingCompany staff uses the checklist created by the network designer to build the prototype network.

Testing the Prototype Network

Refer to **Packet Tracer Activity** for this chapter

After the prototype network is built, the staff executes basic connectivity tests to ensure that the network is configured correctly. They then create a network baseline.

Baseline Measurements

It is important to develop the baseline measurements of the prototype network. The results observed during the various tests are then compared to the original configuration. In this way, the staff can identify and record any processes or functions that increase processor usage or decrease available bandwidth.

To simulate traffic on the network, the designer recommends running a traffic generator on one of the attached PCs. A traffic generator is a testing tool that simulates various levels of network use. In the case of the server farm prototype, the designer intends to use the tool to simulate network traffic to the web server.

Packet Tracer Activity

Using the checklist created by the network designer, build the prototype network. Perform the Basic Connectivity Test according to the test plan.

Refer to **Lab Activity** for this chapter

The following documents should be downloaded to perform the Packet Tracer activity:

1. Stadium Basic Connectivity Test Plan

2. Installation Checklist

Lab Activity

Create a server farm test plan and prototype installation checklist for the FilmCompany.

The following documents should be downloaded to perform the lab activity:

1. Server Farm Design Test Plan

2. Installation Checklist

7.3.3 Validating Device and Topology Selection

The proposed data center design for the stadium network uses a redundant hierarchical topology for the server farm.

Refer to **Figure** in online course

LAN Simulation

In the LAN simulation tests, the routed links usually converged faster than the STP links in the event of a failure. The network designer therefore chooses to prototype the switched links with Rapid Spanning Tree Protocol (*RSTP*) to test how quickly the server farm network recovers from a failure. The designer reviews the operation of RSTP with the network technicians before setting up the test.

RSTP provides rapid connectivity following the failure of a switch, a switch port, or a LAN. RSTP enables switch port configuration so that the ports can transition to forwarding directly when the switch reinitializes.

Per VLAN Rapid Spanning Tree Plus

The RSTP (802.1w) standard assumes only one spanning-tree instance for the entire switched network. This is regardless of the number of VLANs. The Cisco implementation of RSTP is Per VLAN Rapid Spanning Tree Plus (PVRST+). PVRST+ defines a Spanning Tree Protocol that has one instance of RSTP per VLAN. Cisco documentation often refers to this implementation as RSTP.

Refer to **Figure** in online course

Port Roles

RSTP defines the following port roles:

- *Root-* A forwarding port elected for every non-root switch that gives the least-cost path to the root switch.

- *Designated-* A forwarding port elected for every switched LAN segment based on the best bridge protocol data unit (*BPDU*). This port is the least-cost path to the root switch from the LAN segment.

- *Alternate-* An alternate path to the root switch for a non-root switch that is different from the path that the root port takes. This port is blocked for forwarding traffic.

- *Backup-* A backup path that provides a redundant, but less desirable, connection to a segment to which another port on the non-root switch already connects. This port is blocked. (Backup ports can only exist where two ports are connected together in a loopback by a point-to-point link or bridge with two or more connections to a shared LAN segment.)

- *Disabled-* A port that has no role within the operation of spanning tree.

Root and designated port roles include the port in the active topology. Alternate and backup port roles exclude the port from the active topology.

Refer to
Figure
in online course

Stadium Network

The network designer reviews the RSTP operation with the NetworkingCompany staff. The designer creates an installation checklist and a test plan to verify that the switched links can provide the required resiliency.

Following the details outlined on the checklist, the NetworkingCompany staff sets up a per-VLAN rapid spanning tree on the Access Layer switches. The staff designates the primary and secondary root bridges to ensure that the network remains stable if new switches are added to the topology. They then introduce failures into the switched topology to observe the results.

Refer to
Interactive Graphic
in online course.

Full Screen **Activity**

Drag the port state to the appropriate port role, then click Check.

Refer to
Lab Activity
for this chapter

Lab Activity

Configure and test RSTP in a prototype network.

7.3.4 Validating the Security Plan

Refer to
Figure
in online course

Availability and security are two primary requirements for the stadium server farm network.

Availability Requirements

The network designer addresses availability requirements by using redundant links and components where possible. Configuring RSTP for Layer 2 and using EIGRP for Layer 3 ensures quick convergence of the network in the event of a failure.

Multilayer Security

The proposed design for the server farm implements multiple layers of security. Utilities and programs protect the servers from viruses and worm attacks and also provide host-based intrusion prevention. Authentication mechanisms allow only authorized users access.

At the Access Layer, employing port security and disabling unused ports help prevent the network from unauthorized access.

ACLs filter traffic and prevent *spoof*ed, or un-requested, traffic from reaching the servers. The ACLs are placed at the point where the server farm connects into the stadium network.

Firewalls

Firewalls and firewall feature sets in the Cisco IOS Software provide stateful firewall capability. IPSs protect the network from known threats and abnormal traffic patterns.

Refer to **Figure** in online course

Testing the ACL Design

The network designer decides to test the ACL design and placement because it has the most potential for variability. The designer creates a test plan that lists all of the filtering rules and methods for testing. The designer suggests using a network simulator, rather than a prototype network. The simulator can be configured quickly to contain all of the proposed devices and links.

Refer to **Packet Tracer Activity** for this chapter

Packet Tracer Activity

Using a prototype network, apply and test ACLs designed to protect the stadium network server farm from attack and unauthorized access.

The following document should be downloaded to perform the Packet Tracer activity:

1. Stadium ACL Test Plan

7.3.5 Verify Design Meets Business Goals

Refer to **Lab Activity** for this chapter

Lab Activity

Build the FilmCompany prototype network, and perform the tests according to the test plan created in the *Creating a Server Farm Test Plan* lab activity.

Then analyze the results to determine the success or failure of the tests and complete the Actual Results section of the test plan.

7.3.6 Identify Risks and Weaknesses

Refer to **Figure** in online course

At the conclusion of the server farm prototype and simulation testing, some areas of concern with the proposed design are identified. The network designer is satisfied that the network performs as expected. However, the stadium needs to consider some design changes as the network grows and matures.

Identified Weakness

The tests show that the ACLs at the Distribution Layer prevent unauthorized traffic from entering the server farm but are not effective at filtering the traffic within the VLANs themselves. The test traffic between servers in the same VLAN is not restricted.

Recommendations

The network design supports server farm and data center growth. The designer recommends that the stadium management consider using multilayer switches at the Access Layer. Multilayer switches provide more flexibility than Layer 2 switches in separating and filtering traffic from users outside the data center. Additionally, multilayer switches provide more flexibility than Layer 2 switches in separating and filtering traffic from devices within the data center itself.

Refer to **Lab Activity** for this chapter

Lab Activity

Analyze the results of the FilmCompany prototype test and document any risks or weaknesses in the design. Complete the Conclusions section of the test plan.

Summary

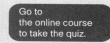

Quiz

Take the chapter quiz to check your knowledge.

Your Chapter Notes

CHAPTER 8

Prototyping the WAN

Introduction

Refer to
Figure
in online course

8.1 Prototyping Remote Connectivity

Refer to
Figure
in online course

8.1.1 Describe Remote Connectivity Testing Methods

The results of the prototype testing of the LAN validate the design choices made by the NetworkingCompany designer. The new design elements that provide WAN connectivity to remote sites and workers need to be tested. Testing remote connectivity options may be more difficult than testing the LAN design.

Remote connectivity usually requires the use of transmission facilities that are not owned or managed by the customer. These facilities, Frame Relay networks, T1 connections, or even DSL links, are usually not available to the designer for testing purposes. As a result, the designer must consider ways to test the proposed design without having access to the actual transmission facilities.

The designer can use three different methods to test remote connectivity designs:

- Simulation software
- Prototype testing using simulated links
- Pilot testing in the actual environment

8.1.2 Testing WAN Connectivity with Simulation Software

Refer to
Figure
in online course

Simulated environments can provide a way to test device configuration and operation. After the design is verified in the simulated environment, remote connectivity can be further tested in a pilot installation.

Network Simulation Software

Computer software programs offer the designer a tool to test configurations before implementing them on actual equipment. The benefits of using a simulation software package are:

- *Lower overall cost -* Test networks are expensive to build and maintain. Networking device capabilities and configuration options change frequently. As a result, keeping a lab environment up-to-date can be difficult.

■ *Flexibility* - Simulation software can support many different types of devices and connectivity options. Changing configurations and topologies is usually much quicker and easier in a simulation than when using actual equipment.

■ *Scalability* - Building a large or complex network in a lab environment is time-consuming and error-prone. Using a simulation program permits testing of large networks in a reduced amount of time.

■ *Control* - Using simulation software allows the designer to control the entire network operation at once. The network designer can determine the types of traffic to send across the network and the rate at which the traffic is sent. The designer can also stop the simulation to capture and examine packets at various points in the network.

Refer to **Figure** in online course

Software Limitations

Using simulation software programs to validate the network designs has a few disadvantages:

■ *Limited functionality* - Software programs are designed and written long before they are available to the public and can quickly become out-of-date. In addition, the software may support only some of the capabilities of the actual equipment.

■ *Unrealistic performance* - It is difficult, if not impossible, for the software programmers to anticipate and simulate all of the conditions that can occur in an actual network. Therefore, relying on the timing and performance estimates obtained from simulation software is risky.

Despite these disadvantages, using simulation software to test the configurations is an excellent way to uncover design flaws.

Refer to **Packet Tracer Activity** for this chapter

Packet Tracer Activity

Use Packet Tracer to simulate a multirouter serial WAN using PPP.

8.1.3 Simulating WAN Connectivity in a Lab Environment

Refer to **Figure** in online course

In addition to network simulation software, other methods are available to simulate remote connectivity in a test environment.

Almost all WAN technologies require an intermediary device to convert the WAN signals to either serial or Ethernet signals at the customer premise. These devices include various types of modems and *CSU/DSU*s. An exception to this is Metro Ethernet,

which does not require the intermediary device.

Simulating a DSL or Cable Connection

To simulate a DSL or cable WAN connection, an Ethernet connection can be used. Most Ethernet interfaces can be set to provide a 10-Mb connection, which is similar to the type of connectivity provided over DSL or cable. The routers are connected using an Ethernet *crossover cable*. Routing protocol metrics can be adjusted to simulate the metrics of a lower-speed link by using the **bandwidth** command on the interface. Static route preference can be manually configured by adjusting the *administrative distance* assigned to the route.

Refer to **Figure** in online course

Simulating Serial Connectivity

There are two common methods used to simulate serial connectivity:

■ CSU/DSUs or serial modems

- V.35 cables

Using CSU/DSUs or Modems

If CSU/DSUs or modems are available, the documentation included with the device usually includes the wiring diagram necessary to create a crossover cable. If the diagram is not included, a search of the Internet can usually uncover the correct pinouts to use. This crossover cable can be used to connect two like devices to simulate the link provided by the telecommunications service provider (*TSP*).

One CSU/DSU or modem is configured to provide the *DCE* function. The other device is configured as a *DTE* device. The routers are then connected and configured just as they would be in the actual WAN environment. The CSU/DSU or modem provides the clocking for the link.

Refer to
Figure
in online course

Using V.35 Cables

In the NetworkingCompany prototype lab environment, it is possible to simulate a point-to-point WAN connection using two serial V.35 cables. One cable must be a V.35 DCE cable, and the other cable must be a V.35 DTE cable. By connecting the two cables, a V.35 crossover cable is created. Interconnecting the routers with these two cables creates a circuit. Eliminating the CSU/DSU or modem from the connection removes the clocking function on the circuit. As a result, one of the routers must be configured as a DCE device, using the `clock rate` command on the interface. In actual implementations, routers and other CPE devices rarely, if ever, provide the DCE function on a circuit.

Setting various clock rates enables the network designer and the NetworkingCompany staff doing the testing to simulate different connection speeds.

The advantage of using simulated serial WAN connections is that the configuration of the serial interfaces can be tested and verified. The disadvantage of doing this type of simulated testing is that the actual network factors of the telecommunications provider cannot be evaluated.

After the configurations are tested in a simulated manner, it is recommended that additional testing be done using a pilot installation.

Refer to
Lab Activity
for this chapter

Lab Activity

Connect two routers using a DCE and a DTE v.35 cable. Configure one device to provide the clocking for the interface.

8.2 Prototyping WAN Connectivity

8.2.1 Identify WAN Goals and Requirements

Refer to
Figure
in online course

Connectivity to the remote sites is a major issue in the existing stadium network. A high-priority goal for the stadium management is to extend the new IP telephony system and the video surveillance network to current remote sites. These services cannot be supported over the existing WAN.

In the stadium network, the two current remote sites access the main network using virtual private network (*VPN*) connections across the Internet. These VPN connections use DSL lines. The ISP does not offer a guarantee of bandwidth or QoS. The proposed design includes an upgrade to dedicated Frame Relay WAN connectivity. The network designer recommends using Frame Relay to connect the new remote office for Team A and the FilmCompany office.

The existing VPNs through the Internet remain in the new design to backup the new WAN.

The designer decides to build a prototype to simulate the WAN connectivity. This prototype tests the configurations and the failover in case of a link failure. It is not possible to simulate the entire TSP packet-switched network using either a prototype or simulation software. The actual Frame Relay connection through the TSP network can only be tested in a pilot. After the prototype is completed and the design accepted, a pilot installation is planned for the souvenir shop.

8.2.2 Creating the Test Plan

Refer to
Figure
in online course

The performance through the TSP network cannot be tested in the prototype. However, other important elements of the design can be tested in the prototype WAN network:

- Frame Relay local loop configuration

- Mechanisms to activate the VPN backup link in the event of a Frame Relay failure

- Static routing configuration

- ACLs that filter traffic to and from the WAN sites

- SSH configuration to enable remote management

To prototype the WAN connectivity, the network designer recommends using a Cisco router to simulate a Frame Relay switch. This simulation enables the local loop configurations to be tested without having to physically connect to the TSP network. To build the WAN prototype, the designer needs four routers to test all of the functionality.

The designer creates the test topology diagram, the installation checklist, and the test plan to demonstrate the Frame Relay connectivity.

Refer to
Figure
in online course

The topology for the Frame Relay WAN test requires a different type of connectivity than the earlier prototypes. In an actual implementation, a Frame Relay local loop usually connects to a CSU/DSU at the customer premise. From the CSU/DSU, a serial connection is made to the customer premise equipment (*CPE*) router.

The DCE function on the local loop is provided by either the TSP or the CSU/DSU. The clocking for the serial connection between the CSU/DSU and the CPE router is provided by the CSU/DSU. All of the connections at the router are DTE connections and use DTE cable.

In the prototype test network, a true *T1* or *E1* connection to a Frame Relay switch does not exist. It has to be simulated using a Cisco router acting as the Frame Relay switch. This router is identified as FR1. It connects to the other routers in the topology using a crossover connection. At the NetworkingCompany, this crossover function is created by connecting one V.35 DTE cable directly to a V.35 DCE cable. Because no CSU/DSU exists in the test topology, the FR1 router interfaces are configured with a clock rate to provide the DCE function.

Refer to
Lab Activity
for this chapter

Lab Activity

Create a test plan to prototype the WAN connectivity between the FilmCompany and the stadium.

The following document should be downloaded to perform the lab activity:

1. WAN Design Test Plan

8.2.3 Validating the Choice of Devices and Topologies

Refer to
Figure
in online course

The Frame Relay topology recommended in the proposed WAN design is radically different from the existing VPN connectivity managed by the ISP. There are many options available when using

Frame Relay. It is a recommended practice for the network designer to review the design and operation of the WAN with the NetworkingCompany staff before they set up the prototype.

Frame Relay

Frame Relay is a high-performance WAN protocol that was standardized by the International Telecommunication Union *ITU-T*. It is widely used in the United States. Many people think of a Frame Relay link as a physical connection between two sites. In reality, a Frame Relay link is a virtual circuit that spans a series of connections.

Every Frame Relay link has at least three components:

- The local point-to-point circuit that connects the local CPE router to the TSP Frame Relay switch

- The TSP packet-switched network

- The remote point-to-point circuit that connects the remote site into the TSP network

Configuring Frame Relay on the CPE router consists of configuring only the settings for the point-to-point link with the TSP Frame Relay switch. These point-to-point links are usually T1/E1 or fractional T1/E1 circuits. The TSP configures the virtual circuit through the packet-switched network.

Refer to
Figure
in online course

Frame Relay terminology and configuration can easily become confusing. To explain the configuration options to the NetworkingCompany staff, the network designer starts with the link between the planned new stadium CPE router and a TSP Frame Relay switch.

The Local Loop

The proposed connection between the stadium CPE router and the Frame Relay switch at the TSP is a T1 circuit. This connection is referred to as a *local loop*. The local loop connects the provider Frame Relay switch to the CSU/DSU on the stadium premises. The connection then terminates on the serial port of the CPE router. The clock speed (port speed) of the local loop connection to the Frame Relay cloud is known as the *local access rate*. The local access rate defines the rate at which data can travel into or out of the provider packet-switched network, regardless of other settings.

Data-link Connection Identifier

More than one virtual circuit can be carried on a single physical local loop circuit. Each virtual circuit endpoint is identified by a data-link connection identifier (*DLCI*). A DLCI is usually significant only on the local loop. In other words, DLCI numbers are unique within a single Frame Relay switch. However, because there can be many Frame Relay switches within the network, DLCI numbers can be duplicated on other switches.

Refer to
Figure
in online course

Some of the services offered by the Frame Relay switch impact the quality of the data transmissions through the telecommunications provider network.

Guaranteed Data Rates

Frame Relay providers offer services with guaranteed average data transfer rates through the provider packet-switched network. This committed information rate (*CIR*) specifies the maximum average data rate that the network delivers under normal conditions. The CIR is less than or equal to the local access rate. A CIR is assigned to each DLCI that is carried on the local loop. If the stadium attempts to send data at a faster rate than the CIR, the provider network flags some frames with a discard eligible (*DE*) bit in the frame address header. The network attempts to deliver all frames. However, if there is congestion, it discards any frames marked with the DE bit.

Zero CIR

Many inexpensive Frame Relay services are based on a CIR of zero. A *zero CIR* means that every frame is a DE frame, and the network can throw any frame away when there is congestion. There is no guarantee of service with a CIR set to zero, so these services are not good choices for mission-critical data.

Local Management Interface

Local Management Interface (*LMI*) is a signaling standard between the router (DTE device) and the local Frame Relay switch (DCE device). LMI is responsible for managing the connection and maintaining status between the router and the Frame Relay switch. For example, LMI uses *keepalive* messages to monitor the status of network connections. LMI Frame Relay adds a set of enhancements, referred to as extensions, to basic Frame Relay. One important LMI extension is the ability to report the status of the virtual circuit as well as the status of the physical connection. LMI standards can differ between networks. Cisco routers support three LMI types: Cisco, ANSI Annex D, and ITU-T Q.933 Annex A.

Congestion Control

To help manage traffic flows in the network, Frame Relay implements two mechanisms:

- Forward-explicit congestion notification (*FECN*)
- Backward-explicit congestion notification (*BECN*)

FECNs and BECNs are controlled by a single bit contained in the Frame Relay frame header.

FECN

FECN informs the destination device about congestion on the network path. The FECN bit is part of the Address field in the Frame Relay frame header. The FECN mechanism works in the following way:

1. A DTE device sends Frame Relay frames into the network.

2. If the network is congested, the DCE devices (switches) set the value of the FECN bit to 1.

3. The frames reach the remote destination DTE device.

4. The DTE device reads the Address field with the FECN bit set to 1.

5. This setting indicates that the frame experienced congestion in the path from source to destination.

BECN

BECN informs the source device about congestion on the network path. The BECN bit is also part of the Address field in the Frame Relay frame header. A BECN works in the following way:

1. A Frame Relay switch detects congestion in the network.

2. It sets the BECN bit to 1 in frames headed in the opposite direction from the frames marked with the FECN bit.

3. This setting informs the source DTE device that a particular path through the network is congested.

Full Screen **Activity**

Drag each definition to the appropriate Frame Relay term, then click Check.

8.2.4 Prototype the WAN

To configure the Frame Relay WAN prototype, the NetworkingCompany staff first configures the router FR1 to act as the Frame Relay switch. The staff uses the command `frame-relay switching` to begin the configuration. This command tells the router to act as the DCE device and to emulate a Frame Relay switch. Additional **frame-relay route** configuration commands are applied to the router to enable it to switch the DLCIs from each interface.

The two serial interfaces on FR1 can now be configured as the Frame Relay DCE devices. Frame Relay encapsulation must be specified on each interface. The two possible Frame Relay encapsulations are **ietf** and **cisco**. The default encapsulation is **cisco**. The **cisco** method is proprietary and should not be used if the router is connected to a non-Cisco router across a Frame Relay WAN.

The network designer configures Frame Relay by configuring the Layer 3 IP address on the interface and setting the encapsulation type to Frame Relay. Encapsulation is set using the following command:

```
Router(config-if)#encapsulation frame-relay {cisco ¦ ietf}
```

The CPE routers do not need to be configured as Frame Relay switches. However, the CPE router serial interface needs to be configured with Frame Relay encapsulation and an IP address. The designer uses the names of the planned devices and their addresses during the test.

In the prototype network, there is no CSU/DSU device to provide the clocking. Therefore, it is important to configure a clock rate on the serial interfaces of FR1.

Refer to **Figure** in online course

During the prototype test, the router FR1 acts as the Frame Relay switch at the service provider. This simulates the connectivity through the Frame Relay cloud. A virtual circuit is created between the Edge2 and BR3 routers. This circuit behaves the same as a directly connected link.

Inverse ARP and Frame Relay Maps

Inverse Address Resolution Protocol (*Inverse ARP*) provides a mechanism to create dynamic DLCI-to-Layer 3 address maps. Inverse ARP works similarly to ARP on an Ethernet local network. With ARP, the sending device knows the Layer 3 IP address. It sends broadcasts to learn the remote data link MAC address. With Inverse ARP, the router learns the Layer 2 address, which is the DLCI. It sends requests for the remote Layer 3 IP address.

When an interface on a Cisco router is configured to use Frame Relay encapsulation, Inverse ARP is on by default. It is possible to manually configure a static mapping for a specific DLCI. Static mapping is used if the router at the other end does not support Inverse ARP.

Refer to **Figure** in online course

An advantage of Frame Relay connectivity is that one physical interface can support multiple virtual circuits. Frame Relay enables one connection into the provider packet-switched network to provide connectivity to multiple remote sites. This type of *multi-access* WAN is less expensive than one that requires dedicated point-to-point links between sites.

Multiple links sharing a single interface can cause problems for distance vector routing protocol updates. Frame Relay is a nonbroadcast multi-access (*NBMA*) protocol. This means that each virtual circuit on an interface is treated as a separate local network. *Split horizon* stops routing table updates from going out of the same interface on which they were received. Because of this, if one remote site sends a routing protocol update, that update does not get sent out on the other virtual circuits that share the same physical interface.

To avoid the problems caused by split horizon, the physical interface is divided into logical *subinterface*s. The two types of Frame Relay subinterfaces are point to point and multipoint.

Point-to-point

With point-to-point subinterfaces, a single subinterface is used to establish one permanent virtual circuit (PVC) connection to another physical interface or subinterface on a remote router. Each pair of interfaces is in its own subnet, and each interface has a single DLCI. Broadcasts are not a problem in this environment because the routers are connected in a point-to-point manner and act like leased lines.

Multipoint

With multipoint subinterfaces, a single subinterface is used to establish multiple PVC connections to multiple physical interfaces or subinterfaces on remote routers. This configuration does not solve the problems with split horizon. Split horizon must be turned off for distance vector routing protocols to work with multipoint links.

Refer to
Figure
in online course

Once the Frame Relay WAN is configured, it is necessary to verify that it is operating as expected. On the CPE router, there are a number of **show** commands that display information about the status of the Frame Relay local loop and the PVC circuit.

The **show interfaces serial** command displays the status of the interfaces, as well as details about the encapsulation, DLCI, LMI type and the LMI statistics. In normal operation of Frame Relay, the show interface serial command output should indicate that the interface is up and line protocol is up.

To verify that LMI messages are being exchanged between the CPE router and the local Frame Relay switch, use the **show frame-relay lmi** command.

The **show frame-relay pvc** [**interface** *interface*] [**dlci**] command shows the status of each configured PVC as well as traffic statistics. This command is also useful for viewing the number of BECN and FECN packets received by the router.

Use the **show frame-relay map** command to display the current entries learned through Inverse ARP, statically configured maps, and information about the connections.

To clear dynamically created Frame Relay maps, which are created using Inverse ARP, use the **clear frame-relay-inarp** command.

Refer to
Interactive Graphic
in online course.

Full Screen

8.2.5 Troubleshooting Frame Relay Operation

Refer to
Figure
in online course

After testing the basic Frame Relay connectivity, the network designer and NetworkingCompany staff decide to test the backup capabilities. They set up Ethernet connections between the routers. These Ethernet connections are intended to simulate the existing VPNs between the remote sites and the main stadium network. Another router, called ISPX, is added to the topology to simulate the ISP connectivity.

Configuring the Backup Link

Routing on the two CPE routers must be configured so that the backup link is used if the Frame Relay link fails. One way to configure the routers to use the backup is to create *floating static route*s.

A floating static route is a static route that has an administrative distance greater than the administrative distance of the corresponding dynamic routes. The staff can configure a static route using the Fast Ethernet interfaces. The configuration specifies a higher administrative distance than the Frame Relay route, using the following command:

`Edge2(config)#`**`ip route 172.18.225.0 255.255.255.0 172.18.0.250 130`**

This route, with an administrative distance of 130, is only installed into the routing table if the other route is lost due to a link failure or some other cause. In this way, as long as the route using the Frame Relay connection is available, the Fast Ethernet interface is not used.

The designer creates a test plan to verify the performance of the backup links in the event of a failure.

Refer to
Figure
in online course

Troubleshooting a Primary Link Failure

In a WAN design, the network designer must ensure that there are backup links, and that they function correctly in the event of a primary link failure. Frame Relay and other WAN technologies are generally very reliable services. There are times however, when the WAN network may perform at less than expected levels, or the circuit may be down. A backup link can carry traffic during these times, as well as during the time it takes to troubleshoot and repair the primary connection failure.

Troubleshooting a Frame-Relay circuit is a multi-step process that encompasses Layer 1, 2 and 3 functionality.

Checking Frame Relay Interface Status

The first step in verifying or troubleshooting Frame Relay configuration issues is to use the **show interface serial** command. If the output of the **show interface serial** command indicates that both the interface and the line protocol are down, it typically indicates a problem at Layer 1. There may be a problem with the cable or CSU/DSU that needs to be corrected.

The interface may also show a down condition if the DLCI is incorrectly statically configured. To check for this, use the **show frame-relay pvc** command. A PVC status of **DELETED** can indicate that the DLCI configured on the CPE device does not match the DLCI assigned to the circuit.

Verify LMI Operation

When the output of a **show interface serial** command indicates that the interface is up, but the line protocol is down, there can be problem at Layer 2. The serial interface may not be receiving the LMI keep alive messages from the Frame Relay switch. The next step in troubleshooting the Frame Relay circuit is to verify that LMI messages are being sent and received correctly. Use the **show frame-relay lmi** command and look for a non-zero value in any of the **Invalid** counters. Also make sure that the LMI type is correct for the circuit.

Refer to
Figure
in online course

Debugging the LMI Exchange

If the LMI type is correct for the circuit, but invalid messages are indicated, the **debug frame-relay lmi** command can provide more information. The **debug** command output shows the LMI messages as they are being sent and received between the Frame Relay switch and the CPE router in real time.

LMI status messages sent by the router are indicated by the (**out**) output. The (**in**) output indicates a message received from the Frame Relay switch.

A **type 0** message is a full LMI status message. Within the status message, the **dlci 110, status 0x2** output indicates that **DLCI 110** is active. The common values of the DLCI status field are:

0x0: Added and inactive - the switch has this DLCI programmed but it is not usable.

0x2: Added and active - the Frame Relay switch has the DLCI and everything is operational.

0x4: Deleted - the Frame Relay switch does not have this DLCI programmed for the router. This status can happen if the DLCIs are reversed on the router or if the PVC was deleted in the Frame Relay cloud.

A **type 1** message indicates a keepalive LMI exchange.

Checking Layer 3 Functionality

At times, the Layer 1 and 2 functions are operational, but IP communication is not occurring over the PVC. For a router to reach a remote router across the Frame Relay network, it must map the IP address of the remote router with the correct local DLCI. If the IP address of the remote router does not appear in the Frame Relay mapping table, it may not support Inverse ARP. It may require the IP address-to-DLCI mapping to be configured using the **frame-relay map ip** {*ip address*}{*dlci*} [**broadcast**] command.

In addition, it is necessary to verify that no access control lists or IP routing table issues exist, as well. Although these types of issues are not directly related to the WAN circuit operation, they can make it appear as though the circuit is not functioning correctly.

Packet Tracer Activity

Using the test plan and the prototype network, configure the backup links and verify that the failover works as expected.

The following document should be downloaded to perform the Packet Tracer activity:

1. Stadium Redundancy Test Plan

Lab Activity

Using the test plan and the FilmCompany prototype network, configure the backup links and verify that the failover works as expected.

8.2.6 Identifying Risks and Weaknesses

After completing the prototype testing of the WAN, the network designer and the Networking-Company staff discuss the results of the testing. The Frame Relay configuration performs as expected and the backup links protect the WAN connectivity in the event the Frame Relay link fails.

However, there are a couple of risks involved with the Frame Relay configuration that must be communicated to the stadium management.

Areas of Risk

The most critical area of risk is the performance of the VPN links functioning correctly when used as backups. When the voice and video components of the network are added to the existing WAN traffic, there may be a quality of service issue if the VPN connection must be used. The current VPN through the ISP does not have a guaranteed level of service. Furthermore, it does not have mechanisms to provide QoS. As a result, the backup links can only provide limited connectivity in the event of a failure.

It is not possible to test the performance through the actual TSP Frame Relay network; therefore, there is a risk associated with the design. The final acceptance of the design cannot be done until the results of the pilot installation are known.

Lab Activity

Analyze the results of the FilmCompany prototype test and document any risks or weaknesses in the design. Complete the Conclusions section of the test plan.

8.3 Prototyping Remote Worker Support

8.3.1 Identifying VPN Goals and Requirements

A high-priority business goal of the stadium network design is to offer additional services to stadium vendors and customers to improve the stadium experience.

Team Office Requirements

The team offices are requesting a secure method for their scouts to connect to the team servers. The scouts need to transmit prospect information to the team servers when they are away from the stadium. Because this information is extremely confidential, the team wants the scouts to be able to connect remotely via a VPN. A VPN is an extension of the internal private network. VPNs transmit information securely across shared or public networks, like the Internet. The network designer needs to consider the network impact of providing this service.

How a VPN Works

A VPN emulates a point-to-point link. The VPN encapsulates the data with a header that provides routing information. This format enables the data to traverse the public network to reach its destination. To emulate a private link, the encapsulated data is encrypted for confidentiality. Encryption algorithms ensure that if packets are intercepted on the public network, they cannot be read without the encryption keys.

The team scouts, as well as others working at home or on the road, can use VPN connections to establish remote access to servers located at the stadium. From the perspective of the users, the VPN is a point-to-point connection between their computer (the VPN client) and a VPN endpoint (the VPN server or VPN concentrator) at the stadium.

There is risk when extending the private LAN to include remote workers.

Refer to **Figure** in online course

VPN Security

In many businesses, remote workers accessing resources at the central site through a VPN are considered "trusted" users, just like those workers who actually work on site. Unlike the on-site workers, VPN users may be accessing the network from devices that are not fully secured or from insecure locations in public areas. Extra care needs to be taken to ensure that these remote workers do not have access to resources or areas of the network that they do not need to do their jobs.

VPN Server Location

The network designer knows that encrypted data cannot be filtered until it is unencrypted at the VPN server endpoint. For that reason, the location of the VPN server in the network is very important. It must be located at a point where incoming packets can be examined and filtered before being delivered to the internal network resources.

8.3.2 Creating the Test Plan

Refer to **Figure** in online course

What Needs to Be Tested?

The stadium uses VPN networks to connect to the souvenir shop and the ticket outlet. These VPNs are site-to-site VPNs managed by the ISP and do not need to be tested.

Team Scout Support

Two options are available to support the team scout VPN requirements for the remote clients:

- **Option 1**: The stadium management can request additional VPN services from the current ISP.
- **Option 2**: The VPN server can be installed on the stadium network.

VPN Server Management

The designer suggests using split tunneling to allow users to send traffic that is destined for the corporate network across the VPN tunnel, while allowing all other traffic to be sent out to the Internet through the local LAN of the VPN client. The designer must determine if a VPN server can be configured and managed by the existing stadium personnel. To do this, the designer decides to test the ease of configuring and installing the VPN server and client software. After configuring the VPN, the designer tests the ACLs for filtering traffic coming through the VPN and the placement of the VPN server in the network.

Cisco EasyVPN

The designer decides that Cisco EasyVPN is the best option to use for configuring and managing remote user VPN connectivity. EasyVPN is a Cisco IOS software tool. It facilitates the configuration of a Cisco security appliance or router as a VPN server or endpoint.

For the prototype, the designer selects the IP Advanced Security feature set for the 1841 router. The Cisco *SDM* interface on the 1841 can be used to configure the EasyVPN Server for the remote clients.

Refer to
Figure
in online course

The Cisco EasyVPN Solution

To ensure that the VPN can support the mobile team scouts, ease of deployment is important. There are two components of Cisco EasyVPN:

- *Cisco EasyVPN Server -* This server can be a router or a dedicated VPN gateway, such as a PIX firewall or a VPN concentrator. A VPN gateway using Cisco EasyVPN Server software can terminate remote access VPNs and site-to-site VPN connections.

- *Cisco EasyVPN Remote -* Cisco EasyVPN Remote enables remote devices to receive security policies from a Cisco EasyVPN Server. This minimizes configuration requirements at the remote VPN location. Cisco EasyVPN Remote allows the VPN parameters to be pushed from the server to the remote device. VPN parameters include internal IP addresses, internal subnet masks, and DHCP server addresses.

The network designer creates a test plan to verify the use of Cisco EasyVPN to configure a VPN server for the stadium and to set up the client software.

Refer to
Lab Activity
for this chapter

Lab Activity

Create a test plan for configuring and testing a VPN client configuration for the FilmCompany.

The following document should be downloaded to perform the lab activity:

1. VPN Design Test Plan

8.3.3 Validate Choice of VPN Topology, Devices and Topologies

Refer to
Figure
in online course

Before testing the VPN prototype configuration, the network designer needs to consider many different protocols, algorithms, and options.

VPN Components

VPNs have two important components:

- Tunneling to create the virtual network

- Encryption to enable privacy and security

Virtual Network

To build a virtual network, a *tunnel* is created between the two endpoints. In a *site-to-site VPN*, hosts send and receive normal TCP/IP traffic through a VPN gateway. A gateway can be a router, firewall, *VPN concentrator*, or security appliance. The gateway is responsible for encapsulating outbound traffic from one site and sending it through a tunnel over a network to a peer gateway at the remote site. A tunnel by itself may not guarantee security. The tunnel simply creates an extension of the local network across the WAN or public network. Tunnels can carry either encrypted or unencrypted content. Upon receipt, the remote peer gateway strips the headers, decrypts the packet, and relays it toward the target host inside its private network. In a *remote-access VPN*, the VPN client on the user computer contacts the gateway to set up the tunnel.

VPN Tunnel Protocols

VPN tunnels are created using a number of different encapsulation protocols. These protocols include:

- Generic Routing Encapsulation (*GRE*)

- IP Security (*IPSec*)

- Layer 2 Forwarding (*L2F*) Protocol

- Point-to-Point Tunneling Protocol (*PPTP*)

- Layer 2 Tunneling Protocol (*L2TP*)

Not all protocols offer the same level of security.

Refer to
Figure
in online course

VPN technologies use encryption algorithms that prevent data from being read if it is intercepted. An encryption algorithm is a mathematical function that combines the message with a string of digits called a key. The output is an unreadable *cipher string*. Decryption is extremely difficult or impossible without the correct key. The most common encryption methods used for VPNs are Data Encryption Standard (*DES*), Triple DES (*3DES*), Advanced Encryption Standard (*AES*), and Rivest, Shamir, and Adleman (*RSA*).

Encryption Algorithms

Encryption algorithms, such as DES and 3DES, require a symmetric, shared secret key to perform encryption and decryption. The network administrator can manually configure keys.

Alternatively, keys can be configured through the use of a key exchange method. The Diffie-Hellman (*DH*) key agreement is a public key exchange method. It provides a way for two peers to establish a shared secret key, which only they recognize, while communicating over an unsecured channel. Diffie-Hellman groups specify the type of *cryptography* to be used:

- *DH GROUP 1 -* Uses 768-bit cryptography.

- *DH GROUP 2 -* Cisco IOS, PIX Firewall, and Cisco Adaptive Security Appliances (ASA) devices only. Specifies to use 1024-bit cryptography.

- *DH GROUP 5 -* Supported if the software system requirements are met. Specifies to use 1536-bit cryptography.

Refer to
Figure
in online course

To guard against the interception and modification of VPN data, a *data integrity* algorithm can be used. A data integrity algorithm adds a *hash* to the message. If the transmitted hash matches the received hash, the received message is accepted as an exact copy of the transmitted message. Keyed Hashed Message Authentication Code (*HMAC*) is a data integrity algorithm that guarantees the integrity of the message. There are two common HMAC algorithms:

- HMAC-Message Digest 5 (*MD5*) - This algorithm uses a 128-bit shared secret key. The variable length message and 128-bit shared secret key are combined and run through the HMAC-MD5 hash algorithm. The output is a 128-bit hash. The hash is appended to the original message and forwarded to the remote end.

- HMAC-Secure Hash Algorithm 1 (*HMAC-SHA-1*) - This algorithm uses a 160-bit secret key. The variable length message and the 160-bit shared secret key are combined and run through the HMAC-SHA-1 hash algorithm. The output is a 160-bit hash. The hash is appended to the original message and forwarded to the remote end.

Refer to
Interactive Graphic
in online course.

Full Screen Activity

Complete this crossword puzzle based on VPN information discussed in this topic.

8.3.4 Prototype VPN Connectivity for Remote Workers

Refer to
Figure
in online course

In the proposed stadium network, the network designer chooses IPSec technology for the remote access VPNs.

IPSec

IPSec is a framework of open standards. It provides data confidentiality, data integrity, and data authentication between participating peers. IPSec provides these security services at Layer 3.

IPSec relies on existing algorithms to implement the encryption, authentication, and key exchange. When configuring the VPN server, the following settings must be configured:

- *An IPSec protocol* - The choices are Encapsulating Security Payload (*ESP*), Authentication Header (*AH*), or ESP with AH.

- *An encryption algorithm that is appropriate for the desired level of security* - The choices are DES, 3DES, or AES.

- *An authentication algorithm to provide data integrity* - The choices are MD5 or SHA.

- *A Diffie-Hellman group* - The choices are DH1, DH2, and DH5, if supported.

IPSec can use Internet Key Exchange (*IKE*) to handle negotiation of protocols and algorithms. IKE can also generate the encryption and authentication keys that IPSec uses.

Refer to
Figure
in online course

VPN clients receive a logical network interface with an IPv4 address that is significant on the central site internal network. This IPv4 address typically comes from a private IP address range. As a result, VPN users may not be able to access their local resources, such as printers and servers.

Split Tunnels

In a basic VPN client scenario, all traffic from the VPN client is encrypted using the logical network interface. It is then sent to the VPN server, regardless of where the traffic is destined to go.

Split tunneling allows users to send only the traffic that is destined for the corporate network across the tunnel. All other traffic is sent out to the Internet via the local LAN of the VPN client. Examples of other traffic include instant messaging, email, and casual web browsing. If split tunneling is configured on the VPN server, Cisco VPN client software can be configured for split tunnels by enabling the Allow Local LAN Access option. Split tunneling increases security risks, because an attack can come from the Internet side of the client into the secured network.

Refer to
Lab Activity
for this chapter

Lab Activity

Using the Cisco SDM, explore the configuration options to create a Cisco EasyVPN Server.

Refer to
Lab Activity
for this chapter

Lab Activity

Using the test plan, configure and test the VPN client.

8.3.5 Validate Placement of VPN Server

Refer to
Figure
in online course

The network designer must decide where to place the VPN server before determining how and where to filter and control traffic.

VPN Server Placement

Often, VPN servers are placed at the WAN edge of a network. In these cases, firewalls or ACLs are used to ensure that VPN users have access only to appropriate network resources.

If the stadium management chooses to install a local VPN server, the designer recommends placing the VPN server on the same device that is providing firewall filtering for servers. The remote user traffic can be decrypted and filtered before being sent to the server.

The designer creates a test topology that is similar to the topology used in the server farm prototype testing. The designer then creates an installation checklist and a test plan to test the operation of the VPN and the ACL filtering.

8.3.6 Identify Risks or Weaknesses

Refer to
Figure
in online course

Upon completion of the testing, the network designer analyzes the results to determine the level of risk in the design.

VPN Design Risks

In the VPN design to support the remote team personnel, the main risk relates to the ability of the current IT support staff to configure and maintain the VPN server. Configuring clients as the need arises is also a risk.

Using Cisco EasyVPN and SDM proves to be the correct choice for configuring and maintaining the remote access VPN for the stadium network. It is relatively easy to create secure connectivity for the remote workers.

With the entire prototype testing complete, the designer can work with the rest of the Networking-Company staff to prepare the final design presentation for the stadium network upgrade.

Refer to
Interactive Graphic
in online course.

Full Screen **Activity**

Determine whether each acronym represents a tunnelling term or an encryption term. Drag each term to the correct security category, then click Check.

Summary

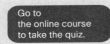

Quiz

Take the chapter quiz to check your knowledge.

Your Chapter Notes

CHAPTER 9

Preparing the Proposal

Introduction

Refer to **Figure** in online course

9.1 Assembling the Existing Proposal Information

Refer to **Figure** in online course

9.1.1 Organizing the Existing Information

After testing the proposed network design, the network designer collects the information gathered from the RFP and previous PPDIOO steps into a network proposal. The proposal typically contains the following sections:

- Executive Summary
- Network Requirements
- Current Network Environment
- Proposed Physical Design
- Proposed Logical Design
- Implementation Plan
- Cost Estimate

If the proposal is in response to an RFP, the proposal components and Table of Contents are assembled to strictly follow the format requested in the RFP.

If there is no written RFP, or if the written RFP does not specify an outline or format, the designer can determine the layout and design of the proposal. In such cases, the proposal layout should be highly readable and aid the reader in locating information. Graphics enhance the readability of a proposal and convey information as well. Text should be legible, typically a serif typeface such as Times Roman, at 10-point to 12-point type. Page margins should be at least 0.5 inches, and page numbers should be included at the top or bottom of each page.

Refer to **Interactive Graphic** in online course.

Full Screen Activity

9.1.2 Integrating the Existing Information

Refer to **Figure** in online course

At this point in the stadium project, the NetworkingCompany account manager and the network designer develop a proposal to respond to the RFP of the StadiumCompany. Most source material for the proposal is already available, except for the implementation plan and the cost estimate.

The designer edits and organizes the existing information prior to developing the implementation plan and the cost estimate.

Executive Summary

Usually, the Executive Summary is written by the account manager assigned to the customer account. It is written from the perspective of the customer and emphasizes how the proposed network creates benefits for the customer organization. The previously identified and prioritized project goals as well as the project scope information are the basis for the Executive Summary.

Network Requirements and Current Network Environment

These sections contain information from the Design Requirements document created and approved earlier in the PPDIOO process. The information is included so that the customer can verify that the proposed design meets the agreed-upon requirements.

Physical and Logical Design

The designer develops the proposed physical and logical design sections from the proposed design diagrams and the results from the prototype and pilot testing. It is important to include any identified risks in this section, as well as strategies to mitigate the risks. This information helps the customer make informed choices about various design elements.

Refer to
Figure
in online course

During the proposal assembly process, the network designer and account manager review all of the materials to ensure that they are complete. It is important that the StadiumCompany management and technical staff are able to easily find and understand the material contained in the proposal. A disorganized or incomplete proposal can cause the customer to choose another contractor to complete the project.

The designer and account manager work together to complete the implementation planning and to create the cost proposal.

Refer to
Lab Activity
for this chapter

Lab Activity

Prepare an outline for the FilmCompany network proposal.

9.2 Developing the Implementation Plan

9.2.1 The Implementation Plan

Refer to
Figure
in online course

In the PPDIOO process, the next step after completing the network design is to develop the implementation and migration plan. It is crucial to include as much detail as possible for the network engineers and technicians.

Implementing the Network Design

Implementing a network design includes installing hardware, configuring systems, testing the network, and launching the network into production. Each task consists of several steps. Each task also requires the following documentation:

- A description of the task
- References to design documents
- Detailed implementation guidelines
- Detailed rollback guidelines in case of failure
- The estimated time required for implementation

Stadium Design

For all aspects of the stadium network design, success and failure criteria have been identified and integrated into the design documentation.

When implementing a design, the network designer must consider the possibility of a failure, even after a successful pilot or prototype network test. At every step during the implementation, additional testing may be required to ensure that the network operates as designed.

Refer to **Figure** in online course

Customer Approval

The stadium implementation plan details the work required to accomplish the project goals. The plan includes the customer expectations and the success criteria, for customer approval and project sign-off.

As soon as customer approval of the implementation plan is obtained, the installation can begin.

The customer is given a detailed list of all devices required and the work to be completed. This list forms part of the implementation plan. A signed copy of this list is maintained by the network designer and account manager.

Upon completion of each task, the customer is required to sign off that the work was completed and that the results are as expected.

Refer to **Interactive Graphic** in online course.

Full Screen Activity

Refer to **Lab Activity** for this chapter

Lab Activity

Create an Implementation Plan for the FilmCompany installation.

9.2.2 Determining the Best Installation Method

Refer to **Figure** in online course

There are three installation methods that may be used for the implementation:

- *New installation-* commonly referred to as a *green field installation*
- *Phased installation-* install components into an existing, functioning network
- *Complete replacement-* commonly referred to as a *fork-lift upgrade*

New Installation

In a new installation, there are no current users or currently running applications. This scenario offers many advantages:

- All of the equipment and services can be installed and tested at the same time.
- The implementation plan for a new network is not as complex as for the other two types of installations.
- Schedules are more flexible than when an existing network is in place.
- There is minimal disruption to the company.

Phased Installation into Existing Network

In a phased installation, portions of the network upgrade are implemented in isolation from other, currently running portions.

When installing new network components or technologies into an existing network, great care must be taken not to disrupt services unnecessarily. A phased implementation requires more detailed planning with the customer. The network upgrade is divided into smaller pieces that can be installed and tested quickly. Installing the upgrade in smaller phases causes the least amount of downtime.

The disadvantage of this method is that it may require more time and funds to complete.

Refer to **Figure** in online course

Complete Network Replacement

Sometimes it is necessary to completely replace an existing network. Complete network replacement usually occurs when the network is outdated and cannot be upgraded. In this scenario, the new network is often built alongside the existing network. When the new network is functional, there may be a period of time during which it is tested in parallel with the old network. A date is set to switch over to the new network, and the old network is then dismantled.

Stadium Installation Method

Determining the best installation method begins early in the network design phase. The network designer gathers and assesses information on business goals, technical requirements, and design constraints.

Two of the StadiumCompany requirements emerge as the main factors that affect the installation method:

- The stadium network services must be available during the upgrade.

- Existing equipment must be used in the new network design.

As a result, the NetworkingCompany designer recommends a phased installation approach.

Refer to **Lab Activity** for this chapter

Lab Activity

Create a plan using the phased installation approach for the FilmCompany.

9.2.3 Estimating Timelines and Resources

Refer to **Figure** in online course

The project duration is part of the contractual agreement. To meet the deadlines of the customer the network designer creates a project timeline. The availability of materials, the schedule of the contractor, and the schedule of the customer all affect the start date and the completion date.

When creating a project timeline, the network designer must consider the possibility that the project might not begin on the proposed start date.

The stadium RFP states that the project must be completed during the off-season for the two teams. This requirement gives the project a timeline of four months.

NetworkingCompany Resources

Given the required sets of tasks, the designer estimates what resources are needed to implement the network. To meet the 4-month deadline, the NetworkingCompany may have to increase the number of technicians assigned to the project. It may also be necessary to adjust the sequence of tasks to accommodate the delivery of specific pieces of equipment or the availability of TSP services.

Refer to **Figure** in online course

Estimated Timeline

The network designer considers several factors when developing a project timeline:

- Equipment order and delivery

- Service installation, such as WAN links

- Customer schedule, including available maintenance and downtime windows

- Availability of appropriate technical personnel

Customer-caused Delays

Customers often make changes to the requirements during the installation of a project. When changes occur, the vendor uses the timeline to make adjustments to personnel and other available resources.

The network designer can also use the timeline documentation to show a customer how delays affect the project completion date.

Project Management Software

Project management tools can be used to create a project timeline.

Using a software program can prove valuable for:

- Tracking the progress of the project
- Keeping the project on schedule
- Identifying milestones
- Tracking labor assignments and costs
- Alerting the designer if the project is falling behind schedule.

Refer to **Lab Activity** for this chapter

Lab Activity

Create a timeline for the FilmCompany network installation.

9.2.4 Maintenance Windows and Downtime Planning

Refer to **Figure** in online course

Maintenance Windows and Downtime

Maintenance windows and planned downtime need to be included in the installation timeline. If only a few hours a day are available to make network changes, the project timeline must reflect this constraint. Otherwise, the time estimates are not accurate and the project may be late. Scheduling downtime for the network needs to be carefully planned to prevent a major disruption for the customer.

Sometimes it is not possible to complete all of the required tasks during an approved maintenance window. If an installation task requires the network, or part of the network, to be down during normal business hours, it is important to obtain permission from the customer. As soon as the time frame is determined and approved, all the people involved need to be notified accordingly.

Refer to **Lab Activity** for this chapter

Lab Activity

Create a maintenance schedule for the FilmCompany network installation.

9.3 Planning for the Installation

9.3.1 Creating the Bill of Material

Refer to **Figure** in online course

One of the most important sections of the proposal to the stadium management is the cost estimate.

To prepare the cost estimate, the network designer creates a Bill Of Material (*BOM*). A BOM is a document that details all of the required hardware and components necessary to implement the proposed upgrade. It consists of an itemized list of hardware, software, and other items that must be ordered and installed. The designer uses this list to obtain quotations and to create the equipment orders.

Ordering Parts

The designer uses the BOM to order new equipment as well as replacement parts for existing equipment. Therefore, every required item must be included in this list. For example, some routers and switches do not come with mounting brackets. These brackets must be purchased separately. If this information is not included in the BOM, the mounting brackets may be left off the order, which delays the device installation.

Refer to
Figure
in online course

To create the BOM, the network designer looks at each section of the network to determine what pieces of networking equipment are required and what capabilities are needed in each device. There are 21 separate locations within the stadium where networking equipment is to be installed or upgraded:

- 16 wiring closets

- 4 WAN locations

- 1 new data center

In addition, the wireless design shows 33 locations for AP installation.

Identifying Additional Devices

By looking at each area of the network separately, the designer can easily identify any additional devices that are necessary. The list of required new equipment includes:

- 6 Distribution Layer switches

- 2 Core switches

- 1 router for WAN connectivity

- 4 routers for WAN sites

- 2 wireless LAN controllers

- 33 lightweight APs

When deciding on new equipment, the designer must keep the budget in mind at all times. The designer reviews the choices of equipment with the account manager assigned to the stadium account. This collaboration ensures that the equipment models selected are within the stadium budget constraints and meet current and future business goals.

Upgrades to Existing Devices

Existing Cisco Catalyst 2960 switches are incorporated into the proposed design. Each of the 16 wiring closets contains one of these switches. The 2960 switches require redundant fiber connectivity to the Distribution Layer devices. Adding the redundant connections requires purchasing an additional fiber transceiver for each switch. These 16 additional transceivers must be listed on the BOM and included in the proposal.

Refer to
Figure
in online course

Software Requirements

During the early stages of the stadium design phase, the customer gave the network designer a list of applications that were currently installed. From this information and the network audit, the designer can identify all existing applications.

Existing Applications

The list of current applications includes:

- *Network applications* - Microsoft file sharing, printing, DNS, Web Server, scanning and recognition software

- *Specialized applications* - Ticket scanning and recognition software

- *Business applications* - Accounting, payroll, event scheduling, lease and rental management, marketing and customer relationship management (*CRM*) software

New Applications

The new applications include:

- *Network applications* - Network management software

- *Specialized applications* - Ticket printing, IP security cameras and viewing stations, e-commerce site for ticket purchasing and souvenir sales

The new applications, installation costs, and required training are added to the BOM with the identified hardware. The designer considers whether the network upgrade requires additional licenses to be purchased for existing software applications.

9.3.2 Recommending SMARTnet Services

Refer to **Figure** in online course

Warranties

All new equipment automatically comes with a *warranty* that covers the device. A standard warranty provides the following benefits:

- **Hardware-**Guarantees that the hardware is free of defects in material and workmanship under normal use

- **Software-**Guarantees that the physical media is free of defects and the software performs to the published specifications.

However, warranties are limited in duration and in the services that they provide. For example, a software warranty usually guarantees that the software conforms to the published specifications for the product. It is explicitly sold "as is" and does not include any new software releases. Most warranties are limited to the replacement of the defective product and do not include technical or on-site support.

Additional Service Contracts

The proposed stadium network includes a mix of both new and older networking equipment. The warranties on some of the older equipment may have expired. To protect the StadiumCompany investment, and to extend the life of the existing equipment, the NetworkingCompany account manager recommends that the stadium management purchase additional maintenance and support contracts.

Refer to **Figure** in online course

SMARTnet Agreements

The SMARTnet program is part of a suite of services that Cisco Technical Support Services provides. The SMARTnet program offers the customer service enhancements and maintenance support resources during the term of the contract.

A SMARTnet agreement includes:

- Software support on the licensed operating system software

- Access to the Cisco Technical Assistance Center (TAC) 24 hours a day, 7 days a week

- Registered access to Cisco.com for easy access to online technical information and service request management

- Advanced replacement of hardware parts

Hardware Replacement Times

Under the SMARTnet agreement, hardware replacement times can vary depending on the urgency of the customer need and the coverage selected. For example, with a 24x7x2 agreement, replacement parts are delivered within two hours of determining that a part replacement is required. This 2-hour replacement agreement applies any day or time in the week.

Benefits

The NetworkingCompany account manager prepares a chart comparing the various SMARTnet agreements to the basic warranty. This comparison is included in the proposal to show the benefits to the customer.

Full Screen **Activity**

Refer to
Interactive Graphic
in online course.

9.3.3 Cisco Technical Services and Support

Refer to
Figure
in online course

The stadium network upgrade must not require an increase in the number of IT support personnel. The NetworkingCompany account manager and network designer agree that external support options should be presented to the stadium management.

Cisco Focused Technical Support Services

Cisco Focused Technical Support Services consists of three levels of coverage that provide a variety of options for the customer.

The NetworkingCompany account manager includes information about the Level 2 contract, Cisco High-Touch Technical Support Service, in conjunction with SMARTnet agreements. This Level 2 contract provides priority access to a designated team of engineers who have received in-depth training on the stadium business operations. The engineers use the Cisco Lifecycle as the approach to providing services from the time the stadium design is placed into operation throughout its lifecycle.

With a firm knowledge of the stadium network infrastructure and service history, the engineers would be able to speed up the resolution of network issues.

9.3.4 Software IOS Services and Support

Refer to
Figure
in online course

One of the business goals of the stadium management company is to simplify the day-to-day management of the stadium network. To accomplish this goal, the NetworkingCompany staff recommends that network management software be installed.

Software Application Support Services

Implementing a CiscoWorks Network Management application or a Cisco IP Telephony solution requires Cisco software products in addition to the networking hardware. Cisco offers Software Application Support Services (SAS) to support the application software.

SAS services include around-the-clock access to technical support, application software updates, and a wealth of technical information on Cisco.com. SAS services are designed specifically for Cisco software applications and provide services in addition to the operating system software support.

The costs of these software support options, as well as any software licensing costs, are included in the proposal.

Refer to
Lab Activity
for this chapter

Lab Activity

Create the BOM and enter the appropriate information into the Costs section of the FilmCompany proposal.

9.4 Creating and Presenting the Proposal

9.4.1 Finalizing the Proposal

Refer to
Figure
in online course

The NetworkingCompany account manager uses information from the completed implementation and costing sections to update the Executive Summary. The proposal components are arranged in a binder, based on the order cited in the Table of Contents.

A cover page is included at the beginning of the proposal. The cover page contains relevant information describing the proposal, including the RFP or solicitation number and date, the customer contact information, and the vendor name and contact information.

The terms of agreement and an acceptance page for customer signatures are included at the end of the proposal. The terms and conditions describe all relevant legal terms and contracts that will be required. These terms and conditions support the supply of goods and services related to network improvements and installations.

Important clauses in the terms and conditions include:

- Details about the proposal expiration date

- Obligations of the customer to obtain permission or other consents within their organization

- Obligations of the vendor to provide services and equipment with care and skill

- Dates when completed milestone deliverables are payable

- Interest charged on outstanding payments

- The amount of notice the customer must give to cancel any equipment and service orders

- Details about guarantees (if any) provided by the vendor

- Details about escalating and resolving complaints or issues

If the proposal is accepted by the customer, an appropriate customer representative signs the Terms and Signatures page.

Refer to
Lab Activity
for this chapter

Lab Activity

Compile implementation and costing information created for the FilmCompany.

9.4.2 Presenting the Proposal

Refer to
Figure
in online course

After compiling the proposal, the network designer reviews the entire proposal with the NetworkingCompany management. During this stage of the design proposal, the designer must sell the concept to internal NetworkingCompany management and then to the customer.

The designer typically develops a presentation to illustrate the proposal. A proposal presentation includes slides or other visual aids to graphically represent the proposal. The presentation, along with the proposal document, is vital to ensuring a successful meeting and increasing the probability of a customer sign-off.

The Presentation

The content and presentation format are quite important in a business environment.

Presentation tips:

- Every slide should contain a title that summarizes the information presented on the slide.
- Computer presentations should not contain full paragraphs of text. Use a bulleted list or outline format and elaborate on the points during the delivery.
- All type should be legible. Use large fonts, because small fonts are often hard to read.
- Use contrasting colors - either a dark background with light text or a light background with dark text.
- Avoid backgrounds that make the text hard to read. Keep the background simple.
- Do not use ALL CAPS! Their use is unprofessional and they can be difficult to read.
- Include a combination of words, pictures, and graphics. Variety keeps the presentation interesting.

After the presentation, the customer can accept the proposal in its entirety, request changes, or decline the proposal altogether.

Remember that proper preparation before the presentation can mean the difference between customer sign-off and losing the project.

Refer to
Lab Activity
for this chapter

Lab Activity

Present the project proposal to the instructor and the class. Be available to respond to questions from the instructors and students.

Summary

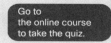

Quiz

Take the chapter quiz to check your knowledge.

Your Chapter Notes

CHAPTER 10

Course Summary

10.0 Putting It All Together

10.0.1 Summary

Refer to
Figure
in online course

Networks are essential to almost all successful modern organizations. This is true in nearly every industry you can imagine including healthcare, sports, government agencies, and ISPs. The pre-sales and network design skills you have developed in this course provide the basis for supporting any IT or networking organization, from a small consulting business to a large corporate enterprise.

As an IT professional, it will be your job to deliver these vital network services efficiently and without disruption to the business. By competently performing the many networking roles in a professional manner, you will become a valuable contributor to any enterprise.

The IT industry is constantly improving and expanding. A successful IT career requires a commitment to lifelong learning. The Cisco Networking Academy offers several courses, such as Cisco Certified Networking Professional (CCNP), that provide the ongoing training that you will need.

10.0.2 Finding the Right Networking Job

Refer to
Figure
in online course

The final two activities in this curriculum are designed to support your networking job search. The portfolio that you created during this course will help you evaluate your skills and interests. It will also serve as documentation and reference material during your networking career.

Many resources are available to help your career search including books, websites, classes, and consultants. Most educational institutions have resources available to help students write resumes, find job openings, and practice interviewing.

Employers around the world respect the CCNA curriculum and CCNA certification exam training. As a qualified CCNA, you may want to consider accepting a position outside your own country or a position that requires travel to other countries. Another option is to start your own business.

In your job search, you should include these steps:

- Evaluate your skills and strengths.

- Research the types of jobs available that require your strengths.

- Create your resume.

- Send your resume to potential employers and post it with online job search websites.

- Talk with people who work in the type of job you are interested in.

- Talk with people who work for companies that you find desirable.

- Apply and interview for available jobs.

Refer to
Lab Activity
for this chapter

Refer to
Figure
in online course

Lab Activity

Research networking jobs that match your skills, strengths, and interests.

Create and submit a resume with a cover letter for a networking job that you are interested in.

Imagine that you have submitted your resume to a company and that they have asked you for an interview.

Question Types

Expect your interviewer to ask many different types of questions, for example:

- *Behavioral -* How you interact with people and the workplace culture: "Are you available to work longer hours when needed?"

- *Hypothetical -* How you would handle a particular situation: "What would you do if the building lost power?"

- *Leading -* A series of questions directed to a specific type of situation: "Have you ever worked in a lab setting?"

- *Open-ended -* A short question requiring an extended response: "Tell me about your job experience."

Interview Methods

Many different methods are used for interviews. Common methods include:

- A screening interview over the telephone

- An interview at a career fair

- An interview with one or more people at the hiring company site

An informational interview is one where you talk with someone at a particular company. You learn about the company and the interviewer learns about you. There is no specific job opening being discussed during an informational interview.

By treating every interview as a valuable learning experience, you will increase your job interview skills and your knowledge of hiring practices. After the interview, reflect on what you learned, what went well, and what you want to improve for your next interview.

10.0.3 Preparing for the CCNA Exam and Lifelong Learning

Full Screen summary.

Your Chapter Notes

3DES
Triple Data Encryption Standard

Procedure to secure data by first separating it into 64-bit blocks. Each block is then processed three times, each time with an independent 56-bit key. 3DES uses a total key of 168-bits to ensure strong encryption. 3DES is a variant of the 56-bit data encryption standard.

802.1Q
IEEE standard that is designed to enable traffic between virtual LANs. IEEE 802.1Q uses an internal tagging mechanism which inserts a four-byte tag field in the original Ethernet frame between the source address and type/length fields. Because the frame is altered, the trunking device recomputes the frame check sequence on the modified frame.

ABR
area border router

Routing device that connects one or more OSPF areas to a backbone network. An ABR maintains routing tables for the backbone and the attached areas of an OSPF.

access control list
See ACL.

Access Layer
Level of the hierarchical Cisco internetworking model that encompass the hosts that are the point of entry into the network. Access Layer devices include switches, hubs, workstations, servers, IP phones, web cameras, and access points.

access link
Connection between a DTE, such as a router, to the nearest point-of-presence of a service provider through a DCE, such as a modem in a Frame Relay network.

access point
See AP.

access port
Pathway to a device that does not create loops in a switched network and always transitions to forwarding if a host is attached.

ACK
acknowledgment

Notification sent between network devices when an event has occurred. For example, a destination device sends an ACK to a source device when a message is received.

acknowledgment
See ACK.

ACL
access control list

List kept by a network device, such as a router, to manage access to or from the router for a number of services. For example, an ACL can be used to prevent packets with a certain IP address or protocol from leaving a particular interface on the router.

active topology
RSTP network design that transition ports to the forwarding state if they are not discarding or are blocked.

AD
1) advertised distance

Distance that is broadcast by an upstream neighbor.

2) administrative distance

Rating of trustworthiness of a routing information source. For a Cisco router, an administrative distance is expressed as a numerical value between 0 and 255. The higher the value, the lower the trustworthiness rating.

adaptive cut-through
Type of switching when the flow reverts back to fast-forward mode when the number of errors drops below the threshold value to an acceptable level.

address
Data structure used to identify a unique entity, such as a particular process or network device. An IP address is a string of characters assigned by an administrator. A MAC address is burned into a device and cannot be changed.

address mask
Bit combination used to identify the part of an address that refers to the network or subnet, and the part that refers to the host.

adjacencies
See adjacency.

adjacency
Relationship between neighboring routers and end nodes for the purpose of exchanging routing information. Adjacency is based on the use of a common media segment.

administrative distance
See AD.

Advanced Encryption Standard
See AES.

advanced replacement
Part of a SMARTnet agreement offered as part of a customer service enhancement.

advertised distance
See AD.

advertisement request
VLAN information that a VTP client requires if the switch has been reset or the VTP domain name has been changed.

advertising
Router process in which routing or service updates containing lists of usable routes are sent at specified intervals to routers on the network .

AES
Advanced Encryption Standard

Specifications for a symmetric 128-bit block cipher that is the current cryptographic standard for the United States adopted by the National Institute of Standards and Techonology. The algorithm must be used with key sizes of 128 bits, 192 bits, or 256 bits, depending on the application security requirement.

aging timer
Period of time in which an entry must be used before a switch deletes it from the MAC address table.

AH
Authentication Header

Security protocol that provides data authentication and optional anti-replay services. AH is embedded in the data to be protected.

algorithm
Well-defined rule or mathematical process for solving a problem. In networking, an algorithm is commonly used to determine the best route for traffic from a source to a destination.

anycast
Type of IPv6 network addressing and routing scheme where data is routed to a destination considered to be the best or closest by the routing topology. An anycast address is formatted the same as an IPv6 global unicast address.

AP
access point

Access Layer device that connects to a wired network and relays data between wireless and wired devices. An AP connects wireless communication devices to form a wireless network to allow roaming.

application characterization
Collecting information about network bandwidth usage and response times of an application. Some of the considerations for application characterization include how the application works and interacts on a network, and the technical requirements.

Application Layer
Layer 7 of the OSI Reference Model. The Application Layer provides services to application processes such as email, file transfer, and terminal emulation that are outside of the OSI Reference Model. It identifies and establishes the availability of intended communication partners and the resources required to connect with them, synchronizes cooperating applications, and establishes agreement on procedures for error recovery and control of data integrity.

application-specific integrated circuit (ASIC)
See ASIC.

area
Logical set of either CLNS-, DECnet-, or OSPF-based network segments, and all attached devices. Areas are usually connected through routers, creating a single autonomous system.

Area 0
Area at the beginning of an OSPF network. An OSPF network must have at least one area, which is area 0. As the network expands, other areas are created adjacent to Area 0.

Area 0 is also known as the backbone area.

area border router
See ABR.

area ID
Identification of the OSPF area to which the network belongs.

AS
autonomous system.

Collection of networks under a common administration sharing a common routing strategy. Autonomous systems are subdivided by areas. An autonomous system must be assigned a unique 16-bit number by the IANA.

ASA
Cisco adaptive security appliance

Hardware device that integrates firewall, Unified Communications security, SSL and IPsec VPN, IPS, and content security services. An example of an ASA is a Cisco ASA 5500 series.

ASBR
autonomous system boundary router

Area border router located between an OSPF autonomous system and a non-OSPF network. An ASBR runs the OSPF routing protocol and another routing protocol, such as RIP. An ASBR must reside in a nonstub OSPF area.

as-built
Diagram that shows the original design and any changes that have been made to a network topology.

ASIC
application-specific integrated circuit

Circuit that gives precise instructions for the functionality of a device during Layer 3 switching.

asymmetric
When one function on a network takes a greater length of time than the reverse function. An example of an asymmetric function is the compression and decompression of data.

Asynchronous Transfer Mode
See ATM.

ATM
Asynchronous Transfer Mode

International standard for the cell relay of service types, such as voice, video, or data. In ATM, the services are conveyed in fixed-length, 53-byte cells. Fixed-length cells reduce transit delays because cell processing occurs in the hardware. ATM is designed for high-speed transmission media such as E3, SONET, and T3.

atomic transaction
Process that guarantees that either all or none of the tasks of a transaction are performed in a database system. An atomic transaction is void if it is not fully processed.

authentication
Security measure designed to control access to network resources by verifying the identity of a person or process.

Authentication Header
See AH.

authentication server
Server that controls the frequency and timing of challenges to prevent attacks on a network.

authority zone
Section of the domain-name tree for which one name server is the authority. Authority zone is associated with DNS.

auto mode
Designation of a port on a device as a trunk port if the other end is set to either trunk or desirable mode.

autonomous system
See AS.

autonomous system boundary router
See ASBR.

AutoQoS
Feature that automates consistent deployment of QoS features across Cisco routers and switches to ensure high-quality application performance. AutoQoS configures the device with QoS features and variables that are based on Cisco best-practice recommendations. A user is able to adjust parameters that are generated by Cisco AutoQoS.

availability
Condition of accessibility.

baby giant
Ethernet frame on a network that has been tagged as too large. A baby giant is dropped and logged as an error.

back end
Application that performs final or hidden functions in a process.

backbone cabling
Physical media that connects wiring closets to each other, wiring closets and the POP, and buildings that are part of the same LAN.

BackboneFast
Feature on the switches of a bridge network that provides fast convergence after a spanning tree topology change. BackboneFast is used at the Distribution and Core Layers to restore backbone connectivity. BackboneFast is Cisco proprietary.

backup designated router
See BDR.

backward explicit congestion notification
See BECN.

bandwidth
Rated throughput capacity of a given network medium or protocol. Bandwidth is the difference between the highest and lowest frequencies available for network signals.

bandwidth reservation
Process of assigning bandwidth to users and applications served by a network. Bandwidth reservation involves assigning priority to different flows of traffic based on critical and delay-sensitive characteristics. If the network becomes congested, lower-priority traffic can be dropped.

Bandwidth reservation is also known as bandwidth allocation.

banner motd
banner motd

Command used to configure a message of the day, or motd. The message is displayed at login. A banner motd is useful for conveying messages, such as an impending system shutdown, that affects all network users.

baseline
A quantitative expression of planned costs, schedules, and technical requirements for a defined project. A baseline is established to describe the 'normal' status of network or computer system performance. The status can then be compared with the baseline at any point to measure the variation from the 'normal' operation condition.

basic configuration
Minimal configuration information entered when a router, switch, or other configurable device is installed on a network. For example, the basic configuration for a LightStream 2020 ATM switch includes the IP addresses, date, and parameters for at least one trunk line. The

basic configuration enables the switch to receive a full configuration from the Network Management System.

baud
Unit of signaling speed equal to the number of discrete signal elements transmitted per second. Baud is synonymous with bits per second, if each signal element represents exactly one bit.

Bc
committed burst

Maximum amount of data, in bits, that a Frame Relay internetwork is committed to accept and transmit at the CIR. Bc is a negotiated tariff metric.

BCP
business continuity plan

Steps to be taken to continue business operations when there is a natural or man-made disaster.

BDR
backup designated router

Router that is identified to take over if the designated router fails.

Be
excess burst

Number of bits that a Frame Relay internetwork will attempt to transmit after Bc is accommodated. Be data is, in general, delivered with a lower probability than Bc data because Be data can be marked as DE by the network. Be is a negotiated tariff metric.

BECN
backward explicit congestion notification

Signal in a frame travelling in the opposite direction of frames that have encountered a congested path in a Frame Relay network. The DTE that receives the frame with the BECN signal can request that higher-level protocols take appropriate flow-control action.

BGP
Border Gateway Protocol

Routing standard used to connect a SP to and from the Internet.

BGP is also known as exterior gateway protocol.

BID
bridge ID

Identification of the root bridge which is the focal point in an STP network.

Bill Of Material
See BOM.

bit-oriented
In networking, data is transmitted using individual bits, instead of the entire byte.

block cipher
Method of encrypting a group of bits together as a single unit.

blocked port
See blocking.

blocking
1) Condition in a switching system in which no paths are available to complete a circuit.

2) Condition when one activity cannot begin until another has been completed.

BOM
Bill Of Material

Itemized list of hardware, software, and other items necessary to build a network. The BOM is used to obtain price quotations and to order equipment.

Boolean ANDing
Clears a pattern of bits; if you AND a bit with zero, it will clear it to zero, while ANDing with one will leave the bit unchanged, leaving it a "1".

bootup process

Activity of starting a computer-based device. The bootup process has three steps. First, the internal components are tested. Then, the operating system is located and started. Finally, the initial configuration is loaded. After the bootup process is complete a device is in an operational state.

border gateway

Router that communicates with routers in other autonomous systems.

Border Gateway Protocol

See BGP.

bottom-up

Troubleshooting technique that begins by examining the lower levels of a hierarchical model first.

bounded update

Feature associated with a link-state routing protocols, such as EIGRP. A bounded update contains specific parameters and is delivered only to routers that require the information.

BPDU

bridge protocol data unit

Spanning Tree Protocol hello packet that is sent out at configurable intervals to exchange information among bridges in the network.

bridge

Device that connects and passes packets between two network segments that use the same communications protocol. A bridge operates at the Data Link Layer of the OSI reference model. In general, it filters, forwards, or floods an incoming frame based on the MAC address of that frame.

bridge ID

See BID.

bridge protocol data unit

See BPDU.

broadcast

Set of devices that receive broadcast frames originating from any of the devices within the set. A broadcast domain is typically bounded by routers because routers do not forward broadcast frames.

broadcast address

Address reserved for sending a message to all stations. Generally, a broadcast address is a MAC destination address consisting of all ones.

broadcast domain

Set of devices that receive broadcast frames originating from any of the devices within the set. A broadcast domain is typically bounded by routers because routers do not forward broadcast frames.

broadcast multi-access

Type of Ethernet link identified by OSPF, which is a standard for a multi-access network that forwards broadcast traffic.

broadcast storm

Undesirable network event in which many broadcasts are sent simultaneously across all network segments. A broadcast storm uses substantial network bandwidth and typically causes network time-outs.

BSP

business security plan

Physical, system, and organizational control measures to be taken to protect network and information assets.

buffer

Storage area used for handling data in transit. A buffer is used in internetworking to compensate for differences in processing speed between network devices. Bursts of data can be stored in a buffer until the data can be handled by slower processing devices.

A buffer is also known as a packet buffer.

business case

Structured design document to justify the financial investment required to implement a technology change.

business continuity

Ability to continue business operations if there is a natural or man-made disaster.

business continuity plan

See BCP.

business enterprise
Large corporate environment with many users and locations, or with many systems.

business security plan
Physical, system, and organizational control measures to be taken to protect network and information assets.

cache
Act of storing data, or the location of stored data.

call agent
Control device that processes calls and administers gateways in IP telephony. A call agent performs functions similar to a switchboard in a traditional telephone system. Examples of call agents include the Cisco Unified Communications Manager and the Cisco Unified Communications Manager Express.

CAM
content addressable memory

MAC address table maintained by a switch. A CAM is recreated every time a switch is activated.

carrier
Electromagnetic wave or alternating current of a single frequency that is suitable for modulation by another data-bearing signal.

carrier wave
Signal on which data is modulated and then demodulated in an analog connection.

Catalyst Workgroup Switch
Series of Cisco workgroup switches that enhance the network performance of Ethernet client/server workgroups. The Catalyst Workgroup Switch integrates software enhancements for network management and provides a 100 Mbps interface to servers and dedicated Ethernet-to-desktop workstations.

CBWFQ
class-based weighted fair queueing

Network packet prioritizing technique based on the standard practice of weighted fair queuing. CBWFQ has additional QoS functionality that assigns packets to user-defined traffic classes. Each class is given a level of priority based on

matching criteria including protocols, ACLs, and input interfaces.

CCITT
Consultative Committee for International Telegraph and Telephone

International organization responsible for the development of communications standards. The CCITT is now referred to as the ITU-T.

CDP
Cisco Discovery Protocol

Protocol on Cisco-manufactured equipment, including routers, access servers, bridges, and switches, that enables a device to communicate with other devices on the LAN or on the remote side of a WAN. CDP runs on LANs, Frame Relay, and ATM media.

Cell-switched networks
Data communication scheme based on fixed-length cell structure. In a cell-switched network, the fixed-length cell achieves a faster speed of transmission than those using variable-length packets. ATM is an example of a switched technology on a network that provides full bandwidth of the link when a station communicates to the switch.

central office
See CO.

Challenge Handshake Authentication Protocol
See CHAP.

challenge message
Response sent by a router to establish the identity of the sender.

channel
Communication path that can be multiplexed over a single cable.

channel service unit
See CSU.

channel service unit/data service unit
See CSU/DSU.

CHAP
Challenge Handshake Authentication Protocol

Security feature supported on lines that use PPP encapsulation to prevent unauthorized access by identifying the remote user. CHAP is a three-way handshake with encryption and enables the router or access server to determine whether a user is allowed access.

child route
Subnet route on an EIGRP network.

CIDR
classless inter-domain routing

Technique based on route aggregation and supported by Border Gateway Protocol v4 that allows routers to group routes to reduce the quantity of information carried by the core routers. When using CIDR, multiple IP networks appear as a single, larger entity to networks outside of the group.

cipher string
Encrypted form of plain text.

CIR
committed information rate

Speed, measured in bits per second and is averaged over a minimum increment of time, that a Frame Relay network transfers information. CIR is a negotiated tariff metric.

circuit
Communication path between two or more points.

circuit switching
System in which a dedicated physical circuit path exists between sender and receiver for the duration of the connection. Circuit switching is often used in a telephone company network.

Cisco adaptive security appliance
See ASA.

Cisco Discovery Protocol
See CDP.

Cisco Enterprise Architectures
Combination of core network infrastructure with productivity-enhancing advanced technologies including IP communications, mobil-

ity, and advanced security. Cisco Enterprise Network Architecture divides the three-layer hierarchical design into modular areas. The modules represent different physical or logical connectivity. They also designate where different functions occur in the network. The modularity of the Cisco Enterprise Network Architecture allows flexibility in network design and facilitates implementation and troubleshooting.

Cisco Internetwork Operating System software
See Cisco IOS software.

Cisco IOS software
Cisco Internetwork Operating System software

Application that provides common functionality, scalability, and security for all Cisco products. Cisco IOS software allows centralized, integrated, and automated installation and management of internetworks, while ensuring support for a wide variety of protocols, media, services, and platforms.

Cisco Security Agent
Consists of host-based agents, deployed on mission-critical desktops and servers that report to the Cisco Management Center for Cisco Security Agents. The Management Center runs as a standalone application performing configuration of Cisco Security Agent deployments. Cisco Security Agents provide threat protection for servers, desktops, and laptops.

Cisco Security Device Management
See SDM.

Cisco switch clustering
Management of up to 16 switches simultaneously through a single IP address. To create redundancy in Cisco switch clustering, a network administrator assigns an IP address to a second switch. If the primary command switch fails, the backup or secondary command switch seamlessly takes over the management of the cluster. A user can still access the cluster through the virtual IP address.

Cisco switch clustering technology is featured in Catalyst 3500 XL, 2900 XL, 2955/2950, 2970, 3550, 3560, 3750, 4500, and Catalyst 1900/2820 Standard and Enterprise Edition switches.

Cisco Unified Communications Manager
IP-based PBX in an IP telephony solution. Cisco Unified Communications Manager acts as a call agent for IP phones and MGCP gateways. It can interact with H.323 or SIP devices using the protocols of the devices.

Cisco Unified Communications Manager is also known as Cisco Unified CallManager or CallManager.

CiscoView
GUI-based management application that provides dynamic status, statistics, and comprehensive configuration information for Cisco internetworking devices. In addition to displaying a physical view of Cisco device chassis, CiscoView also provides device monitoring functions and basic troubleshooting capabilities, and can be integrated with several SNMP-based network management platforms.

CiscoWorks
Series of SNMP-based internetwork management applications for monitoring router and access server status, managing configuration files, and troubleshooting network problems. CiscoWorks applications are integrated on several platforms including SunNet Manager, HP OpenView, and IBM NetView.

class-based weighted fair queueing
See CBWFQ.

classful
Type of subnetting that uses the extension of the subnet mask. An example of classful subnetting is IPv4.

classful boundary
Designation of subnets as a single Class A, B, or C network by protocols such as RIP and EIGRP.

classful routing
Selecting a path on a network without including subnet mask information. In classful routing, variable-length subnet masks are not supported.

classless inter-domain routing
See CIDR.

classless routing
Feature of a protocol where the subnet mask is sent with all routing update packets. Classless routing protocols include RIPv2, EIGRP, and OSPF.

Classless Routing Protocol
Standard that instructs data to send a subnet mask with all routing update packets. A classless routing protocol is necessary when the mask cannot be assumed or determined by the value of the first octet. Classless routing protocols include RIPv2, EIGRP, and OSPF.

CLI
command line interface

Ability to interact with the operating system that requires the user to enter commands and optional arguments on a command line.

client
Device requesting services or information.

client-to-client
From one end station to another end station on a network.

client-to-distributed server
From an end station to the server.

client-to-enterprise edge
From an end station to the perimeter of the enterprise before entering the Internet.

client-to-server farm
From an end user to a location with a number of servers.

clocking
Rate at which data moves onto the local loop.

clocking signal
Indicator of the rate at which data moves onto the local loop.

cluster
Network of servers used as a single unit. The redundancy of technology that occurs when clustering improves performance because of load balancing and failover among devices.

clustered
See cluster.

CO
central office

Strategically located environment that accommodates vital devices on a network topology.

coding
Electrical technique used to convey binary signals.

collapsed backbone
Physical media system in which all network segments are interconnected by an internetworking device. An example of a collapsed backbone is a virtual network segment that exists in a device such as a hub, router, or switch.

collision
Result when two or more devices transmit frames simultaneously which impact and become damaged when they meet on the physical media.

collision domain
Network area in Ethernet where frames that have collided are propagated. Repeaters and hubs have collision domains. LAN switches, bridges, and routers do not.

co-located
To also be present at a site. A secondary server may be co-located at the same SP for backup.

command line interface
See CLI.

committed burst
See Bc.

committed information rate
See CIR.

committed time
See Tc.

composite metric
Method used on an EIGRP network to calculate the best route for loop-free routing and rapid convergence.

Configuration Builder
Microsoft Windows application that enables the administrator to configure multiple routers at once. Configuration Builder automatically detects the model, software version, image type, and the number and type of installed interfaces on the router being configured. It quickly imports predefined priority queuing lists, access lists, and filters into multiple configuration files.

configuration register
16-bit, user-configurable value in Cisco routers that determines how the router functions during initialization. The configuration register can be stored in hardware or software. In hardware, the value for each bit position is set using jumpers. In software, the values for bit positions are set by specifying a hexadecimal value using configuration commands.

congestion
Traffic in excess of network capacity.

Consultative Committee for International Telegraph
See CCITT.

content addressable memory
See CAM.

content networking
Infrastructure that delivers static, streaming, and dynamic content to an end user in a reliable, scalable, and secure manner. Content networking offers efficient bandwidth management and content distribution for complex, high-bandwidth content, and the flexibility to accommodate new content and services.

Content networking is also known as content delivery networking or Internet content networking.

contiguous
Location of a neighboring device. Contiguous means adjacent or next.

control plane
Collection of processes that run at the process level on the route processor. Control plane processes collectively provide high-level control for most Cisco IOS functions.

converged
Condition where the speed and ability of a group of internetworking devices running a specific routing protocol agree on the topology of the internetwork after a change in the topology.

converged network
A network capable of carrying voice, video and digital data.

convergence
Condition where the speed and ability of a group of internetworking devices running a specific routing protocol moves towards agreement on the topology of the internetwork after a change in the topology.

convergence time
Condition where the speed and ability of a group of internetworking devices running a specific routing protocol react after a change in the topology. The faster the convergence time, the quicker a network can adapt to the new topology.

Core Layer
Layer in a three-layer hierarchical design with the Access Layer and Distrubution Layer. The Core Layer is a high-speed backbone layer between geographically dispersed end networks.

core router
Router in a packet-switched star topology that is part of the backbone. The core router serves as the single pipe through which all traffic from peripheral networks must pass on the way to other peripheral networks.

cost
Value, typically based on hop count, media bandwidth, or other measures, that is assigned by a network administrator and used to compare various paths through an internetwork environment. Costs are used by routing protocols to determine the most favorable path to a particular destination. The lower the cost, the better the path.

Cost is also known as path cost.

CPE
customer premises equipment

Terminating equipment, such as terminals, telephones, and modems, supplied by the telephone company, installed at a customer site, and connected to the telephone company network.

CQ
custom queuing

Method that guarantees bandwidth for traffic by assigning space to each protocol.

CRC
cyclic redundancy check

Store and Forward error checking technique that counts the number of packets the checksum generates by far end device and compares it to the checksum calculated from the data received. A CRC error may indicate noise, gain hits, or transmission problems on the data link or interface.

CRM
customer relationship management

Software used to help organizations attract and retain customers for their growth and expansion.

crossover cable
Style of connecting switches and hubs to be able to send and receive data.

cryptography
Process of transforming plain text into scrambled cipher text.

CSU
channel service unit

Digital interface device that connects end-user equipment to the local digital telephone loop. Often referred to with DSU, as CSU/DSU.

CSU/DSU
channel service unit/data service unit

Network devices that connect an organization to a digital circuit.

custom queuing
See CQ.

customer premise equipment
See CPE.

customer relationship management
See CRM.

cut-through packet switching
Process where data is streamed through a switch so that the leading edge of a packet exits the switch at the output port before the packet finishes entering the input port. Cut-through packet switching enables a device to read, process, and forward packets as soon as the destination address is looked up, and the outgoing port determined.

Cut-through packet switching is also known as on-the-fly packet switching. Contrast with store and forward packet switching.

cut-through switching
Process where data is streamed through a switch so that the leading edge of a packet exits the switch at the output port before the packet finishes entering the input port. Cut-through packet switching enables a device to read, process, and forward packets as soon as the destination address is looked up, and the outgoing port determined.

Cut-through packet switching is also known as on-the-fly packet switching. Contrast with store and forward packet switching.

cycle
Process that is repeated.

cyclic redundancy check
See CRC.

data center
Central management location that monitors all network resources.

A data center is also known as a NOC.

data communications equipment
See DCE.

Data Encryption Standard
See DES.

data integrity
Process, strategy, and technology that ensures data is unchanged from creation to reception.

data service unit
See DSU.

data terminal equipment
See DTE.

datagram
Unit of information on a network that contains the source and destination addresses.

A datagram is also known as a message, packet, segment, or frame.

data-link connection identifier
See DLCI.

DCA
dynamic channel assignment

Open radio frequency that is selected when an access point identifies an unused channel on a WLAN.

DCE
data communications equipment

Physcal connection to a communications network in an EIA expansion environment. The DCE forwards traffic, and provides a clocking signal used to synchronize data transmission between DCE and DTE devices. Examples of DCE devices include a modem and an interface card.

DCE is also known as data circuit-terminating equipment when used in an ITU-T expansion environment.

DE
discard eligible

Designation of a packet in Frame Relay networking. A packet with the DE bit set will be dropped first when a router detects network congestion. The DE bit is set on oversubscribed traffic, which is traffic that was received after the CIR was set.

de facto standard
Format, language, or protocol that becomes a standard because it is widely used. De jure standard, in contrast, is one that exists because of approval by an official standards body.

dead interval
Period of time, in seconds, that a router will wait to hear a Hello from a neighbor before declaring the neighbor down.

dedicated LAN
dedicated local area network

Network segment allocated to a single device. Dedicated LAN technology is used in LAN-switched network topologies.

dedicated line
Bandwidth on a communications line that is indefinitely reserved for transmissions rather than switched when transmission is required.

dedicated local area network
See dedicated LAN.

default gateway
Path of a packet on a network used by default, or as the gateway of last resort, when the destination hosts are not listed in the routing table.

default route
Path of a packet on a network used by default, or as the gateway of last resort, when the destination hosts are not listed in the routing table.

delay
1) Length of time between the initiation of a transaction by a sender and the first response received by the sender. 2) Length of time required to move a packet from source to destination over a given path.

demarc
Indicated point between carrier equipment and CPE.

demilitarized zone
See DMZ.

demodulation
Process of returning a modulated signal to its original form. A modem performs demodulation by taking an analog signal and returning it to its digital form.

demultiplexing
Act of separating a common physical signal into multiple output streams.

Denial of Service
See DoS.

denies
Rejection of data on a network.

dense wavelength division multiplexing
See DWDM.

DES
Data Encryption Standard

Symmetric key cryptosystem that uses a 56-bit key to ensure high-performance encryption. DES is a cryptographic algorithm developed by the U.S. National Bureau of Standards. Today, DES is no longer considered a strong encryption algorithm by the U.S. government.

designated port
Interface on a device that forwards traffic toward the root bridge but does not connect to the least cost path.

designated router
See DR.

desirable mode
Designation of a port on a device as trunk port if the other end is set to trunk, desirable, or auto mode.

deterministic network
System that is designed for data transmission to follow a pre-defined path for an exact duration.

DH
Diffie-Hellman

Public key exchange method that provides a way for two peers to establish a shared secret key over an insecure communications path.

DHCP
Dynamic Host Configuration Protocol

Standard used by a software utility that requests and assigns an IP address, default gateway, and DNS server address to a network host. DHCP allocates an IP address for a host dynamically so the address can be reused when hosts no longer needs it.

dial backup
Feature on a Cisco router that provides protection against WAN downtime by allowing the network administrator to configure a backup serial line through a circuit-switched connection.

dial-up line
Communications circuit that is established by a switched-circuit connection using a telephone company network.

Differentiated Services Code Point
See DSCP.

Diffie-Hellman
See DH.

diffusing update algorithm
See DUAL.

digital signal level 0
See DS0.

digital signal level 1
See DS1.

digital signal level 3
See DS3.

digital subscriber line
See DSL.

Dijkstra's Algorithm
Process used in a SPF to dentify all paths to each destination and the total cost of each path.

discard eligible
See DE.

discarding
State of a port in an RSTP network where the server does not send a reply. A solid amber LED signifies discarding is in process.

discontiguous
Address on a network that is separated by a network or subnet from other subnets.

discontiguous network
Networking system with non-adjacent subnets, or subnets that are separated from other subnets by other networks.

discontiguous subnet
Address on a network that is separated by a network or subnet from other subnets.

distance vector
Type of routing protocol that periodically informs directly-connected routers of changes on the network.

Distance Vector Multicast Routing Protocol
See DVMRP.

distance vector protocol
Type of standards that uses distance to select the best path. Examples of a distance vector protocol include RIP, IGRP, and EIGRP.

distance vector routing algorithm
Mathematical process that uses the number of hops in a route to find the shortest path to a destination. Distance vector routing algorithms call for each router to send its entire routing table in each update, but only to its neighbors. Distance vector routing algorithms can be prone to routing loops, but are computationally simpler than link-state routing algorithms.

distributed collaborative information system
Database and application programs that support online asynchronous collaborative activities.

Distribution Layer
Layer in a hierarchical design between the Access layer and Core layer. The Distribution layer interconnects access layer hosts and switches, and provides security and traffic management for the Core Layer.

divide-and-conquer
Troubleshooting technique to resolve a network issue by breaking down the problem into smaller parts that are more manageable.

DLCI
data-link connection identifier

Layer 2 address that is required for each virtual circuit to reach a destination on an NBMA network. The DLCI is stored in the address field of every frame transmitted. The DLCI usually has only local significance and may be different at each end of a virtual circuit.

DMZ
demilitarized zone

Area in a network design that is located between the internal network and external network, usually the Internet. The DMZ is accessible to devices on the Internet, such as a web server, FTP server, SMTP server, and DNS.

DNS
Domain Name System

System used in the Internet for translating names of network nodes into IP addresses

domain
Portion of the naming hierarchy tree that refers to general groupings of networks based on the type of organization or geography.

Domain Name System
See DNS.

DoS
Denial of Service

Attack by a single system on a network that floods the bandwidth or resources of a targeted system, such as a web server, with the purpose of shutting it down.

dot1q
See IEEE 802.1Q.

downtime
Percentage of time in which a network is unavailable because of administrative shutdown or equipment failure.

DR
Router that is designated by the OSPF Hello protocol on an OSPF network that has at least two attached routers. A designated router generates LSAs. It enables a reduction in the number of adjacencies required which reduces the amount of routing protocol traffic and the size of the topological database.

DRAM
dynamic random access memory

This non-permanent working memory on a Cisco router includes primary DRAM used for holding routing tables and the running configuration, and shared DRAM used for supporting packet buffering.

DROther
Any router on an OSPF network that is not the DR or BDR.

DS0
digital signal level 0

Framing specification when transmitting digital signals over a single channel at 64-kbps on a T1 facility.

DS1
digital signal level 1

Framing specification when transmitting digital signals at 1.544-Mbps on a T1 facility in the United States, or at 2.108-Mbps on an E1 facility in Europe.

DS3
digital signal level 3

Framing specification when transmitting digital signals at 44.736-Mbps on a T3 facility.

DSCP
Differentiated Services Code Point

Field in an IP packet that enables different levels of service to be assigned to network traffic. DSCP can be assigned by the router or switch. The first six bits in the ToS byte in the header is the DSCP.

DSL
Public network service that delivers high bandwidth at limited distances over the copper wiring of conventional telephone lines that run between the CPE and the DSLAM of a SP. DSL incorporates technology that enables devices to immediately connect to the Internet when they are powered on. DSL is a physical layer transmission technology similar to dial, cable, or wireless technologies.

DSU
data service unit

Digital transmission device that adapts the physical interface on a DTE to a transmission facility such as T1 or E1. The DSU is also responsible for functions such as signal timing. Often referred to with CSU, as CSU/DSU.

DTE
data terminal equipment

Physical connection to the user end in an EIA expansion environment. The DTE serves as a data source, destination, or both. It connects to a data network through a DCE device, such as a modem, and typically uses clocking signals generated by the DCE. Examples of DTE devices include computers, protocol translators, and multiplexers.

DUAL
diffusing update algorithm

Mathematical process used in EIGRP that provides loop-free operation at every instant throughout a route computation. DUAL allows routers involved in a topology change to synchronize at the same time, while not involving routers that are unaffected by the change.

dual stack
Two similar protocol systems operating concurrently on one device. For example, a strategy for IPv4 transitioning to IPv6 is to run both protocol stacks on the same device. This enables IPv4 and IPv6 to coexist.

DVMRP
Distance Vector Multicast Routing Protocol

Internetwork gateway protocol largely based on RIP that implements a typical dense mode IP multicast scheme. DVMRP uses IGMP to exchange routing datagrams with its neighbors.

DWDM
dense wavelength division multiplexing

Process that assigns incoming optical signals to specific frequencies or wavelengths of light. DWDM can amplify these wavelengths to boost the signal strength. It can multiplex more than 80 different wavelengths or channels of data onto a single piece of fiber. Each channel is capable of carrying a multiplexed signal at 2.5 Gbps.

Dynamic ACL
An ACL that requires a user to use Telnet to connect to the router and authenticate. An extended ACL initially blocks traffic through the router. Users that want to traverse the router are blocked by the extended ACL until they Telnet to the router and are authenticated. The Telnet connection then drops, and a single-entry dynamic ACL entry is added to the existing extended ACL. This entry permits traffic for a particular time period; idle and absolute timeouts are possible. Dynamic ACLs are sometimes referred to as "lock and key" because the user is required to login in order to obtain access.

dynamic channel assignment
dynamic channel assignment

Open radio frequency that is selected when an access point identifies an unused channel on a WLAN.

Dynamic Host Configuration Protocol
See DHCP.

dynamic NAT
dynamic network address translation

Network Address Translation process that converts a local IP address to a global IP address by assigning the first available IP address in a pool of public addresses to an inside host. The host uses the assigned global IP address for the length of a session. When the session ends, the global address returns to the pool for use by another host.

dynamic network address translation
See dynamic NAT.

dynamic routing
Process of finding a path that adjusts automatically to network topology or traffic changes.

Dynamic routing is also known as adaptive routing.

E1

Wide-area digital transmission scheme used predominantly in Europe that carries data at a rate of 2.048 Mbps. E1 lines can be leased for private use from common carriers.

E2

Route outside of the OSPF routing domain, redistributed into OSPF.

E3

Wide-area digital transmission scheme used predominantly in Europe that carries data at a rate of 34.368 Mbps. E3 lines can be leased for private use from common carriers.

ECNM

Enterprise Composite Network Model

Cisco network design that divides the network into functional components while still maintaining the concept of Core, Distribution, and Access layers. The functional components are the Enterprise Campus, Enterprise Edge, and Service Provider Edge.

edge device

Filter on the perimeter of an enterprise network where incoming packets are passed. Examples of edge devices include firewall and DMZ. Edge devices may be equipped with IDS and IPS to examine and block unwanted traffic.

EGP

Exterior Gateway Protocol

Standards for exchanging routing information between autonomous systems. EGP is an obsolete protocol that was replaced by Border Gateway Protocol.

EIGRP

Enhanced Interior Gateway Routing Protocol

Proprietary Cisco routing protocol that combines distance vector routing protocol standards and link-state routing protocol standards. EIGRP uses the DUAL algorithm to determine routing.

EIGRP is also known as Enhanced IGRP.

EIR

excess information rate

Average rate above the CIR that a VC can support when no network congestion exists.

electromagnetic interference

See EMI.

electronic mail

See email.

email

electronic mail

1) Widely used network application in which mail messages are transmitted electronically between end users over a network using various network protocols. 2) Exchange of computer-stored messages by network communication.

Email is also written e-mail.

EMI

electromagnetic interference

Disturbance in an electronic circuit from an external electrical source.

Encapsulating Security Payload

See ESP.

encapsulation

Transmission of one network protocol within another. Tunneling is the basis of several IP security systems, including IPsec used in VPNs.

encoder

Device that modifies information into a required transmission format.

encoding

Process used to represent bits as voltages in wires or pulses of light in fiber optics.

encryption

Application of a specific algorithm that protects data by scrambling the information as it is sent and unscrambling the data when it is delivered.

end of transmission

See EOT.

Enhanced Interior Gateway Routing Protocol
See EIGRP.

Enhanced Rapid Spanning Tree Protocol
See RSTP+.

enterprise
Corporation, business, or other entity that uses computers in a networked environment. An enterprise usually refers to large companies or organizations with complex networks.

Enterprise Composite Network model
See ECNM.

enterprise network
Network that integrates all systems within a company or organization. An enterprise network differs from a WAN because it is privately owned and maintained.

Enterprise Network Architectures
See enterprise network.

EOT
end of transmission

Character that signifies that the transfer of data has ended.

equal cost
See equal cost load balancing.

equal cost load balancing
Packet distribution technique supported by EIGRP to prevent overloading a network route.

ESP
Encapsulating Security Payload

Security protocol that encapsulates data to be protected. ESP provides a framework for encrypting, authenticating, and securing data. ESP offers data privacy services, optional data authentication, and anti-replay services.

EtherChannel
EtherChannel allows multiple physical Ethernet links to combine into one logical channel. This allows load balancing of traffic among the links in the channel as well as redundancy in the event that one or more links in the channel fail.

EtherChannel can support Layer 2 or Layer 3 LAN ports.

Ethernet
Baseband LAN specification invented by Xerox Corporation and developed jointly by Xerox, Intel, and Digital Equipment Corporation. An Ethernet network uses the Carrier Sense Multiple Access/Collision Detection method and runs on cable types of 10 Mbps or more. Ethernet is similar to the IEEE 802.3 series of standards.

EUI-64
extended universal identifier-64 address

IPv6 address format created by taking an interface of the MAC address, which is 48 bits in length, and inserting another 16-bit hexadecimal string, FFFE, between the OUI, first 24 bits and the unique serial number, last 24 bits, of the MAC address. To ensure that the chosen address is from a unique Ethernet MAC address, the seventh bit in the high-order byte is set to 1 to indicate the uniqueness of the 48-bit address.

excess burst
See Be.

excess rate
Traffic on a network that is greater than the insured rate for a given connection. Excess traffic is delivered only if network resources are available, and may be discarded during periods of congestion. The excess rate equals the maximum rate minus the insured rate.

exit interface
Location on a router that the data passes through to move closer to the destination.

extended ACL
Type of access control list that filters source IP addresses, destination IP addresses, MAC addresses, protocol, and port numbers. The identification number assigned to an extended ACL can be from 100 to 199 and from 2000 to 2699.

extended star
Star topology that is expanded to include additional networking devices.

extended universal identifier-64 address
See EUI-64.

Exterior Gateway Protocol
See EGP.

external traffic
Data communication to and from a private network.

extranet
Network that provides access to information or operations of an organization to suppliers, vendors, partners, customers, or other businesses. Extranet is a private network using Internet protocols and the public telecommunication system to share internal resources. It may be considered an extension of an intranet.

faceplate
Protective component usually installed in the front of a device.

failover
Occurance of a redundant network device performing the load or function of another device automatically if the initial device fails. The failover scheme creates a backup system for mission-critical hardware and software. The objective is to reduce the impact of system failure to a minimum by actively monitoring and identifying system failure.

failure domain
Area of a network that is affected when a networking device malfunctions or fails. A properly designed network minimizes the size of failure domains.

Fast Ethernet
100BaseT-type Ethernet specification that offers speed 10 times greater than the standard 10BASE-T Ethernet specification while preserving such qualities as frame format, MAC mechanisms, and MTU. Based on an extension to the IEEE 802.3 specification.

fast switching
Feature developed by Cisco that uses a high-speed switching cache to expedite packet switching in IP routing. Destination IP addresses are stored in the cache to accelerate the packet forwarding process.

fast-forward
Cut-through switching method where the switch forwards the frame before all of frame is received. Using the fast-forward method, the switch forwards the frame out of the destination port immediately when the destination MAC address is read. The switch does not calculate or check the CRC value. The fast-forward method has lowest latency but may forward collision fragments and damaged frames. This method of switching works best in a stable network with few errors.

FCS
frame check sequence

Characters added to a frame for error control purposes. FCS is used in HDLC, Frame Relay, and other Data Link Layer protocols.

FD
feasible distance

Most desireable EIGRP metric along the path to the destination from the router.

feasible distance
See FD.

feasible successor
Backup route identified in a topology table. A feasible successor becomes a successor route if a primary route fails. The feasible successor must have a lower reported distance than the feasible distance of the current successor distance to the destination.

Feature Navigator
Web-based tool on Cisco website that helps to determine which features are supported by a specific IOS software image. Feature Navigator can also be used to find which IOS software images support a specific feature.

FECN
forward explicit congestion notification

Signal in a Frame Relay network to inform DTE that is receiving the frame that congestion was experienced in the path from source to destination. The DTE that receives the FECN signal can request that higher-level protocols take flow-control action as appropriate.

fiber-optic cable
Physical medium capable of conducting modulated light transmission. Compared with other transmission media, fiber-optic cable is more expensive and is capable of higher data rates, but is not susceptible to electromagnetic interference.

Fiber-optic cable is also known as optical fiber.

file transfer
Network application used to move files from one network device to another.

File Transfer Protocol
See FTP.

filter
Process or device that screens network traffic for certain characteristics such as source address, destination address, or protocol, and determines whether to forward or discard traffic based on the established criteria.

firewall
One or more router or access servers designated as a buffer between any connected public networks and a private network. A firewall router uses access lists and other methods to ensure the security of the private network.

firewall rule set
Set of configuration commands put into an access list on a Cisco security appliance or Cisco router that perform firewall functions. Source and destination IP addresses, protocols, or functions of a protocol can be affected by firewall rules.

first mile
Section of physical medium leading from the location of the customer to the central office of a service provider.

fixed configuration
Rules that are set and cannot be altered. An example of fixed configuration is a Layer 2 switch that has the number of ports and type of ports, such as FastEthernet and gigabit Ethernet, that are preconfigured in the factory.

flapping
Problem in routing when an advertised route between two devices alternates between two paths due to intermittent failures on a network.

flash memory
Memory used to store and run the Cisco IOS software. When a router is powered down, the contents of flash memory are not lost. Depending on the router model, flash memory can be implemented on erasable programmable read-only memory (EPROM) chips, or in external compact flash memory cards. (It is called flash memory, since the contents of the EPROMs can be upgraded by "flashing" the chip.)

flash update
Routing information sent asynchronously in response to a change in the network topology.

flat network
System where all stations can be reached without having to pass through a device such as a router.

floating static route
Path that is manually configured and entered into the routing table that has an administrative distance set greater than the administrative distance of a dynamic route. This route is only used if the existing dynamic route becomes unavailable.

flooding
Technique used by switches to pass traffic that is received on an interface to all other interfaces of the device except the interface on which the information was originally received.

flow control
Ability to maintain the rate of activity on a network.

form factor
Physical size and shape of computer components. Components that share the same form factor are physically interchangeable.

forward explicit congestion notification
See FECN.

forwarding
Process of sending a frame out of a port toward the destination by way of an internetworking device. Examples of devices that forward frames are hosts, repeaters, bridges, and routers.

fractional E1
Portion of a high-bandwidth E1 connection offered to a customer by a service provider.

fractional T1
Portion of a high-bandwidth T1 connection offered to a customer by a service provider.

FRAD
Frame Relay access device

Network device that provides a connection between a LAN and a Frame Relay WAN. A FRAD adds and removes headers and trailers for incoming packets.

fragment
Piece of a packet that has been broken down to smaller units.

fragmentation
Process of breaking a packet into smaller units when transmitting over a network medium that cannot support the size of the packet.

fragment-free
A switching technique that forwards a frame after the first 64 bytes are received. Fragment-free switching has a higher latency than fast-forward switching.

frame check sequence
See FCS.

Frame Relay
Industry-standard, switched, WAN standard that operates at the Physical Layer and Data Link Layer of the OSI Reference Model. Frame Relay handles multiple virtual circuits using HDLC encapsulation between connected devices. It is more efficient than the X.25 protocol that it replaced.

Frame Relay access device
See FRAD.

Frame Relay access support
See FRAS.

Frame Relay bridging
Technique described in RFC 1490 that uses the same spanning-tree algorithm as other bridging functions, but allows packets to be encapsulated for transmission across a Frame Relay network.

frame tagging
Method used by a Cisco Catalyst switch to identify the VLAN a frame belongs to. When a frame enters a switch it is encapsulated with a header that tags it with a VLAN identification.

FRAS
Frame Relay access support

Cisco IOS software feature that allows SDLC, Token Ring, Ethernet, and Frame Relay IBM devices to connect to other IBM devices across a Frame Relay network.

FTP
File Transfer Protocol

Defined in RFC 959, set of standards for transferring files between network nodes. FTP is commonly used to transfer webpages and download programs and other files to a computer.

full mesh
Network topolgy where each device connects to all others using either a physical or virtual circuit. Full mesh provides redundancy in the functionality of the network. It is usually reserved for network backbones because of the high cost of implementation.

gateway
Device that performs an application layer conversion of information from one protocol stack to another. An example of a gateway is the device that connects a traditional PSTN or analog phone to an IP network in VoIP.

Gateway Discovery Protocol
See GDP.

Gateway of Last Resort
Final stop on a route within an enterprise for packets that cannot be matched. Information about the packets appears in the routing tables of all routers.

GDP
Gateway Discovery Protocol

Cisco standard that allows a host to dynamically detect the arrival of a new router as well as determine when a router disconnects. GDP is based on UDP.

Generic Routing Encapsulation
See GRE.

Gigabit Ethernet
Data transmission bandwidth of 1000Mbps on a LAN. Gigabit Ethernet is the standard for high-speed Ethernet, approved by the IEEE 802.3z standards committee in 1996.

global unicast address
Unique IPv6 unicast address that can be routed worldwide with no modification. A global unicast address shares the same address format as an IPv6 anycast address. A global unicast address is assigned by IANA.

GMT
Greenwich Mean Time

Time zone located at 0 degrees longitude that sets the standard for all time zones.

GRE
Generic Routing Encapsulation

Cisco tunneling protocol used to encapsulate different protocols into a standard Internet protocol for transmission.

Greenwich Mean Time
See GMT.

hash
One-way encryption algorithm that takes an input message of arbitrary length and produces unique, fixed-length output text.

Hash-based Message Authentication Code
See HMAC.

Hashed Message Authentication Code-Message Digest
See HMAC-MD5.

Hashed Message Authentication Code-Secure Hash Alg
See HMAC-SHA-1.

HCC
horizontal cross-connect

Wiring closet where the horizontal cabling connects to a patch panel which is connected by backbone cabling to the main distribution facility.

HDLC
High-Level Data Link Control

Bit-oriented synchronous Data Link Layer protocol developed by ISO. HDLC specifies a data encapsulation method on synchronous serial links using frame characters and checksums.

header
Control information placed before data when the data is encapsulated for network transmission. Examples of a header information are the IP addresses of the sender and recipient.

hello interval
Period of time, in seconds, that a router keeps a Hello packet from a neighbor.

hello packet
Packet that is multicast to detect devices on a network and to test the connections. A hello packet is used by a router to determine the best connection available.

Hello Protocol
Standard used by OSPF systems for establishing and maintaining neighbor relationships. The Hello Protocol is an interior protocol that uses a routing metric based on the length of time it takes a packet to make the trip between the source and the destination.

helper address
Router configuration used to forward broadcast network traffic from a client computer on one subnet to a server in another subnet. A helper address is configured on an interface.

heterogeneous network
System of dissimilar devices that run dissimilar protocols and may support various functions or applications that are able to work together.

hexadecimal
Base 16 numbering system. Hexadecimal is a number representation using the digits 0 through 9, with their common meaning, plus the letters A through F to represent hexadecimal digits with values of 10 to 15. In a hexadecimal system, the right-most digit counts ones, the next counts multiples of 16, such as $16^2=256$.

hierarchical design model
Representation of a network featuring an access layer, a distribution layer, and a core layer.

hierarchical network
Design technique that divides the network into layers to prevent congestion and reduce the size of failure domains. The Cisco hierarchal design model uses core, distribution, and access layers.

hierarchical network design
See hierarchical network.

hierarchical routing
Transfer of data on a system that assigns network addresses based on the role or position of the network device or host.

hierarchical star topology
System on a network where a central switch or router is connected to other switches or routers. The layout of a hierarchical star topology is similar to the hub and spoke of a wheel.

High-Level Data Link Control
See HDLC.

High-Speed Serial Interface
See HSSI.

high-speed WAN interface card
See HWIC.

hijacking
When a hacker illegally gains access to a system through an authenticated connection.

HMAC
Hashed Message Authentication Code

Algorithm using cryptographic hash functions to encrypt code. HMAC can be used with any iterative cryptographic hash function, such as MD5 or SHA-1, in combination with a secret shared key.

HMAC-MD5
Hashed Message Authentication Code - Message Digest 5

Algorithm that uses a specific cryptographic hash function called MD5, with a secret key. The output is a 128-bit hash string that can be used to verify the data integrity and the authenticity of a message simultaneously.

HMAC-SHA-1
Hashed Message Authentication Code - Secure Hash Algorithm 1

HMAC-SHA-1 computes a Hash-based Message Authentication Code (HMAC) using the SHA1 hash function. The output is a 160-bit hash string that can be used to verify the data integrity and the authenticity of a message simultaneously.

hold time
Maximum time a router waits to receive the next hello packet or routing update. Once the hold time counter expires, the route becomes unreachable.

holddown
Placing a router in a state that will neither advertise nor accept routes for a specific length of time, called the holddown period. Holddown is used to remove bad information about a route from all routers in the network. A route is typically placed in holddown when a link in that route fails.

Holddown is also known as a holddown period.

holddown period
See holddown timer.

Holddown timer

Timers that a route is placed in so that routers neither advertise the route nor accept advertisements about the route for a specific length of time (the holddown period). Holddown is used to flush bad information about a route from all routers in the network. A route typically is placed in holddown when a link in that route fails.

hop

Transfer of a data packet between two network devices, such as routers.

hop count

Routing metric that tracks the number of legs that a data packets traverses between a source and a destination. RIP uses hop count as its sole metric.

horizontal cross-connect

See HCC.

host number

Section of an IP address that designates the node on the subnetwork is being addressed.

A host number is also known as a host address.

Hot Standby Router Protocol

See HSRP.

hot-swappable

Ability for a component to be installed or removed without having to turn off the power first. Installing or removing a hot-swappable component will not disturb the operation of other components in a device.

HSRP

Hot Standby Router Protocol

Standard that provides the ability to communicate on an internetwork if a default router becomes unavailable. HSRP provides high network availability and transparent network topology changes.

HSSI

High-Speed Serial Interface

Protocol that establishes the codes and electrical parameters that the router and the CSU/DSU use to communicate with each other.

HTTP

Hypertext Transfer Protocol

Standard used to transfer or convey information on the World Wide Web. HTTP is a communication protocol that establishes a request/response connection on the Internet.

HWIC

high-speed WAN interface card

Optional module for a series of Cisco routers that provides high-speed WAN connectivity.

hybrid network

Internetwork made up of more than one type of network technology, such as a LAN and WAN.

Hypertext Transfer Protocol

See HTTP.

IANA

Internet Assigned Numbers Authority

Entity that keeps records of the autonomous system numbers and is a registry for IP addresses and protocol numbers.

ICMP

Internet Control Message Protocol

Standard for network layer testing and troubleshooting. ICMP provides the ability to report diagnostic and error messages. The ping command is part of the ICMP utility.

IDF

intermediate distribution facility

Secondary communications room for a building that uses a star networking topology. An IDF has a frame that cross-connects the user cable media to individual user line circuits and may serve as a distribution point for multipair cables from the main distribution frame. The IDF is dependent on the MDF.

IDS

intrusion detection system

Combination of a sensor, console, and central engine in a single device installed on a network to protect against attacks missed by a conventional firewall. IDS inspects all inbound and outbound network activity and identifies suspicious patterns that may indicate a network or system attack. It is configured to send an alarm to network administrators when such attack is encountered.

IEEE
Professional organization whose activities include the development of communications and network standards. IEEE LAN standards are the predominant LAN standards today.

IEEE 802.1Q
IEEE standard that is designed to enable traffic between virtual LANs. IEEE 802.1Q uses an internal tagging mechanism which inserts a four-byte tag field in the original Ethernet frame between the source address and type/length fields. Because the frame is altered, the trunking device recomputes the frame check sequence on the modified frame.

IETF
Internet Engineering Task Force

Task force consisting of over 80 working groups responsible for developing Internet standards. The IETF is part of the Internet Society, or ISOC, organization.

IETF format
Task force consisting of over 80 working groups responsible for developing Internet standards. The IETF is part of the Internet Society, or ISOC, organization.

IGMP
Internet Group Management Protocol

Standard used by IP hosts to report a multicast group membership to an adjacent multicast router. IGMP can be used to access online video and gaming more efficiently.

IGP
Interior Gateway Protocol

Standard used to exchange routing information within an autonomous system. Examples of an Internet IGP includes EIGRP, OSPF, and RIP.

IKE
Internet Key Exchange

Hybrid protocol obtained from ISAKMP and Oakley standards that provides utility services for IPSec which include authentication of the IPSec peers, negotiation of IKE and IPSec security associations, and establishment of keys for encryption algorithms used by IPSec.

implicit deny
Last statement of an ACL inserted to block the accidental entry of unwanted traffic.

in-band
Management technique for connecting a computer to a network device. In-band management is used to monitor and make configuration changes to a network device over a network connection.

inbound
One of two directions a packet will travel on a network through an interface. An inbound packet is enteiring a device.

inside global address
Public-routable IP address of an inside host as it appears to the outside network. An inside global address is an IP address translated by NAT.

inside local address
Private IP address configured on a host on an inside network. An inside local address must be translated before it can travel outside the local addressing structure to the Internet.

inside local network
Privately addressed network space connected to a router interface. Inside local network is used to overcome shortages of public IP addressing.

Institute of Electrical and Electronics Engineers
See IEEE.

insured burst
Largest transfer of data above the insured rate that will be temporarily allowed on a permanent virtual circuit. An insured burst is not tagged to be dropped in the case of network congestion. An insured burst is specified in bytes or cells.

insured traffic
Data transfer at the rate specified for the PVC. Insured traffic should not be dropped by the network under normal network conditions.

interactive voice response
See IVR.

inter-area routing
Transfer of data between two or more logical areas.

interface
1) Connection between two systems or devices. 2) In routing terminology, a network connection. 3) In telephony, a shared boundary defined by common physical interconnection characteristics, signal characteristics, and meanings of interchanged signals. 4) The boundary between adjacent layers of the OSI model.

Interior Gateway Protocol
See IGP.

intermediate distribution facility
See IDF.

Intermediate System-to-Intermediate System
See IS-IS.

internal traffic
Data transmitted within a private, trusted network.

International Telecommunication Union
See ITU-T.

Internet Assigned Numbers Authority
See IANA.

Internet Control Message Protocol
See ICMP.

Internet Engineering Task Force
See IETF.

Internet Group Management Protocol
See IGMP.

Internet Key Exchange
See IKE.

Internet Protocol address
See IP address.

Internet Protocol address pool
See IP address pool.

Internet Protocol Control Protocol
See IPCP.

Internet Protocol multicast
See IP multicast.

Internet Protocol phone
See IP phone.

Internet Protocol security
See IPSec.

Internet Protocol telephony
See IP telephony.

Internet Protocol version 4
See IPv4.

Internet Protocol version 6
See IPv6.

internetwork
Collection of networks interconnected by routers and other devices that functions as a single network.

Internetwork operating system file naming system
See IOS file naming convention.

Internetwork Packet Exchange Control Protocol
See IPXCP.

Inter-Switch Link
See ISL.

inter-VLAN
Routing within a virtual LAN. Specific configuration to switches and routers is necessary.

intra-area routing
Transfer of data within a logical area when the source and destination are in the same area.

intranet
Networks accessible internal users of an organization. An intranet is used to share internal information and computing resources.

intrusion detection system
See IDS.

intrusion prevention system
See IPS.

inverse
Having the reverse effect.

Inverse Address Resolution Protocol
See Inverse ARP.

inverse ARP
Inverse Address Resolution Protocol

Method of building dynamic routes in a network. Inverse ARP allows an access server to discover the network address of a device associated with a virtual circuit.

Inverse ARP is also known as Reverse ARP or RARP.

IOS file naming convention
internetwork operating system file naming system

Cisco IOS software image name that represents the hardware, feature set, format, maintenance release, individual release, and T release, in that order.

IP address
Internet Protocol address

32-bit address in IPv4 that is assigned to hosts that use TCP/IP. An IP address belongs to one of five classes: A, B, C, D, or E.

It is written with four octets in the dot address format <a.b.c.d>. Each address consists of a network number, an optional subnetwork number, and a host number. The network and subnetwork numbers together are used for routing. The host number is used to address an individual host within the network or subnetwork. A subnet mask is used to extract network and subnetwork information from the IP address.

IP address pool
Internet Protocol address pool

Range of registered IP addresses to be used with NAT.

IP multicast
Internet Protocol multicast

Routing technique where one packet is sent to a multicast group identified by a single IP destination group address. IP multicast saves network bandwidth because packets are transmitted as one stream over the backbone and only split apart to the target stations by the router at the end of the path.

IP network
A network that uses the IP protocol, which is part of TCP/IP.

IP phone
Telephone that supports voice calls over an IP network.

IP Security
see IPSec.

IP telephony
Telephone that supports voice calls over an IP network.

IPCP
IP Control Protocol

Standard for establishing and configuring IP over PPP. IPCP is responsible for configuring, enabling, and disabling IP protocol modules on both ends of the point-to-point link.

IPS
intrusion prevention system

Active device in the traffic path that monitors network traffic and permits or denies flows and packets into the network. All traffic passes through an IPS for inspection. When the IPS detects malicious traffic, it sends an alert to the management station and blocks the malicious traffic immediately. IPS proactively prevents attacks by blocking the original and subsequent malicious traffic.

IPSec
IP Security

Framework of open standards that provides data confidentiality, data integrity, and data authentication between participating peers. IPSec provides security services at the IP layer. IPSec uses IKE to handle the negotiation of protocols and algorithms based on local policy and to generate the encryption and authentication keys to be used by IPSec. IPSec can protect one or more data flows between a pair of hosts, between a pair of security gateways, or between a security gateway and a host.

IPv4
Internet Protocol version 4

Current network layer standard for packet-switched internetworks. The IP address of IPv4 is 32 bits.

IPv6
Internet Protocol version 6

Network layer standard for packet-switched internetworks. IPv6 is the successor of IPv4 for general use on the Internet.

IPXCP
Internetwork Packet Exchange Control Protocol

Standard that establishes and configures IPX over PPP.

IS-IS
Intermediate System-to-Intermediate System

Standard for OSI link-state hierarchical routing based on DECnet Phase V routing. Routers exchange information based on a single metric to determine network topology.

ISL
Inter-Switch Link

Cisco protocol for tagging frames on an IEEE 802.1q network.

ITU-T
International Telecommunication Union Telecommunication Standardization Sector

International organization that develops communication standards.

ITU-T was formerly known as the Committee for International Telegraph and Telephone.

IVR
interactive voice response

A system that provides information in the form of recorded messages over telephone lines in response to user input in the form of spoken words or dual-tone multifrequencysignaling. An examples of IVR includes the ability to check a bank account balance from a telephone.

jabber
1) Error condition in which a network device continually transmits random and meaningless data onto the network. 2) Data packet that exceeds the length prescribed in the IEEE 802.3 standard.

jitter
Analog communication line distortion. Jitter can be caused by the variation of a signal from the reference timing positions, network congestion, or route changes. It can cause data loss, particularly at high speeds.

K value
Numeric value for a composite metric formula in EIGRP to determine the best path to a destination. K1 and K3 are set to 1. K2, K4, and K5 are set to 0. The value of 1 designates that bandwidth and delay have equal weight.

keepalive
Broadcast sent by one network device to inform another network device that the virtual circuit between the two is still active.

keepalive interval
Period of time that the client waits before sending a keepalive message on a TCP connection.

keepalive message
Broadcast sent by one network device to inform another network device that the virtual circuit between the two is still active.

key
Authentication code that passes between routers in plain text form.

key exchange
Method for two peers to establish a shared secret key, which only they recognize, while communicating over an unsecured channel.

key ID
Identification of code used between devices.

L2F
Layer 2 Forwarding Protocol

Layer 2 Forwarding (L2F) is a protocol developed by Cisco that supports the creation of secure virtual private dialup networks over the Internet by tunneling Layer 2 frames.

L2TP
Layer 2 Tunneling Protocol

Standard for tunneling PPP through a public network. L2TP provides a method to implement Virtual Private Dialup Network based on L2F and Point-to-point Tunneling protocols. L2TP is an Internet Engineering Task Force standard track protocol defined in RFC 2661.

LAN
local area network

High-speed, low-error data transfer system that encompasses a small geographic area. A LAN connects workstations, peripherals, terminals, and other devices in a single building or other geographically limited area. LAN standards specify cabling and signaling at the Physical Layer and the Data Link Layer of the OSI Reference Model. Examples of LAN technologies are Ethernet, FDDI, and Token Ring.

LAN switch
local area network switch

Device that forwards packets between data-link segments at a high speed. A LAN switch usually uses the MAC address to determine where to forward traffic. Some LAN switches operate at the network core, others operate at a workgroup level.

LAP
Lightweight Access Point

The access points used in the Cisco Unified Wireless Network architecture. LAPs are dependent on a Cisco wireless LAN controller for configuration and security information.

latency
1) Delay between the time when a device receives a frame and the time that frame is forwarded out the destination port. 2) Data latency is the time between a query and the results displaying on the screen.

Layer 2 Forwarding Protocol
See L2F Protocol.

Layer 2 Tunneling Protocol
See L2TP.

Layer 3 switching
Process on a router that uses cut-through techniques to increase the speed of packet inspection and forwarding.

LCP
Link Control Protocol

Standard that establishes, configures, and tests data-link connections for use by PPP. LCP checks the identity of the linked device, determines the acceptable packet size, searches for errors and can terminate the link if it exceeds the requirements.

learning
One of four states that a port cycles through when a switch powers on an STP network. The switch uses information learned to forward a packet.

leased line
Bandwidth on a communications line reserved by a communications carrier for the private use of a customer. A leased line is a type of dedicated line.

least cost path
Calculation of a switch to find a path that uses the least amount of bandwidth for each link required to reach the root bridge.

legacy
Older styles of hardware or software that are still being used.

Light Weight Access Point Protocol
See LWAPP.

Lightweight Access Point
See LWAP.

link
Network communications channel that includes a circuit or transmission path and all related equipment between a sender and a receiver.

A link is also known as a line or a transmission link.

Link Control Protocol
See LCP.

link-state advertisement
See LSA.

link-state protocol
Type of standards, such as OSPF and IS-IS, used in a hierarchical network design. Link-state protocols help manage the packet-switching processes in large networks.

link-state routing algorithm
Mathematical process in which each router broadcasts or multicasts information regarding the cost of reaching each of its neighbors. A link-state routing algorithm creates a consistent view of the network and is not prone to routing loops. Examples of link-state algorithms are OSPF and IS-IS.

listening
One of four states that a port cycles through when a switch powers on an STP network. The switch listens for BPDUs from neighboring switches.

LLQ
low latency queueing

Strict-priority ordered list that allows delay-sensitive data such as voice to be taken out of sequence and sent first. A voice packet is sent to the priority queue part where it has a fixed bandwidth allocation and is served first. A data packet enters the CBWFQ system directly and is assigned priority to determine how the data is treated. LLQ provides strict priority queuing to CBWFQ.

LMI
Local Management Interface

Standard that enhances the basic Frame Relay specification. LMI includes support for a global addressing, and support for keepalive, multicast, and status mechanisms.

load
Amount of traffic on a network.

load balances
See load balancing.

load balancing
Ability of a router to distribute traffic over all network interfaces that are the same distance from the destination address. Load balancing increases the use of network segments which improves bandwidth. A load-balancing algorithm may use both line speed and reliability information.

local access rate
Clock speed, or port speed, of the local loop connection to the Frame Relay cloud.

local area network
See LAN.

local area network switch
See LAN switch.

local loop
Physical line from the premises or demarcation point of a telephone subscriber to the edge of the carrier or telephone company central office.

A local loop is also known as a subscriber line.

Local Management Interface
See LMI.

logging
Process to recording and accessing details about packets on a network that have been permitted or denied.

logical topology
Map of the flow of data on a network that shows how devices communicate with each other.

loop
Route on a network where a packet never reaches its destination. A loop carries data repeatedly through a constant series of network nodes.

loopback interface
Connection between devices that share the same type of routing.

Low Latency Queuing
See LLQ.

LSA
link-state advertisement

Broadcast packet used by a link-state protocol. An LSA contains information about neighbors and path costs. It is used by the receiving routers to maintain routing tables.

A LSA is also known as link-state packet.

LWAP
Lightweight Access Point

Access point used in the Cisco Unified Wireless Network architecture. LWAPs depend on a Cisco WLAN controller for configuration and security information.

LWAPP
Light Weight Access Point Protocol

LWAPP is a draft protocol standard that defines how lightweight access points communicate with a centralized WLAN intelligence. LWAPP is used to manage security, mobility, QoS, and other functions essential to WLAN operations over an entire wireless enterprise.

MAC address
Media Access Control Address

Standardized data link layer address that is required for every port or device that connects to a LAN. Other devices in the network use these addresses to locate specific ports in the network and to create and update routing tables and data structures. MAC addresses are 6 bytes long and are controlled by the IEEE.

MAC address is also known as a hardware address, a MAC-layer address, or a physical address.

main cross-connect
See MCC.

main distribution facility
See MDF.

manageability
Ability of a system to be administered.

management domain
Information included on a message that each switch advertises on its trunk ports.

management information base
See MIB.

management virtual local area network
See management VLAN.

management VLAN
management virtual local area network

VLAN1 on a switch. The IP address of VLAN1 is used to access and configure the switch remotely and to exchange information with other network devices.

manual summarization
Feature on an EIGRP route where the administrator determines which subnets on which interfaces are advertised as summary routes. Manual summarization is done on a per-interface basis and gives the network administrator complete control. A manually summarized route appears in the routing table as an EIGRP route sourced from a logical interface.

maximum transmission unit
See MTU.

MCC
main cross-connect

Wiring closet that serves as the most central point in a star topology. An MCC is where LAN backbone cabling connects to the Internet.

MCU
multipoint control unit

Device used to support multiple-party conference calls. Members of the conference call can send media to the MCU which mixes the media and then sends it to all participants.

MD5
Message Digest 5

Method of authentication that requires that each router has a unique key and key ID. The router uses an algorithm that processes the key, the OSPF packet, and the key ID to generate an encrypted number. Each OSPF packet includes that encrypted number. The key is never transmitted.

MDF
main distribution facility

Primary communications room for a building. An MDF is the central point of a star networking topology where patch panels, hubs, and routers are located. It is used to connect public or private lines coming into the building to internal networks.

Media Access Control Address
See MAC Address.

media converter
Data Link Layer process on a router that changes a frame to Ethernet if it is on a LAN and to a WAN interface if it exits the LAN and enters the Internet.

mesh
Network topology where devices are organized in a segmented manner with interconnections strategically placed between network nodes.

Message Digest 5
See MD5.

metric
Information a routing algorithm uses to determine the best route on a network. Metrics are stored in a routing table. Metrics include bandwidth, communication cost, delay, hop count, load, MTU, path cost, and reliability.

Metro Ethernet
Network system based on Ethernet technology that covers a metropolitan area.

MIB
management information base

Database of network management information that is used and maintained by a network man-
agement protocol such as SNMP or Common Management Information Protocol, also known as CMIP. The value of a MIB object can be changed or retrieved using SNMP or CMIP commands. MIB objects are organized in a tree structure that includes public, or standard, and private, or proprietary, branches.

microprocessor
Chip that contains the central processing unit for the device.

microsegment
See microsegmentation.

microsegmentation
Division of a network into smaller segments, usually with the intention of increasing aggregate bandwidth to network devices.

Microsoft Visio
Diagramming application software published by Microsoft.

mission-critical
Type of network or computing process that is vital to an organization. Mission-critical applications that are halted often or for too long may have negative consequences.

Mobile Internet Protocol
See mobile IP.

Mobile IP
Mobile Internet Protocol

IETF standard for IPv4 and IPv6 which enables a mobile device to move without breaking the connection. Mobility is a feature of IPv6.

modem
Device that converts digital computer signals into a format that is sent and received over an analog telephone line. Modem is the common term for modulator-demodulator.

modular block diagram
Illustration of the major functions of a network in modular form. A modular block diagram helps a designer determine the underlying architecture on which the network is built.

modulated
See modulation.

modulates
See modulation.

modulation
Process where the characteristics of an electrical signal is transformed to represent information. Types of modulation include amplitude modulation, frequency modulation, and pulse amplitude modulation.

MOSPF
Multicast Open Shortest Path First

Intradomain multicast routing protocol used in Open Shortest Path First networks. An extension is applied to the base OSPF unicast protocol to support IP multicast routing. Multicast information is included in OSPF link-state advertisements. MOSPF builds a distribution tree for each group and computes a tree for active sources sent to the group. The tree state is cached and must be recomputed when a link-state change occurs or when the cache times out.

MOSPF is also known as multicast OSPF.

MPLS
Multiprotocol Label Switching

Standard used to increase the speed of traffic flow on a network. The MPLS process marks each packet with the path sequence to the destination instead of using a routing table. Packet switching is done at Layer 2 of the OSI Reference Model. MPLS supports protocols such as IP, ATM, and Frame Relay.

MS Visio
Diagramming application software published by Microsoft.

MTU
maximum transmission unit

Maximum packet size, in bytes, that a particular interface can handle.

multi-access
Type of network that allows multiple devices to connect and communicate simultaneously.

multicast
Single packets copied by the network and sent to a specific subset of network addresses. Multicast addresses are specified in the destination address field.

Multicast Open Shortest Path First
See MOSPF.

multilayer switch
Device that filters and forwards packets based on MAC addresses and network addresses. A layer 2/layer 3 switch is a multilayer switch.

multilayer switching
Device that filters and forwards packets based on MAC addresses and network addresses. A layer 2/layer 3 switch is a multilayer switch.

multiplexing
Scheme that allows multiple logical signals to be transmitted simultaneously across a single physical channel. The signals are then seperated at the receiving end.

multipoint control unit
See MCU.

Multiprotocol Label Switching
See MPLS.

NAC
network admission control

Method of preventing a virus from infecting a computer by controlling access to a network. NAC uses protocols and software products to assess a host that tries to log onto a network. NAC determines the condition, called the posture, of the host,. An infected host may be placed in quarantine. A host with outdated virus protection will be directed to obtain an update. An uninfected host with virus protection will be allowed on the network.

Network admission control is also known as network access control.

NACL
named access control list

Standard or extended format that are referenced by a descriptive name rather than a number. When configuring a NACL, the router IOS uses a NACL subcommand mode.

NACL is also known as named ACL.

named access control list
See NACL.

NAS
network attached storage

High-speed, high-capacity data storage that groups large numbers of disk drives that are directly attached to the network and can be used by any server. A NAS device is typically attached to an Ethernet network and is assigned its own IP address.

NAT
Network Address Translation

Standard used to reduce the number of IP addresses necessary for all nodes within the organization to connect to the Internet. NAT allows a large group of private users to access the Internet by converting packet headers for only a small pool of public IP addresses and keeping track of them in a table.

NAT overload
Dynamically translates multiple inside local addresses to a single public address so more than one client can access the connection to the Internet.

native VLAN
Special VLAN that accomodates untagged traffic. Trunk links carry untagged traffic over the native VLAN. On Cisco Catalyst switches, VLAN1 is the native VLAN.

NAT-PT
Network Address Translation-Protocol Translation

Mechanism located between an IPv6 network and an IPv4 network to translate IPv6 packets into IPv4 packets and vice versa.

NBAR
Network Based Application Recognition

Cisco utility that conducts audits and traffic analysis. NBAR is a classification and protocol discovery tool that identifies traffic up to the application layer. It provides interface, protocol, and bi-directional statistics for each traffic flow that traverses an interface. NBAR does sub-port classification, which include looking and identifying beyond application ports. NBAR recognizes web-based and other protocols that use dynamic TCP and UDP port assignments.

NBMA
non-broadcast multi-access

Network that does not support broadcasting, such as X.25, or broadcasting is not possible, such as a SMDS.

NCP
Network Control Protocol

Standard that routes and controls the flow of data between a communications controller, in which it resides, and other network resources.

negotiate parameter
Parameter on a switch that automatically detects the encapsulation type of the neighbor switch.

neighbor
Routers that have interfaces to a common network in OSPF. On a multi-access network, neighbors are dynamically discovered by the OSPF Hello protocol.

neighbor table
One of three interconnected EIGRP router tables. The neighbor table collects and lists information about directly connected neighbor routers. A sequence number records the number of the last received hello from each neighbor and time-stamps the time that the packet arrived. If a hello packet is not received within the hold time, the timer expires and DUAL recalculates the topology. Other router tables include topology and routing tables.

neighboring routers
Routers that have interfaces to a common network in OSPF. On a multi-access network, neighbors are dynamically discovered by the OSPF Hello protocol.

NetFlow
Accounting tool used to analyze and provide details about traffic patterns in a network. NetFlow can be used to capture the traffic classification or precedence associated with each flow.

network access control
Limit access to the physical components of a network.

Network Address Translation
See NAT.

Network Address Translation-Protocol Translation
See NAT-PT.

network admission control
See NAC.

network analyzer
Monitoring device or software application that maintains statistical information about the status of the network and each device attached to it. Some network analyzers are able to detect, define, and fix problems on the network.

network attached storage
See NAS.

network backbone
Core network architecture for an enterprise. Network backbone connects all LAN segments of a system and provides fast switching between subnets.

Network Based Application Recognition
See NBAR.

network baseline
Process that involves monitoring network performance and behavior over a certain period of time to create a point of reference for future network evaluations. Network baseline is used by network administrators to monitor the network and troubleshoot if there is a problem.

network boundary
Location where route summarization occurs on a boundary router.

Network Control Protocol
See NCP.

network diameter
Maximum number of hops between any two end stations in the network. Network diameter is the maximum number of links that must be traversed to send a message to any host along a shortest path.

network discovery
Result of dynamic routing protocols enabling a router to share information about reachability and status, and also to add remote networks to the routing table.

network infrastructure diagram
Illustration of the topology of a network that shows the location, function, and status of devices. A network infrastructure diagram may represent either a physical or logical network.

A network infrastructure diagram is also known as a topology diagrams.

network maintenance plan
See NMP.

network management system
See NMS.

network modularity
Network modularity refers to organizing a network from smaller subsystems or modules that can be designed and implemented independently. The modules can represent areas that have different physical or logical connectivity. They also designate where different functions occur in the network. Modularity allows flexibility in network design, and facilitates implementation and troubleshooting. As network complexity grows, designers can add new functional modules.

network monitoring plan
Information used by a network administrator to evaluate the condition of a network.

network operations center
See NOC.

next hop
Interface on a connected router that moves the data closer to the final destination.

NMP
network maintenance plan

Ensures business continuity by keeping the network running efficiently. Network maintenance must be scheduled during specific time periods, usually nights and weekends, to minimize the impact on business operations.

NMS
network management system

System or application that is used to monitor and control managed network devices, such as CiscoWorks.

NOC
network operations center

Organization responsible for maintaining a network.

non-broadcast multi-access
See NBMA.

non-stub area
OSPF area that carries default, static, intra-area, interarea, and external routes. An non-stub area can have virtual links configured across it and can contain an ASBR.

Null0 interface
EIGRP installs a Null0 summary route in the routing table for each parent route. The Null0 interface indicates that this is not an actual path, but a summary for advertising purposes.

NVRAM
non-volatile random access memory. NVRAM is used as the storage location for the startup configuration file for a Cisco router. After the router loads its IOS image, the settings found in the startup configuration are applied.

OC
optical carrier

Series of physical protocols, such as OC-1, OC-2, OC-3, defined for synchronous optical network optical signal transmissions.

OC signal levels put synchronous transport signal frames onto fiber-optic line at different speeds. The base rate of an OC signal level is 51.84 Mbps for OC-1. Each signal level thereafter operates at a speed multiplied by that number. For example, OC-3 runs at 155.52 Mbps (51.84 x 3 = 155.52).

Open Shortest Path First
See OSPF.

open standard
Protocol or rule available to the public to be applied to a network. An open standard is not proprietary.

optical carrier
See OC.

organizational unique identifier
See OUI.

OSPF
Open Shortest Path First

Routing algorithm for a link-state, hierarchical Interior Gateway Protocol that replaces Routing Information Protocol. OSPF features include least-cost routing, multipath routing, and load balancing.

OUI
Three octets assigned to the hardware manager by the IEEE in a block of 48-bit LAN addresses.

outbound
One of two directions a packet will travel on a network through an interface. An outbound packet is exiting a device.

out-of-band
Transmission using frequencies or channels outside the frequencies or channels normally used for information transfer. Out-of-band signaling is often used for error reporting in situations in which in-band signaling can be affected by whatever problems the network might be experiencing.

outside global address
Public IP address of an external host, as it is referred to on the Internet.

outside global network
Network attached to a router that is external to the LAN and that does not recognize the private addresses assigned to hosts on the internal LAN.

outside local address
IP address of an outside host as it appears to the inside network.

Packet over SONET/SDH
See POS.

packet sniffer
Tool that analyzes traffic flows based on the source and destination of the traffic as well as the type of traffic being sent. Packet sniffer analysis can be used to make decisions on how to manage the traffic more efficiently.

packet switch
WAN device that routes packets along the most efficient path and allows a communications channel to be shared by multiple connections.

Packet switch is also known as a packet switch node.

packet switching
Networking method where nodes share bandwidth by sending packets to each other. Packet switching is a way to direct encoded information in a network from a source to a destination.

packet-switched network
See PSN.

PAP
Password Authentication Protocol

Standard used by PPP peers to authenticate each other on a network. A remote router sends an authentication request when attempting to connect to a local router. PAP passes the password and host name or username. PAP does not prevent unauthorized access, but identifies the remote user. The router or access server then determines if the user is allowed access.

parent route
When default summarization is disabled, updates include subnet information. The routing table installs entries for each of the subnets and also an entry for the summary route. A parent route is announced by the summarizing router as long as at least one specific route in its routing table matches the parent route.

The parent route is called the summary route and the child route is called the subnet route.

partial mesh
Network where devices are organized in a mesh topology with network nodes that are organized in a full mesh, and network nodes that connected to one or two other nodes in the network. A partial mesh does not provide the level of redundancy of a full mesh topology and is less expensive to implement. They are generally used in the peripheral networks that connect to a fully meshed backbone.

Password Authentication Protocol
See PAP.

PAT
Port Address Translation

Standard used to reduce the number of internal private IP addresses to only one or a few external public IP addresses. PAT enables an organization to conserve addresses in the global address pool by allowing source ports in TCP connections or UDP conversations to be translated. Different local addresses then map to the same global address, with PAT providing the unique information. PAT is a subset of NAT functionality.

patch panel
Assembly of pin locations and ports which can be mounted on a rack or wall bracket in the wiring closet. A patch panel acts like a switchboard that connects workstation cables to each other and externally.

PBX
private branch exchange

Digital or analog telephone switchboard located on the subscriber premises and used to connect private and public telephone networks.

PDM
protocol dependent module

Used by EIGRP making decisions about specific routing tasks. Each PDM maintains three tables.

per VLAN Rapid Spanning Tree Plus
See PVRST+.

permanent virtual circuit
See PVC.

permanent virtual path
See PVP.

permits
Allows a process to occur.

physical addressing
See MAC address.

physical topology
Layout of devices on a network. The physical topology shows the way that the devices are connected through the cabling and how cables are arranged.

pilot installation
Small implementation of a new network technology used to test how well the technology meets the design goals.

PIM
Protocol Independent Multicast

Standard for a routing architecture that enables the addition of IP multicast routing on an existing IP network. PIM is unicast routing protocol independent. It can be operated in the dense mode and sparse mode.

PIM dense mode
Protocol Independent Multicast dense mode

When a receiver affected by PIM standards processes large amounts of traffic. Packets are forwarded on all outgoing interfaces until pruning and truncation occurs. It is assumed that the downstream networks will receive and use the datagrams that are forwarded to them. PIM dense mode is driven by data and resembles typical multicast routing protocols.

PIM sparse mode
Protocol Independent Multicast sparse mode

When receivers affected by PIM standards are widely distributed, PIM sparse mode tries to constrain data distribution so that a minimal number of routers in the network receive it.

Packets are sent only if they are explicitly requested at the rendezvous point. It is assumed that downstream networks will not necessarily use the datagrams that are sent to them.

plain old telephone service
See POTS.

PoE
Power over Ethernet

Powering standard of network devices over Ethernet cable. IEEE 802.3af and Cisco specify two different PoE methods. Cisco power sourcing equipment and powered devices support both PoE methods.

Point-of-Presence
See POP.

Point-to-Point Protocol
See PPP.

Point-to-Point T1
WAN connectivity that offers control over the quality of service available.

Point-to-Point Tunneling Protocol
See PPTP.

poisoned reverse
Routing update that indicates that a network or subnet is unreachable, rather than implying that a network is unreachable by not including it in updates. Poison reverse updates are sent to defeat large routing loops. The Cisco IGRP implementation uses poison reverse updates.

policy routing
Scheme that forwards packets on a network to specific interfaces based on user-configured policies. An example of policy routing is that it may specify that traffic sent from a particular network should be forwarded from one interface, while all other traffic should be forwarded from another interface.

POP
Point of Presence

Physical connection between a communication facility provided by an ISP or local telephone company, and an organization's main distribution facility.

port

1) Interface on a networking device, such as a router or a switch. 2) Upper-layer process that receives information from lower layers. 3) Female plug on a patch panel.

Port Address Translation
See PAT.

port density
Amount of ports per RU on a switch.

PortFast
Enhancement to STP that causes an access port to enter the forwarding state immediately, by-passing the listening and learning states. Using PortFast on access ports that are connected to a single workstation or server allows those de-vices to connect to the network immediately,

POS
Packet over SONET/SDH

Type of networking supported by SONET and SDH that moves large amounts of voice and data over great distances through fiber-optic cable.

POST
power-on self test

A process used to test the device hardware after the power is turned on.

POTS
Plain old telephone service. See PSTN.

Power over Ethernet
See PoE.

power-on self test
See POST.

PPDIOO
prepare, plan, design, implement, operate, and optimize

Six-phase Cisco Lifecycle Services approach to support evolving networks. Each phase defines the activities required to successfully deploy and operate Cisco technologies. PPDIOO de-tails how to optimize performance throughout the lifecycle of a network.

PPP
Point-to-point Protocol

Standard that provides router-to-router and host-to-network connections over synchronous and asynchronous circuits.

PPTP
Point-to-Point Tunneling Protocol

Point-to-Point Tunneling Protocol (PPTP) was developed by Microsoft. It is described in RFC2637. PPTP is widely deployed in Windows client software to create VPNs across TCP/IP networks.

PQ
priority queing

Feature in routing in which the characteristics of a frame, such as packet size and interface type, are used to determine the order the frame is sent.

prefix address
Pattern that matches the bits of an IP address. For example, 130.120.0.0/16 matches the first 16 bits of the IP address 130.120.0.0, which is 130.120. In another example, 12.0.0.0/12 matches 12.0.2.3, 12.2.255.240, and 12.15.255.255, but does not match 12.16.0.1.

prefix length
Identifies the number of bits used in the net-work.

A prefix length is also known as a network pre-fix.

prepare, plan, design, implement, operate, and opt
See PPDIOO.

priority queuing
See PQ.

Private addresses
Type of IP address that is reserved for internal use. A private network address is not routed across the public Internet. In IPv4, the range of private network addresses are 10.0.0.0 to 10.255.255.255, 172.16.0.0 to172.31.255.255, and 192.168.0.0 to 192.168.255.255.

private branch exchange
See PBX.

private network address
Portion of an IP address that is reserved for internal use. A private network address is not routed across the public Internet. In IPv4, the range of private network addresses are 10.0.0.0 to 10.255.255.255, 172.16.0.0 to172.31.255.255, and 192.168.0.0 to 192.168.255.255.

proactive maintenance
Method for a network administrator to ensure uptime by monitoring network functionality and taking corrective action immediately. Proactive maintenance is performed on a regular basis to detect weaknesses prior to a critical error that could bring down the network.

process switching
Operation that occurs when a router evaluates the route and per packet load balancing across parallel links before sending a packet. In process switching, a router performs a table lookup for each packet, selects an interface, and looks up the data-link information. Because each routing decision is independent for each packet, all packets going to the same destination are not forced to use the same interface.

proof-of-concept
Proving that a design functions as expected.

propagation delay
Amount of time required for data to travel over a network, from the source to the destination.

proprietary
Device or software that cannot be used with devices or software from other vendors.

Protocol Dependent Module
See PDM.

Protocol Independent Multicast
See PIM.

Protocol Independent Multicast dense mode
See PIM dense mode.

Protocol Independent Multicast sparse mode
See PIM sparse mode.

PSN
packet-switched network

Network that uses packet-switching technology for data transfer.

PSTN
Public Switched Telephone Network

General term referring to the variety of telephone networks and services in place worldwide.

PSTN is also known as plain old telephone service, or POTS.

public network address
IP address that is unique and routable across the public Internet.

Public Switched Telephone Network
See PSTN.

punchdown
Spring-loaded tool used to cut and connect wires in a jack or on a patch panel.

punchdown block
A device that connects telephone or data lines to each other. The solid copper wires are punched down into short open-ended slots to establish connectivity.

PVC
permanent virtual circuit

Connection that saves bandwidth because the circuit is established ahead of time.

PVP
permanent virtual path

Passage that consists of permanent virtual circuits.

PVRST+
Per VLAN Rapid Spanning Tree +

Cisco implementation of one instance of RSTP per VLAN.

Q.922A
ITU-T specification for Frame Relay encapsulation.

QoS
quality of service

Standard for monitoring and maintaining a level of transmission performance and service, such as available data transmission bandwidth and error rate.

QoS policies
Procedures defined and used in the QoS process.

quad zero route
Route where the network address and subnet mask are both specified as 0.0.0.0. The command uses either the next-hop address or the exit interface parameters.

quality of service
See QoS.

query packet
Message used to inquire about the value of some variable or set of variables.

rack unit
See RU.

radio frequency
See RF.

radio frequency interference
See RFI.

RAM
random-access memory

Type of memory that allows any byte of memory to be accessed without affecting preceding bytes. RAM is used for temporary storage by programs. When the computer is shut down, all data stored in RAM is lost.

random-access memory
See RAM.

Rapid Spanning Tree Protocol
See RSTP.

Rapid Transport Protocol
See RTP.

RD
reported distance

Distance to a destination as reported by a neighbor.

read-only memory
See ROM.

Real-Time Transport Control Protocol
See RTCP.

Real-Time Transport Protocol
See RTP.

Receiver Signal Strength Indicator
See RSSI.

recursive lookup
Two steps necessary to determine the exit interface. First a router matches the destination IP address of a packet to the static route. Then the router matches the next hop IP address of the static route to entries in its routing table to determine which interface to use.

redirector
Software that intercepts requests for resources on a remote computer and then sends the requests to the appropriate host to process the transaction more efficiently. The redirector creates a remote-procedure call that is sent to lower-layer protocol software that can satisfy the request.

redistribution
Process of including routing information discovered through one routing protocol in the update messages of another routing protocol.

redlined
Marks on blueprints showing changes in the design.

redundancy
1) Duplication of components on a network, such as devices, services, or connections, for the purpose of maintaining operability if any tool fails. 2) Portion of the total information contained in a message that can be eliminated without losing the context.

redundant link
Secondary connection between network devices to ensure network availability if the primary link fails.

reference bandwidth
Parameter related to the OSPF cost metric which is used to calculate interface cost. The bandwidth value calculation of each interface uses the equation 100,000,000/bandwidth, or 10^8/bandwidth.

Reflexive ACL
An ACL that allows IP packets to be filtered based on upper-layer session information. They are generally used to allow inbound traffic into the network in response to sessions that originate on an inside interface of the router. This mechanism can help reduce exposure to spoofing and denial-of-service attacks. Reflexive ACLs function similarly to the "established" keyword used in extended ACL statements, except that reflexive ACLs can also inspect UDP and ICMP traffic in addition to TCP.

release notes
Documentation that accompanies software when it is distributed. Release notes include the most recent information, such as a user guide.

reliability
Ratio of expected-to-received keepalives from a link. If the ratio of keepalives is high, the line is reliable. Relibility is used as a routing metric.

Reliable Transport Protocol
See RTP.

remote login
See rlogin.

remote monitoring
See RMON.

remote shell protocol
See rsh.

remote-access virtual private network
See remote-access VPN.

remote-access VPN
Connectivity option used to augment or replace a traditional remote access strategy, such as the use of a dial-up link.

remote-access VPN is also known as remote-user VPN.

remote-procedure call
See RPC.

replay attack
Malicious process that allows a hacker to gain access to a router using information that is saved and replayed by the hacker as proof of identity.

reply packet
Information sent when a query packet is received. A reply packet helps DUAL to locate a successor route to the destination network. Queries can be multicast or unicast. Replies are always unicast.

reported distance
See RD.

Request For Proposal
See RFP.

Request For Quotation
See RFQ.

request message
When a router is started, message sent out by each RIP-configured interface requesting that all RIP neighbors send their routing tables.

response message
Reply to a message sent out by each RIP-configured interface requesting that all RIP neighbors send their routing tables.

RF
radio frequency

Electromagnetic waves generated by AC and transmitted to an antenna within the electromagnetic spectrum. Radio, cable TV, and broadband networks use RF technology. WLAN uses RF to transmit data.

RFI
radio frequency interference

Noise that interferes with information being transmitted across unshielded copper cabling.

RFP
Request For Proposal

Formal documentation presented to potential vendors by an organization asking for information on the type of services or products to be provided.

RFQ
Request For Quotation

Formal documentation presented to vendors by an organization asking for a bid or quotation of the cost of providing services or products. An RFQ is issued when the specifications have been determined.

RIP
Routing Information Protocol

Distance vector routing standard that uses hop count as a routing matrix.

RIPng
Routing Information Protocol next generation

Distance vector routing standard with a limit of 15 hops that uses split-horizon and poison reverse to prevent routing loops. It is based on IPv4 RIPv2 and similar to RIPv2, but uses IPv6 for transport. The multicast group address FF02::9 identifies all RIPng enabled routers.

RIPv2
Routing Information Protocol version 2

Distance vector routing standard based on RIPv1 with additional extensions to conform to modern routing environments. RIPv2 supports VLSM, authentication, and multicast updates. RIPv2 is defined in RFC 1723 and supported in IOS versions 11.1 and later.

Rivest, Shamir, and Adleman
See RSA.

rlogin
remote login

Terminal emulation program that is offered in most UNIX implementations to access a device remotely, such as Telnet.

RMON
remote monitoring

Management information base agent specification described in RFC 1271 that defines functions to remotely monitor networked devices. RMON provides monitoring, problem detection, and reporting capabilities.

rogue switch
Unidentified switch on a network.

ROM
read-only memory

ROM is typically used as the memory area from which a Cisco router begins the boot process, supports the Power-On-Self-Test, and supports the ROM Monitor diagnostic environment.

root bridge
Designated packet forwarding device in a spanning-tree implementation that receive topology information and notifies all other bridges in the network when topology changes are required. A root bridge prevents loops and provides a measure of defense against link failure.

Root bridge is also known as root switch.

root port
STP designated port that provides the least cost path back to the root bridge.

root switch
See root bridge.

route
Path between the source and destination devices.

route aggregation
See route summarization.

route map
Method to control and modify routing information on a network. A route map is a complex access list that allows some conditions to be tested against the route in question. If the conditions match, some actions can be taken to modify the route.

route poisoning
Setting the metric for a route to 16 to stop traffic on the route. RIP sends a triggered update immediately, poisoning the route.

route redistribution
Default route is propagated from the edge router to other internal routers.

route summarization
Consolidation of advertised addresses in a routing table. Route summarization reduces the number of routes in the routing table, the routing update traffic, and overall router overhead.

Route summarization is also known as route aggregation.

router
Network layer device that uses one or more metrics to determine the optimal path along which network traffic should be forwarded. Routers forward packets from one network to another based on network layer information.

router ID
IP address determined by a value configured with the router-id command, a value of the highest configured IP address on a loopback interface, or a value of the highest IP address on any active physical interface.

router-on-a-stick
Configuration on the router that determines that if the destination VLAN is on the same switch as the source VLAN, the router forwards the traffic back down to the source switch using the subinterface parameters of the destination VLAN ID.

routing
Process to find a path to a destination host. Routing is complex in large networks because of intermediate destinations a packet might traverse before reaching the final destination host.

routing algorithm
Mathematical formula for procedures used to determine the best route to forward traffic from source to destination.

routing domain
Group of end systems and intermediate systems that operate under the same set of administrative rules. Within each routing domain there are one or more areas, each uniquely identified by an area address.

Routing Information Protocol
See RIP.

Routing Information Protocol next Generation
See RIPng.

Routing Information Protocol version 2
See RIPv2.

routing metric
Standard of measurement that is used by a routing algorithm that determines that one route is better than another. Routing metrics are stored in routing tables and may include bandwidth, communication cost, delays, hop count, load, maximum transmission unit, path cost, and reliability.

routing prefix
Pattern to match some routes in a routing table.

routing protocol
Standard that makes use of the routing algorithm. Examples of routing protocols include EIGRP, OSPF, and RIP.

routing table
Table stored on a router or other internetworking device that keeps track of routes to network destinations and metrics associated with those routes.

Routing Table Protocol
See RTP.

routing update
Message sent from a router to check network access and associated cost information. A routing update is sent at regular intervals and after a change in network topology.

RPC
remote-procedure call

Communication from a local program to a remote program to request temporary use of services available on the remote program.

RSA

Rivest, Shamir, & Adleman

Algorithm for public key asymmetric encryption. RSA was the first algorithm suitable for signing as well as encryption. It was one of the first great advances in public key cryptography.

rsh

remote shell protocol

Standard that allows a user to execute commands on a remote system without having to log in to the system. For example, rsh can be used to remotely examine the status of access servers on a network without having to connect to each communication server to execute the command.

RSSI

Receiver Signal Strength Indicator

Measurement of received RF signal strength in WLAN application.

RSTP

Rapid Spanning Tree Protocol

Update to Spanning Tree Protocol standards that reduces the time for connections to be established to switch ports.

RSTP+

Enhanced Rapid Spanning Tree Protocol

Type of spanning tree protocol with increase convergence speed.

RTCP

Real-Time Transport Control Protocol

Control standard for RTP that monitors and provides feedback on the QoS of a transmission link.

RTP

Routing Table Protocol

VINES routing standard based on RIP that is used to distribute network topology information and assist VINES servers to find neighboring clients, servers, and routers. RTP uses delay as a routing metric.

Rapid Transport Protocol

Standard that provides pacing and error recovery for data as it crosses the APPN network. With RTP, error recovery and flow control are conducted end-to-end rather than at every node. RTP prevents congestion.

Real-Time Transport Protocol

Standard commonly used with IP networks that provides end-to-end network transport functions for applications transmitting real-time data, such as audio, video, or simulation data, over multicast or unicast network services. RTP provides such services as payload type identification, sequence numbering, timestamping, and delivery monitoring to real-time applications.

RU

rack unit

Standard form factor measurement for the vertical space that equipment occupies. A rack unit is equal to the height of 1.75 inches (4.4cm). A device is measured in RUs. If a device is 1.75 inches tall, it is 1RU. If it is 3.5 inches tall, it is 2RU.

runt

Frame that is less than 64 bytes, usually the result of a collision. In fragment-free switching, the switch reads the first 64 bytes of the frame before it begins to forward it out the destination port. Checking the first 64 bytes ensures that the switch does not forward collision fragments.

SAN

storage area network

Data communication platform that interconnects servers and storage at Gigabaud speeds. By combining LAN networking models with server performance and mass storage capacity, SAN eliminates bandwidth issues and scalability limitations created by previous SCSI bus-based architectures.

scalability

Ability of a network design to develop to include new user groups and remote sites. A scalable network design should support new applications without impacting the level of service delivered to existing users.

SDH
Synchronous Digital Hierarchy

European standard that defines a set of rate and format standards that are transmitted using optical signals over fiber. SDH is similar to SONET, with a basic SDH rate of 155.52 Mbps, designated at STM-1.

SDM
Cisco Security Device Management

Web-based device-management tool for a Cisco IOS software-based router. Simplifies router and security configuration through smart wizards used to deploy, configure, and monitor a Cisco router without requiring knowledge of the CLI.

SDRAM
synchronous dynamic random access memory. A form of DRAM.

Secure Shell
See SSH.

security
Protection of data and hardware against unwanted access or damage.

security appliance
Device that protects data and hardware against unwanted access or damage.

security policy
Description of the system, physical, and behavioral protection measures implemented in an organization.

segment
1) Section of network that is bounded by bridges, routers, or switches. 2) Continuous electrical circuit in a LAN using a bus topology, that is often connected to other segments with repeaters. 3) Single, logical transport layer unit of information.

A segment that is a logical unit of information may also be known as a datagram, frame, message, or packet.

segmented data
Small, uniform parts of data that switch quickly and efficiently between nodes.

Serial Line Address Resolution Protocol
See SLARP.

serial transmission
Method of data transmission in which the bits of a data character are transmitted sequentially over a single channel.

serial tunnel
See STUN.

server
Software program or node that provides data or services at the request of clients.

See also back end, client, and front end.

server farm
Collection of servers located in a central facility and maintained by the central group to provide server needs for organizations. A server farm usually has primary and backup server hardware for load balancing, redundancy, and fault tolerance purposes. Server farm architecture provides the operation and maintenance of servers.

service level agreement
See SLA.

service provider
See SP.

Service Set Identifier
See SSID.

setup mode
Interactive menu to create an initial configuration file for a new networking device, or a device that has had the startup-config file from NVRAM erased. Setup mode can also be used to modify an existing configuration.

shared secret
Password known between devices.

Shortest path first algorithm
See SPF algorithm.

Shortest Path Routing
See SPR.

silicon switching
High-speed, dedicated packet switching based on the silicon switching engine, not the silicon switch processor.

Simple Mail Transfer Protocol
See SMTP.

Simple Network Management Protocol
See SNMP.

simple password authentication
Method that offers basic securtiy to a router using a key to gain access.

site-to-site VPN
Connection between sites of an organization or between an organization and a partner site. Site-to-site VPN does not require IPSec client configuration on computer hosts because data is encrypted at the entry point of a site and decrypted at the exit point of the tunnel at the other site.

SLA
service level agreement

Binding contract between a network service provider and the end user who requires a certain level of service.

SLARP
Serial Line Address Resolution Protocol

Standard that assigns an address to the end point of a serial link if the other end is already configured. SLARP assumes that each serial line is a separate IP subnet, and that one end of the line is host number 1 and the other end is host number 2. As long as one end of the serial link is configured, SLARP automatically configures an IP address for the other end.

SMDS
switched multimegabit data service

High-speed, packet-switched, WAN technology offered by a telephone company.

SMTP
Simple Mail Transfer Protocol

Internet standards that provide electronic mail services.

SNMP
Simple Network Management Protocol

Standard that allows monitoring of individual devices on the network. SNMP-compliant devices use agents to monitor a number of predefined parameters for specific conditions. These agents collect information and store it in a MIB.

softphone
Application installed on a computer to support voice calls. An example of softphone is Cisco IP Communicator.

software phone
See softphone.

SONET
Synchronous Optical Network

Up to 2.5 Gbps, high-speed synchronous network specification developed by Bellcore and designed to run on optical fiber. STS-1 is the basic building block of SONET. Approved as an international standard in 1988.

SP
service provider

Organization, such as the local phone or cable company, that provides Internet service.

SPAN
switched port analyzer

Tool used with a Catalyst switch that enables the capture of traffic by mirroring the traffic at one switched segment onto a predefined SPAN port. A network analyzer attached to the SPAN port can monitor traffic from any of the other Catalyst switched ports.

spanning tree
Loop-free subset of a network topology.

Spanning Tree Protocol
See STP.

spanning-tree algorithm
Mathematical process that creates a hierarchical tree to bridge a network.

SPF algorithm
shortest path first algorithm

Mathematical process that uses the length of a path to determine a shortest-path spanning tree. An SPF algorithm is a link-state routing algorithm.

SPF tree
All paths from a source to each destination and the total cost of each path.

SPI
stateful packet inspection

Inspect and permit an incoming response to established communication on an internal network.

split horizon
Routing technique that controls the formation of loops by preventing information from exiting the router interface through the same interface it was received.

split tunneling
Configuration to give a VPN client access to the Internet while tunneled into a Cisco IOS Router. Split tunneling is required to give a VPN client secure access to corporate resources via IPsec as well as allow unsecured access to the Internet.

split-horizon updates
Routing technique in which information about a route is prevented from exiting the router interface through which that information was received. A split-horizon update is used to prevent routing loops.

spoof
1) Method used by a Cisco router to cause a host to handle an interface as if it were running and supporting a session. The router creates false replies to keepalive messages from the host to convince the host that the session still exists. Spoofing is used in a routing environment such as DDR. In DDR, a circuit-switched link is taken down when there is no traffic to save toll charges. 2) When a packet claims to be from an address from which it was not sent. Spoofing is designed to bypass network security mechanisms such as filters and access lists.

SPR
Shortest Path Routing

Algorithm that uses the length of a path to determine a shortest-path spanning tree. Shortest-path routing is commonly used in link-state routing algorithms.

SSH
Secure Shell

In-band protocol used to encrypt username and password information when it is sent.

SSID
Service Set Identifier

32-character code that normally appears in every packet of a Wi-Fi transmission. The SSID contains the network name for the WLAN. All devices on a WLAN use the same SSID. The SSID code can be set by the network administrator, or it can be automatically assigned.

SSL
Secure Sockets Layer

Protocol used for protecting confidential information and private documents across the Internet. SSL uses a cryptographic system that uses two keys to encrypt data: a public key or digital certificate, and a private or secret key known only to the recipient of the message.

stakeholder
Person or organization that has an interest in the success of a process.

standard ACL
Access control list that accepts or denies packets based on the source IP address. Standard ACLs are identified by the number assigned to them. The numbers range from 1 to 99 and from 1300 to 1999.

star
Structure in which devices on a network are connected to a common central switch by point-to-point links. The star topology is the most commonly used physical topology for Ethernet LANs.

stateful packet inspection
See SPI.

Static NAT
static network address translation

Method in which an internal host with a fixed private IP address is mapped with a fixed public IP address all of the time.

static network address translation
See static NAT.

static route
Path that is manually configured and entered into the routing table. A static route take precedence over routes chosen by dynamic routing protocols.

statistical time-division multiplexing
See STDM.

STDM
statistical time-division multiplexing

Technique where information from multiple logical channels is transmitted across a single physical channel. STDM dynamically allocates bandwidth only to active input channels, making better use of available bandwidth and allowing many devices to be connected.

Statistical time-division multiplexing is also known as statistical multiplexing or stat mux.

storage area network
See SAN.

storage networking
Infrastructure that uses SAN and security measures to support the network-based storage needs.

store and forward
See store and forward packet switching.

store and forward packet switching
Technique in which frames are completely processed before being forwarded out of the appropriate port. Store and forward packet switching is a process that includes the calculation of the cyclic redundancy check and the verification of the destination address.

STP
Spanning Tree Protocol

Bridge standards that use the spanning-tree algorithm and enable a bridge to dynamically work around loops in a network topology by creating a spanning tree. A bridge exchanges BPDU messages with other bridges to detect loops, and then removes the loops by shutting down selected bridge interfaces.

streaming video
Multimedia that is continually downloaded to the receiving host as an end-user is viewing the material. The end-user does not fully download the multimedia file to the computer.

Streaming media is also known as live video.

structured cabling
Using an internationally recognized standard to implement a physical network cabling design.

STS-1
Synchronous Transport Signal level 1

SONET format adopted by common carriers for high-speed digital circuits that operate at 51.84 Mbps.

STS-3c
Synchronous Transport Signal level 3, concatenated

SONET format that specifies the frame structure for the 155.52-Mbps lines used to carry Asynchronous Transfer Mode cells.

stub area
OSPF area that carries a default route, intra-area routes, and interarea routes, but does not carry external routes. Virtual links cannot be configured across a stub area, and they cannot contain an autonomous system border router.

stub network
Network that has only a single connection to a router.

STUN
serial tunnel

Router feature that allows two SDLC- or HDLC-compliant devices to connect to each other through an arbitrary multiprotocol topology, with the use of Cisco routers, rather than through a direct serial link.

subinterface
One of a number of virtual interfaces on a single physical interface.

subnet address
Portion of an IP address that is specified as the subnetwork by the subnet mask.

subnet mask
In IPv4, a 32-bit number associated with an IP address to determine where the network portion of an IP address ends and the host portion in an IP address begins.

subnetwork
System in an IP network that shares a particular subnet address. A subnetwork is arbitrarily segmented by a network administrator to provide a multilevel, hierarchical routing structure while shielding the subnetwork from the addressing complexity of attached networks.

subset advertisement
VTP message that contains new VLAN information based on the summary advertisement.

substitution
Troubleshooting technique using functioning parts to test equipment.

sub-subnet
Further division of a subnetted network address.

successor route
Equal cost, primary loop-free path with the lowest metric to the destination determined by the topology and recorded in in the routing table.

summary advertisement
Current VTP domain name and configuration revision number issued periodically by a Catalyst switch.

supernet
See supernetting.

supernetting
Process of summarizing of contiguous class addresses given out by the Internet community. An example of supernetting is when a group of class C addresses 200.100.16.0 through 200.100.31.0 is summarized into the address 200.100.16.0 with a mask of 255.255.224.0.

Also known as classless inter-domain routing.

SVC
switched virtual circuit

Route that is dynamically established on demand and is destroyed when transmission is complete. An SVC is used in situations where data transmission is sporadic.

switch
Network device that filters, forwards, and floods frames based on the destination address of each frame. A switch operates at the data-link layer of the OSI Reference Model.

switch block
Configuration where a router, or multilayer switch, is deployed in pairs, with Access Layer switches evenly divided between them. Each switch block acts independently which prevents the network from going down if a device fails.

A switch block is also known as a building or departmental switch block.

switched multimegabit data service
See SMDS.

switched port analyzer
See SPAN.

switched virtual circuit
See SVC.

switching loop
Causes duplicate frames to be sent throughout a network. A switching loop occurs when there is more than one path between two switches.

symmetric cryptography
Type of of data coding that involves algorithms that use the same key for two separate steps of the process. Examples of symmetric cryptography include encryption and decryption, and signature creation and verification.

symmetric key
Cryptographic key that is used in a symmetric cryptographic algorithm.

Synchronous Digital Hierarchy
See SDH.

Synchronous Optical Network
See SONET.

synchronous transmission
Digital signals that are sent with precise clocking. Synchronous transmission signals have the same frequency, with individual characters encapsulated in start and stop bits, that designate the beginning and end of each character.

Synchronous Transport Signal level 1
See STS-1.

Synchronous Transport Signal level 3, concatenated
See STS-3c.

syslog
Type of message logged and sent to an external server to inform users of various reports in real time.

system-level acceptance testing
Practice of verifying if a network meets the business goals and design requirements. The results of system-level acceptance testing are recorded and are part of the documentation provided to the customer.

T1
Digital WAN carrier facility that transmits DS-1-formatted data at 1.544 Mbps through the telephone-switching network, with the use of AMI or binary 8-zero substitution coding.

T3
Digital WAN carrier facility that transmits DS-3-formatted data at 44.736 Mbps through the telephone switching network.

Tc
committed time

Calculated time interval that data takes to travel a specific distance.

T-carrier
Any of several digitally multiplexed telecommunications carrier systems.

TDM
time division multiplexing

Division of bandwidth to allow multiple logical signals to be transmitted simultaneously across a single physical channel. The signals are then seperated at the receiving end.

telecommunications room
Facility that contains network and telecommunications equipment, vertical and horizontal cable terminations, and cross-connect cables.

Also known as a riser, a distibution facility, or a wiring closet.

Telecommunications Service Provider
See TSP.

telecommuting
Working from a location other than the centralized office.

teleconferencing
Method for a group of people to communicate in real time online.

telephony
Technology designed to convert audio to digital signals, and to transmit the signals over a network, especially packet-switched networks.

teleworker
Employee that works at a location other than the centralized office.

Teleworking
Employee that works at a location other than the centralized office location.

Telnet
TCP/IP protocol that allows a remote user to log on to a host on the network and issue commands remotely.

TFTP
Trivial File Transfer Protocol

Standards that allows files to be transferred from one computer to another over a network. TFTP is a simplified version of FTP .

three-way handshake
Series of synchronization and acknowledgments used by TCP to open a connection.

threshold
Acceptable level of errors on an interface.

threshold value
Maximum number of errors that a switch allows before it will go into store and forwarding switching to slow traffic and correct the problem.

time division multiplexing
See TDM.

time slice
Period of time during which a conversation has complete use of the physical media. Bandwidth is allocated to each channel or time slot. In standard TDM, if a sender has nothing to say, the time slice goes unused, wasting valuable bandwidth. In STDM, it keeps track of conversations that require extra bandwidth. It then dynamically reassigns unused time slices on an as-needed basis to minimize the use of bandwidth.

Time-based ACL
An ACL that permits and denies specified traffic based on the time of day or day of the week. Time-based ACLs are similar to extended ACLs in function, but they support access control based on a time range. A time range is created to define specific times of the day and week for controlling access. The time range relies on the router system clock, and the feature works best with Network Time Protocol (NTP) synchronization.

Top-down
See top-down approach.

top-down approach
Method for testing a network designed to support specific network applications and service requirements. When a design is complete, a

prototype or proof-of-concept test is performed using the top-down approach approach to ensure that the new design functions as expected before it is implemented.

topology
Map of the arrangement of network nodes and media within an enterprise networking infrastructure. Topology can be physical or logical.

topology database
Location on a topology that stores SPF tree information.

topology table
One of three tables on an EIGRP router. The topology table lists all routes learned from each EIGRP neighbor. DUAL takes the information from the neighbor and topology tables and calculates the lowest cost routes to each network. The topology table identifies up to four primary loop-free routes for any one destination.

ToS
type of service

8-bit field used for frame classification located in the IP packet and used by a device to indicate the precedence or priority of a given frame. ToS is not used when a frame is received that contains an 802.1q frame tag.

traffic filtering
Control traffic in various segments of the network. Traffic filtering is the process of analyzing the contents of a packet to determine if the packet should be allowed or blocked.

traffic shaping
Using queues to limit surges that can congest a network. In traffic shaping, data is buffered and then sent into the network in regulated amounts to ensure that the traffic will fit within the promised traffic envelope for the particular connection. Traffic shaping is used in networks such as ATM and Frame Relay.

transceiver
Device that receives and forwards analog and digital signals.

transmit power control
Modify the RF transmission in a wireless LAN by increasing or decreasing the rate of power on a device to improve the link quality and signals received.

transmit queue
See TxQ.

transparent
Not visible or apparent. In networking, a lower layer protocol may make a decision that does not affect or include the upper layers, so the action is invisible, or transparent to the upper layers.

trial-and-error
Troubleshooting technique that relies on experience and testing to solve a problem.

triggered update
Message containing the routing table of a router that is sent to neighboring routers on a network when the router starts up.

triple data encryption standard
See 3DES.

Trivial File Transfer Protocol
See TFTP.

trunk
Point-to-point link that connects a switch to another switch, a router, or a server. A trunk carries traffic for multiple VLANs over the same link. The VLANs are multiplexed over the link with a trunking protocol.

trunk port
A port on a switch or router that connects a switch to another switch, a router, or a server through a trunk. A trunk carries traffic for multiple VLANs over the same link. The VLANs are multiplexed over the link with a trunking protocol.

TSP
Telecommunications Service Provider

Vendor that is authorized by regulatory agencies to operate a telecommunications system and provide telecommunications service.

A telecommunications service provider is also known as a local exchange carrier, telecom carrier, or carrier.

tunnel
Secure communication path between two peers, such as two routers.

tunneling
Method of data transmission over networks with differing protocols. With tunneling, a data packet is encapsulated to form a new packet that conforms to the protocols used over intermediary networks.

two-way handshake
Authentication process used on a PAP. During the two-way handshake, a device looks up the username and password of the calling device to confirm the information matches what is stored in the database.

TxQ
transmit queue

Process of storing traffic on hardware and then sending the packets out in the order they were received.

type field
Extra field in a Cisco HDLC frame which allows multiple protocols to share the same link by identifying the type of protocol carried by the frame.

type of service
See ToS.

UDP
User Datagram Protocol

Standard for connectionless transmission of voice and video traffic. Transmissions using UDP are not affected by the delays caused from acknowledgements and retransmitting lost packets.

unequal cost
Additional bandwidth is needed to forward a packet on certain routes on a network. Some routes may have higher metric values than others.

unequal cost load balancing
Distribution of packets on more than one path using a specified variance in the metric. Distributing the traffic helps prevent a single path from being overloaded.

unicast
Type of message sent to a single network destination. Compare unicast with broadcast and multicast.

Unicast frames
Data packet that is addressed to a single destination.

uninterruptible power supply
See UPS.

untagged
Traffic with no VLAN ID that needs to cross the 802.1q configured link. Examples of untagged traffic include Cisco Discovery Protocol, VTP, and some types of voice traffic. Untagged traffic minimizes the delays associated with inspection of the VLAN ID tag.

update packet
Message about the network topology sent to a neighbor. The update packet is added to the topology table. Several updates are often required to send all of the topology information to a new neighbor.

uplink port
High-speed port that connects to areas that have a higher demand for bandwidth, such as another switch, a server farm, or other networks.

UplinkFast
STP enhancement to minimize downtime during recalculation. STP UplinkFast accelerates choosing a new root port when a link or switch fails, or when an STP is reconfigured. The transition of the root port to the forwarding state occurs immediately, without going through the normal STP procedures of listening and learning.

UPS
uninterruptible power supply

Continuous and reliable power source made available in the event of power failure. UPS is often provided to mission critical servers and network devices.

uptime
Period of time in which a network or a device is fully functional.

User Datagram Protocol
See UDP.

V.35
ITU-T standard describing a synchronous, physical layer protocol used for communications between a network access device and a packet network. V.35 is most commonly used in the United States and in Europe, and is recommended for speeds up to 48 Kbps.

variable-length subnet mask
See VLSM.

variance
Amount multiplied to a route to determine if it is within range of the maximum acceptable metric for use as a path. For example, If the variance value is 2, the router balances the traffic load using any path for which the metric is less than two times the best metric.

VC
virtual circuit

Logical relationship created to ensure reliable communication between two network devices. A virtual circuit is defined by a virtual path identifier/virtual channel identifier pair, and can be either a permanent virtual circuit or switched virtual circuit. Virtual circuits are used in Frame Relay and X.25. In ATM, a virtual circuit is called a virtual channel.

vector
Data segment of an SNA message. A vector consists of a length field, a key that describes the vector type, and vector-specific data.

VID
VLAN ID

Identity of the VLAN inserted into an Ethernet frame as it enters a port on a switch.

Video on Demand
See VoD.

virtual circuit
See VC.

virtual local area network
See VLAN.

virtual path
Logical group of virtual circuits that connect two sites.

virtual path connection
See VPC.

virtual path link
See VPL.

virtual private network
See VPN.

Virtual Trunking Protocol
See VTP.

VLAN
virtual local area network

Group of devices on a network, typically end-user stations, that communicate as if attached to the same network segment even though they may be on different segments. VLANs are configured on workgroup switches. Switches with VLANs may interconnect using VLAN trunking protocols.

VLAN is also known as virtual LAN.

VLAN ID
See VID.

VLAN management policy server (VMPS)
See VMPS.

VLAN number
Number assigned to a VLAN when it is created. The VLAN number is any number from the range available on the switch, except for VLAN1. Naming a VLAN is considered a network management best practice.

VLSM
variable-length subnet mask

Technique used to specify a different subnet mask for the same major network number to identify different subnets. VLSM can help optimize available IP address space.

VMPS
VLAN management policy server

Server with a database that maps MAC addresses to VLAN assignments. When a device plugs into a switch port, the VMPS searches the database for a match of the MAC address and temporarily assigns that port to the appropriate VLAN.

VoD
Video on Demand

Type of system that allow a user to select and watch video content over a network as part of an interactive television system. A VoD system either streams content, allowing viewing while the video is being downloaded, or downloads the content entirely to a set-top box before viewing starts.

Voice over IP
See VoIP.

Voice/WAN interface card
See VWIC.

voice-enabled router
Device that converts analog voice from telephone signals to IP packets. The voice-enabled router forwards IP packets between locations.

VoIP
Voice over Internet Protocol

Standard for transmitting voice data encapsulated in an IP packet on an already implemented IP network without needing its own network infrastructure. In VoIP, the digital signal processor divides the voice signal into frames which are paired in groups of two and stored in voice packets. The voice packets are transported using IP in compliance with ITU-T specification H.323.

VoIP is also known as Voice over IP.

VPC
virtual path connection

Group of virtual channel connections that share one or more contiguous VPLs.

VPL
virtual path link

Group of unidirectional virtual channel links within a virtual path with the same end points. Grouping into a VPL reduces the number of connections to be managed, and as a result, decreases network control overhead and cost.

VPN
virtual private network

Network through which data is sent through a public telecommunication infrastructure while maintaining the privacy of the data by creating a tunnel through the public telecommunication infrastructure.

VPN concentrator
virtual private network concentrator

Gateway on a network that filters all VPN traffic.

VTP
Virtual Trunking Protocol

Cisco proprietary standard that maintains a consistent VLAN configuration across a common administrative domain.

VTP configuration revision number
VLAN Trunking Protocol configuration revision number

Numerical order of multicast messages on a network. The VTP configuration revision number begins at zero. As changes on the network occur, the configuration revision number increases by one. It continues to increment until it reaches 2,147,483,648. If a message has a higher VTP configuration revision number than the one stored in the database, the switch updates its VLAN database with this new information.

VWIC
voice/WAN interface card

Adapter that provides support for voice, data and integrated voice, and data applications. A VWIC facilitates the migration from data only, as well as channelized voice and data, to packet voice solutions which simplifies deployment and management.

WAN
wide area network

Data communication network that serves users across a broad geographic area and often uses transmission devices provided by common carriers. Examples of WAN technologies include Frame Relay, SMDS, and X.25.

WAN interface card
See WIC.

warranty
Guarantee that a product or service is free of defects and performs as advertised. A warranty is limited in duration and in the services provided.

WEP
Wired Equivalent Privacy

Optional security mechanism standard defined within the 802.11 standard designed to make the link integrity of wireless devices equal to that of a cable.

WIC
wide area network interface card

Adapter that connects a system to a WAN link service provider.

wide area network
See WAN.

wide area network interface card
See WIC.

Wi-Fi Protected Access
See WPA.

wildcard mask
32-bit quantity used in conjunction with an IP address to determine which bits in an IP address should be ignored when that address is compared with another IP address. A wildcard mask is specified when access lists are set up. A wildcard mask is used in in IPv4.

wire speed
Rate that packets are forwarded on a network.

Wired Equivalent Privacy
See WEP.

Wireless Access Point
Physical sites connected on a network that transmit signals for wireless devices.

wireless LAN
See WLAN.

wireless LAN controller
Type of module that provides a secure enterprise-class wireless system. A wireless LAN controller enables a smaller organization to cost-effectively and easily deploy and manage a secure WLAN.

wiring closet
Specially designed room used to wire a data or voice network. Wiring closets serve as a central junction point for the wires and wiring equipment that is used to interconnect devices.

WLAN
wireless local area network

Connection between two or more computers without using physical media. WLAN uses radio communication to accomplish the same functionality as a LAN.

WLAN is also known as wireless LAN.

WPA
Wi-Fi Protected Access

Standard based on IEEE 802.11i that was developed to address security issues. WPA provides high levels of security in a wireless network. WPA uses the Temporal Key Integrity Protocol for data protection and 802.1X for authenticated key management.

zero CIR
Excess bandwidth that is discounted when it is available from a Frame Relay service provider. In Zero CIR, a user pays a small fee for the capability to transmit data across a PVC at speeds up to that of the access link. If there is congestion, all DE lableled frames are dropped. There is no guarantee of service with a CIR set to zero.